Keep Laughing

CHRIS McCAUSLAND

THE AUTOBIOGRAPHY

MICHAEL JOSEPH

PENGUIN MICHAEL JOSEPH

UK | USA | Canada | Ireland | Australia
India | New Zealand | South Africa

Penguin Michael Joseph is part of the Penguin Random House group of companies
whose addresses can be found at global.penguinrandomhouse.com

Penguin Random House UK,
One Embassy Gardens, 8 Viaduct Gardens, London SW11 7BW

penguin.co.uk

First published 2025

001

Set in 14/17pt Garamond Premier Pro
Typeset by Penguin Books
Printed and bound in Great Britain by Clays Ltd, Elcograf S.p.A.

The authorised representative in the EEA is Penguin Random House Ireland,
Morrison Chambers, 32 Nassau Street, Dublin D02 YH68

A CIP catalogue record for this book is available from the British Library

HARDBACK ISBN: 978-0-241-77736-7
TRADE PAPERBACK ISBN: 978-0-241-80089-8

Penguin Random House is committed to a sustainable future
for our business, our readers and our planet. This book is made from
Forest Stewardship Council® certified paper.

For Patricia and Sophie

Introduction

It was Wednesday, 4 September 2024, and I was in the back of a car on the way to Elstree Studios to film the opening episode of *Strictly Come Dancing*. This is where our celebrity and dancer pairings would be revealed to the public when it was broadcast in ten days' time, and where we would all be taking part in a group dance number.

Spray tans were the hot topic in the WhatsApp group. You could book yourself in for one and many of the guys were all in on this. I had never had a spray tan in my life, but I had made the decision to try to let myself go a little bit, to just throw myself into the show and get involved with whatever was asked or expected of me. The only issue was that I would need this tan to be super-light, as in a week's time I was filming a stand-up show for the telly and didn't want to be up on stage, and therefore preserved for ever, hosting that show with a glaringly obvious mahogany sheen.

Of course this reminded me of the *Friends* episode where Ross has a bit of a nightmare while getting a spray tan. As you will no doubt remember, he keeps turning in the wrong direction and being sprayed over and over again in the face until he has become way more tanned than he had intended.

I remember watching this on the telly, actually watching, when I could still see enough to do so. It was hilarious, and even replaying the scene in my mind was making me chuckle along to myself whilst sat in the back of that car. I could recall Ross's confusion and frustration as he was sprayed over and over, and ultimately that deep mahogany finish once all the spraying had stopped. It was like re-watching the scene as it was on the telly, a private viewing just for me.

I can't watch anything these days, without two or three questions popping up in my mind that only Google can answer. I wonder if the internet wasn't a thing, whether I would still have these questions being a nuisance in there, or whether I only allow them the consideration because I know I have the means of easily finding out the answers? Also, the act of looking these things up is often a distraction from more important things I should really be doing instead, and my brain loves a distraction.

How old is actor David Schwimmer now?

What was the name of the pet monkey Ross had?

Which series was that tan episode in?

It's not like in those pre-internet days, I would have had to run to a local library and access microfiche archives of historical records and publications to find answers to the questions that, if left unanswered, would have slowly lead to me going mad. It's not like I would have had to find a record of David Schwimmer's birthdate and done the quick maths to work out his current age. It's not like I would have had to comb through back issues of the *TV Times* magazine until I found a reference to that monkey. It's not like I would have had to go into HMV to check the back covers of TV boxsets until I knew the exact series that a specific episode was a part of so that particular itch could be scratched.

The internet is a thing, though, and I was sat in the back of a car with an iPhone, and so had both the time and the means to scratch all of these itches before I arrived at the studio.

He was fifty-seven years old at the time, but is fifty-eight now at the point of publication.

The monkey was called Marcel, of course it was, how the hell did I forget that?

I then looked up the tan episode online to see which series it was part of and couldn't believe it when I saw that 'The One with Ross's Tan' was episode three of series ten. It was first broadcast in the US on Friday, 3 October 2003, and had been shown in the UK just a few weeks later.

The glaringly shocking truth was that I had never seen that episode. Never seen it, as in actually seen it, with my own eyes, not with any level of sight whatsoever. It was broadcast on the telly three months after I had picked up a microphone and tried performing stand-up comedy for the first time. I was blind by that point, well and truly blind. The chances are that I likely didn't even catch it when it was first on the telly, but rather some time afterwards on video with my mate Kev, who is *Friends*-obsessed, collected the whole lot on VHS, and who almost certainly could have answered any of those questions without the need for Google at all.

In that moment I felt as if the rug of what was real had been pulled from under my feet. Like when we find out that

Bruce Willis was actually a ghost all along. Mahogany Ross was in fact just a ghost, an apparition I had conjured up in my mind, and that I had at some point started to believe was real.

I had obviously just listened to the episode, and so evocative was the scene and the comedy that I had created my own movie to go along with the audio I'd heard, and here we were, twenty years later, and I had become convinced that the images I had in my mind were the images that had been on the TV and that we had all experienced together.

My mind is a lie. My visual memory is a fabrication. The truth is that there are probably countless memories I have of things I think I've seen, but that I just haven't. During the process of losing my sight, especially in my late teens and early twenties, my imagination would often just fill a lot of the gaps with what it thought was probably there. As more and more sight disappeared and those gaps got bigger, my imagination had more and more work to do, but I don't think my mind really understood the difference between what was real and what was not, as it filed bits and pieces away for some future time when they might be called upon as part of a memory, or even a book.

When I was in my early twenties I had a fairly imposing rickety old bookcase stood against a wall in the living room. I could see this bookcase, kind of. I could see its dark shape looming in the blurry haze of that current level of minimal vision. Well, I thought I could anyway, because once I had finally got rid of the knackered old thing, condemned it to the local dump, for a while afterwards I could still see it there. Still see the dark imposing shape of the bookcase stood where

I knew it wasn't. I would have to go over to where it had once been to confirm to myself with my hands that it was not there any more, upon which it would instantly evaporate from my vision, until the following day that is, when it would be back again to taunt me.

For how long had I not seen that bookcase? For how long had my imagination been papering over the cracks and filling in those gaps with what I thought should be there? To be honest, I haven't got a clue. I realise that the murky ten-year period from my late teens onwards, when I was losing the dregs of my sight and living with the early years of blindness, is probably full of visual memories that are nothing more than my imagination doing its best to give me something to look at.

These days, my mind still functions extremely visually. I imagine everything around me, but I'm very aware of that. It's not a conscious thing on my part, it doesn't take effort or require intent, it just happens unconsciously as my mind still does its best to provide me with at least some visual sense of what I think should, or might, be there.

I can sit working on a computer, like I am now, and still become convinced that I can see the shapes and shadows of things I know are on the desk. There's the dark shape of the computer in front of me, and I can easily become mesmerised by the blurry colours and shapes of things moving on its screen. I have to remind myself that because my computer talks, I don't even have the screen turned on, and that It is nothing more than a black rectangle of glass that operates as a rather expensive lid for my laptop. This then causes those blurry colours and shapes to disappear from in front of me, until the next time my mind wanders enough to be duped again.

Of course I have visual memories from when I could see pretty well, or half decent at least. From my childhood, through to my mid-teens when I was still able to see to some extent, and these memories do enable me to look back on my earlier years with a greater level of immersion than I can for those in my twenties. I do have all the facts, though, even if I can't trust a lot of the pictures.

So with all that in mind, let's get started and I'll do my best to tell you about as much as I can of the funny and interesting stuff that has happened throughout my life, and how I think that I might remember it.

Chapter One

I was born in Liverpool.

I was born on a Wednesday, just about.

I was born twenty-five minutes before it would have been a Thursday, that particular midnight crossover from one day to the next being exactly slap-bang right in the middle of June 1977.

It seems a bit silly to go back as far as your own birth when writing an autobiography. After all, it's not like we can remember any of it, and surely that's the point of an auto-biography, isn't it? A first-hand account of life's events, experiences, triumphs and tribulations – as best as you can recall them anyway: 'After nine months of solitary confine-ment I caught a glimpse of daylight and decided to make a dash for it. I charged forward, despite the passage ahead seeming much too narrow, but somehow managed to squeeze myself through to freedom before I was immediately ambushed by giants.'

No. Surely any autobiography that bothers to go back this far is at this point, really, just a biography of some baby. A third-hand account of just some baby we have no memory of ever being, but who would one day become us, once we'd finally finished booting up properly and were able to access the hard drive. Only then are we able to start archiving fragments of experience for later inclusion in a book.

So why have I dragged you all back here? Well, I do have a point and this just felt like the best place to make it, so sit tight for a moment and let me try and set the scene as best as I can, for somebody who wasn't actually there, of course.

I did try to look up what the weather was like in Liverpool when I entered the world, but it says there is no recorded data. Considering it was twenty-five minutes to midnight, though, I think it's fairly safe to say that the sun wasn't out and that it was probably pretty dark.

I cried. An owl hooted, something like that.

This particular day happened to be precisely three weeks after Liverpool Football Club had triumphed in their first ever European Cup final, so I can only imagine that I felt incredibly disappointed to have missed the occasion.

The nurses would have announced to the room that I had a penis, counted my fingers and toes, and then whisked me off to be weighed. Eight pounds six, not bad!

'A healthy baby boy!' they would have proclaimed.

Well, almost, but not quite, because unbeknownst to everybody in that room, this baby's eyesight had already started to worsen. It wouldn't happen quickly, it would take about twenty-five years. A slow march over a quarter of a century into a blurry soup of nothingness.

So that is why we're here, because in this particular moment in a Liverpool delivery room in the middle of June 1977, my eyes were the healthiest they would ever be. What a shame that I was just a baby and couldn't really appreciate it, or maybe I could and I just don't remember it.

I would say that the rate at which my eyesight deteriorated was probably fairly consistent, but in a proportional sense, that is.

This is how I see it, pardon the pun . . .

I think it is simplest to think of it as being in an exponential decline, with my sight roughly halving in acuity every five years, always reducing significantly but never with an absolute zero in its grasp. Retinal cells were dying off, but always at that constant rate of about 50 per cent proportional to the amount of them still remaining.

Those first five years would have taken the biggest hit, wiping out about half of normal vision before I could attempt to read a book that had even the bare bones of a story within it. Books were big and bold, though, so this wouldn't be too much of a problem yet, but being able to see the blackboard would be a different matter entirely.

This would also be the first real awareness I would have of my condition, as in those years prior to the age of five I was just too young to notice it happening, or to have any understanding of what was in play or what the hell 'normal' was meant to be anyway. For me, this was where the deterioration really started and my sight was half gone already.

By the age of ten I was down to about 25 per cent. I could read a book, but only if it had large print and I held it close to my face.

I could play hide and seek, but I was shit at it, and when it was my turn to be on base then all of the other kids knew they didn't really need to hide, but just be far enough away so they couldn't be seen in plain sight.

By the age of fifteen I was coping with about 12 per cent acuity. I'd given up reading anything unless I had to, and even then it had to be magnified onto a special TV screen. Reading was a chore and it was neither fun nor enjoyable.

Playing computer games would become an issue, and soon even football, as I started having to relinquish parts of myself due to the ever-encroaching haze.

I lost about 12 per cent of normal vision over those last five years, which was a lot, but it worked out to be about one per cent every five or six months. That's not really something you can notice happening in the moment, or even month by month, but certainly something that presents huge changes over these longer periods of time.

As I hit twenty years old I was running on 6 per cent, completely oblivious to the vast majority of the world around me. Relying on my sight now just got me into more trouble than it was worth. I was essentially blind, but still with just about enough sight to pretend I wasn't, and denial consumed me.

I had to sit so close to the TV to see even the basic movements of people on it that the static played havoc with my hair. It was long by then, but I couldn't see myself in the mirror to tell if it suited me or not. My dad would have said not, but who listens to their dad on these matters?

By the age of twenty-five, just a blurry nothing would cloud everything. I could still see something, but that remaining 3 per cent would just be a 'something' which was nothing of any use.

Eventually I would reach a plateau, the point at which any further decline was no longer noticeable to me, and where any further halves of almost nothing left me with a fairly similar sense of almost nothing. The relentless loss would stop but my imagination would now take over, painting pictures in my mind as compensation for a brain that was still hungry for things to look at.

Finally, though, I would reach a state of unchanging blindness that I could now try to get used to, although acceptance would still take a while.

It's probably all a little more complicated than that, but I hope that gives you a rough idea of what was ahead of this almost very nearly healthy baby boy in that Liverpool delivery room on a Wednesday evening in the middle of June 1977. That initial twenty-five years would contain a lot of loss, frustration and shame, but I also had a blast along the way.

My life would then change for ever when, at the age of twenty-six, I would dare myself to pick up a microphone for the very first time. That would prove to be the most terrifying thing I would ever do, until I was to stick on a pair of dance shoes and try dancing on live TV in front of millions. What the hell was I thinking?

Chapter Two

The first memory I have is of putting my hand into something wet. It's more just a recollection of the sensation, a sliminess, of an initial confusion and surprise, and then of my mum realising that my novelty Donald Duck bubble bath had leaked on the carpet. The Donald-shaped bottle with screw-off head might have begged to be played with, but he evidently wasn't built for such things and much to my anguish poor Donald's insides had ended up on his outside. My mum doesn't remember this, but why would she? This would have been one of countless insignificant things that had happened in her life, whereas for me it must have been a fairly monumental tragedy, I would imagine perhaps on a par with the passing of a close family member.

I think I was somewhere around two and a half to three years old, and in my mind this is the first memory I have of anything happening. We were living in a part of Liverpool called Cantril Farm, first in a flat and then a small house, but I don't remember anything specific about these homes aside from a few faded snapshots of memories that I know definitely occurred while we were living there.

My mum worked behind the bar in the Hare and Hounds

pub in Liverpool's West Derby Village, and in one of those memories I'm toddling along a pavement after the back of her legs as she was leaving for a shift, and my dad is sweeping me up from behind as I cried.

I suppose you could call such moments traumatic, and that's likely why they etched themselves into my memory with such significance that they remain there to this day. It also shows how happy my earliest years must have been when this constitutes trauma: having to say goodbye to my mum as she left for work, and the loss of our beloved Donald, may he rest in peace.

My mum has the same eyesight condition as I do. It's hereditary and it deteriorates significantly more slowly in females than in males. Yes, I have a sexist eyesight condition that hates men. To be honest, it hates women as well, just not with as much vigour as it hates men.

My mum became a housewife and a full-time mum throughout my entire childhood, I was certainly a full-time job, and for the last thirty years she has volunteered, teaching braille to adults who lose their sight later in life.

My mum would have been about twenty-five when she was still working in the pub, the age I was when my sight had completely left me. I would hazard a guess that maybe it deteriorates twice as slowly in females as it does in males, maybe halving every ten years rather than every five. My sister Louise is in her early forties now and her sight is probably where mine was in my early twenties, so this seems to be about right.

These faulty genes were passed on to my mum via my nan, and to my nan via her father, but where they came from before that generation or for how many generations it has existed in our family is anybody's guess. My mum tells me that her grandmother died in childbirth with her tenth child, and her blind grandfather ended up raising nine children on his own, which certainly puts anything I've ever achieved into stark perspective.

Prior to my arrival my dad was working in the Barker & Dobson factory, where they made those lovely Everton Mints. He was also the drummer in a band called Pisces, and they would travel the working men's clubs of northern England with their long hair, moustaches and bright orange crushed-velvet suits with purple trim. My dad tells me that the first time they wore those bright orange suits was for a gig in a Catholic club, which he said didn't go down very well.

There was one eventful show when my dad collapsed off the drums during a performance and had to be rushed to hospital. Talk about living the rock 'n' roll lifestyle! Although it doesn't seem quite so exciting when you learn that he was actually suffering from an acutely inflamed appendix . . . but I would imagine that was probably because of all the booze and women, yeah?

When I was born my dad became a fireman, working in both Huyton and Storrington Avenue stations in Liverpool. As a kid, there was nothing cooler than your dad turning up at home in a fully manned fire engine, which he would do from time to time, because it would instantly command the attention and admiration of all the kids in the neighbourhood, and I would feel like that fire engine belonged to me.

On two occasions during my childhood I needed to call

him out on official business . . . well, kind of. The first was when I was walking with my mum and my nan through our local Croxteth Park and decided to take a shortcut through a wooded area. I was about seven years old at this point as my mum was pushing my sister in a pram, and kids back then were actively encouraged to play in wooded areas whenever an opportunity arose. I had obviously popped out the other side before my mum and my nan had managed to take the long way around, but due to my poor sight I thought I'd seen them ahead of me and followed the backs of two strangers through the park, only realising at the end that I was alone. My mum and my nan had spent some time calling and shouting for me when I hadn't met them as promised, and once they had accepted that I was likely dead they had returned back to my nan's house to phone my dad, who promptly turned up in a fire engine to locate and retrieve my body.

They eventually found me still alive and walking all the way back to where I had started, a bit confused as to why my dad was there with all of his mates, but a lift in a fire engine was a lift in a fire engine so all in all a pretty good day.

A few years later when I was about ten we had to call him out again as I had become ridiculously stuck in a basket. It was a small moulded plastic basket with lots of square holes all over each side. I took my left hand and I pushed all of my fingers through these square holes right up to my knuckles, but the holes pinched them in place so that I was unable to pull them out.

So, what did I do with one hand firmly stuck in a basket?

Well, I pushed the fingers on my other hand through the other side, so that now I had both hands firmly locked into an improvised Chinese-style finger trap. I couldn't budge them loose, and now they were starting to lose blood supply and turn purple. My mum couldn't free them either so, with no other options available to us, she phoned the fire brigade, or rather my dad, who promptly turned up on a fully manned and equipped fire engine to rescue his idiot son from a small plastic basket.

My parents had to put up with a lot from me when I was a kid, as I was naughty and I was noisy and I never ran out of energy. I was climbing the walls at the best of times, but any episode of a favourite show, such as The A-Team or Knight Rider would have me diving over furniture and behind the couch doing my best to re-enact whatever I'd been watching while providing a full range of sound effects and theme-tune accompaniments.

My sister has always been pretty chilled out and good as gold, but she wouldn't turn up until Chapter Five. Even with a seven-year age gap, though, you would have struggled to tell which of us was the oldest from behaviour alone. When she was four and I was eleven we would fight over who might have been occupying the other's half of the TV viewing area. We would sit on the floor in front of the TV and draw an invisible line from the centre of the screen into the room to illustrate by how many centimetres we thought the other had encroached into our own personal space. Honestly, she was so childish. Even now she's trying to encroach into the story three chapters before she should. I rest my case.

Our eyesight condition is possibly called retinitis pigmentosa, which is not as sexy as it sounds, and I say 'possibly' because I'm not entirely sure any more that that is what we have. RP is a genetic condition that comes in many flavours that lead to a variety of ways in which it can be inherited or will reveal its symptoms. Ours is dominant, which means there's a 50:50 chance of inheriting it from a parent who has the condition. If you inherit it, there's a 50:50 chance you can pass it on to any children you have, but if you don't inherit it you can't pass it on. It doesn't hide or skip generations or anything as cunning as that.

About ten years ago I participated in the 100,000 Genomes Project, a humungous undertaking to map and better understand a range of rare genetic diseases. I waited seven whole years for the results of my participation to be posted out to me, and after all that it came back as inconclusive. They were unable to identify any faulty genes and I got the all clear. Seven years to be told they couldn't find anything wrong with me.

Now here's why I say 'possibly'. At some point in the last twenty years I remember being told by a specialist that they thought I had something called cone rod dystrophy, which I assumed was one of those many flavours of RP, a subtype of RP, so to speak. It is only now when writing this book that I have looked up CRD and learned that it's not a type of RP, but something entirely different. Reading about it, though, and CRD does seem to fit the pattern of my family's sight loss more than RP, so there's a chance that that specialist was right. There are no cures or treatments for either, and they are pretty similar, so it doesn't really make a lot of difference, does it?

Because of the family history, sight loss and blindness were always just part of normal life growing up. My nan never let her blindness faze her, well certainly not in front of me anyway. She would laugh about misfortune and frustration and set the tone for how my family would try to relate to our sight loss.

When I was a teenager, probably around thirteen, my dad was cleaning the inside of the living-room windows.

'Here you go, hold this for me,' he said, and I opened my hand to take what he was offering me.

He dropped something small and light into my open hand but I couldn't tell what it was. I fiddled, poked and rolled it between my fingers to see if I could figure it out but I didn't have a clue.

'What is it?' I asked.

'Oh, that? It's a dead wasp.'

My parents broke out in hysterical laughter as I flung the hideous dried corpse as far away from myself as I could manage and ran off to wash my contaminated hands. I hated insects and creepy-crawlies, and the fact that I'd been playing with a dead one trying to work out what it was because I couldn't see it, well, they thought that was the funniest thing in the world. Somebody phone social services.

Even now when I reminded them of this they broke out into almost the same amount of laughter as they did back then. Some people never grow up.

My grandad was a drunk, and although he was fairly

18

harmless, I would imagine he was a lot for my poor nan to put up with. As a kid I would regularly be able to find coins scattered on the floor and under furniture from where he had fallen over the night before.

'Whatever you can find you can keep,' she would say. 'It's his own fault.'

I believe that my other grandparents, on my dad's side, were pretty decent ballroom dancers back in the day, so maybe I inherited a few of those genes from them. My dad's dad died when I was eleven months old and so I have no memory of him. When he died, though, there was a concern that he might have had tuberculosis so I was promptly given my BCG inoculation when I was still in a nappy, which gave me a glorious pass from pain as a teenager when classmates were having to go for the jab. Thanks, Grandad!

We moved from Cantril Farm to a house in West Derby Village when I hadn't yet reached four years old. The house was a two-up two-down that cost fourteen thousand pounds in 1981. It consisted of a living room, a kitchen, with a small bathroom off it, stairs, two bedrooms, and that was it.

I have so many good memories of that house. Despite its tiny size, single-glazed windows, and lack of any heating, aside from a gas fire in the living room, my memories of being there are very warm and cosy indeed, although my mum tells me that it was often bloody freezing.

Its address confused me at first, '2 Craigside Avenue'. I'd only ever heard it said out loud so didn't realise that it was the number two. I remember thinking it was 'To Craigside Avenue' and wondered how the postman would know that the letters were for us if they were only ever addressed 'To' the street.

Each side of the street was one long terrace with the front doors opening straight out onto the pavement. Ours was one of the end houses, and in my opinion the best house on the street. On our side everyone had a small square back garden, while on the other they had a tiny concrete back yard. As one of only two houses occupying an end position on what was clearly the best side, ours had side access via a gate at the front that would take you through a passage at the side of the house through to that back garden. Point proved.

My dad would smoke cigarettes in that tiny house, and it seems nuts now to even think that was the norm for smokers back then, but it was, and a tall standing ashtray was positioned next to the couch.

We would soon have a commemorative photograph album of Prince Charles and Lady Diana's wedding, with a big Union flag on the front, that we had got from my dad's Embassy tokens. Not only was smoking perfectly acceptable indoors back then, but it was rewarded with a whole range of tat you could select from a catalogue when you'd smoked enough to earn the privilege.

Shortly after moving into this house, I met Neil. He was my age, in fact almost exactly. He was just two days older than me in 1981 and remains so to this day. We met when we were fast approaching four and we're still the best of friends as we approach the final lap of our forties.

The story goes that I actually went knocking on all of the doors on my street enquiring as to whether there were any children living there that I could play with – adorable, I know. Neil didn't live on my street but just around the corner, but I believe that it was my proactive efforts to find a friend that led to me being pointed in his direction.

Friends from the age of nearly four. We would do almost everything together over the coming years, including moving to London, going to university, a thousand different concerts, and even having our kids at the same time, although this bit wasn't planned.

Neil is six foot seven and, despite being a skinny waif like me throughout his twenties, he is a lot bigger built, these days. You can see him featuring as my mystery guest on *Would I Lie to You?* during a story about how I accidentally handed my own keys in to a lost property office after I dropped them without realising it, then didn't recognise them as mine when picking them up off the ground.

He loved standing there and trying to keep a straight face as David Mitchell did his best to pretend to know him, while Lee Mack baited David about how there was no chance that anybody like Neil would ever hang around with anybody like David.

One thing we would never do together, though, was attend the same school. Neil's family was Catholic, and mine Church of England, and it was this that determined the schools we attended.

Chapter Three

To say I had a difficult relationship with school from the outset would be a bit of an understatement. On my very first day I point-blank refused to enter the building with all of the other children, so my mum had to pick me up and carry me inside to try and facilitate some kind of hostile handover with the poor lady who was to become my first ever teacher.

Apparently she'd had to do exactly the same thing two years earlier when trying to drop me off at a nursery for the first time. I have no memory of this, but she tells me I also refused to part company on that occasion as well. As my mum and the lovely old lady who ran the nursery had tried to force that particular handover, I reached over, grabbed hold of the lady's blouse with two hands, and then ripped it wide open, sending her buttons pinging off in all directions.

Back in the school, though, and despite all my kicking and screaming, this handover was eventually carried out with everybody's buttons remaining intact, but I wouldn't imagine with anybody really feeling good about any of it.

I do have a few memories of my very first week in school. Of being taught how to sit on the floor with my legs crossed, in the way that kids sit cross-legged on the floor in school. I had honestly never sat like that before and had no idea how to do it, so when the teacher told us to sit on the carpet with our legs crossed I just did exactly what that sounded like. I sat on my bum with my legs stretched perfectly straight in front of me and just crossed at the ankles. I looked around, and all of the other kids were doing something weird and different but I couldn't figure out what it was. Somehow their feet were pulled up and almost tucked underneath them while their bent knees were poking out to the sides.

Where did they learn how to do that? I thought, as my new teacher tried to fold me into the correct position.

I remember the first book I had to read to my teacher. A bit of a search online tells me that it might have been from a series called 'Look and Say' that consisted of various coloured levels with multiple books in each level. Obviously the complexity would build as you worked your way through the various books and levels. Level One was red, and book one of Level One was simply called *Look*.

Look wasn't just the name of the book though. It was the only word written on each and every single page of that book. Every page had a picture of the same boy pointing at something with the word 'Look' written alongside him. I remember standing there at the teacher's desk just saying the word 'Look' over and over again while she turned the pages seemingly riveted to the story, and even at the young age of four I quite clearly remember thinking that this was a rubbish story.

Despite the incredible level of patience my teacher must have been blessed with, I still managed to get into trouble, constantly. I was a disruptive kid in school, disruptive to the class, and I spent quite a lot of my early education just stood up facing a wall. This was often the punishment for lower-value crimes, but for those instances when staring at a wall just wouldn't cut it, a visit to the headmaster was required.

My first trip to see him came in my very first week of school, because I had . . . I am ashamed to say this but I had bitten Gillian Pearce on the hand. I think she tried to wrestle a toy off me during an indoor play time, and as my two hands were busy trying to secure possession of said toy, I mobilised my mouth to get involved.

Sometimes you need to really feel shame to know that something was wrong, and I certainly felt ashamed of myself on that particular day, and I'm pleased to report that I have never bitten anybody since. Well, not unless they've asked me to. That's a kinky-sex joke. Nobody has ever asked me to.

For somebody who ended up in trouble as much as I did, I had an extraordinarily high level of compliance with certain rules when I first started school, specifically when it came to the ways of the toilet.

My issue related to what was allowed, and what was not allowed, when it came to doing a poo at school. Basically, I wouldn't do a poo at school. I would often return home absolutely desperate to go and would sometimes only just make it to the toilet in time before my school uniform would have needed burning in the garden.

My mum couldn't understand why I was returning home so desperate for a sit-down visit to the bathroom when there were toilets in the school.

'Why don't you just go for a poo in school?' she asked.

I told her I wasn't allowed. I told her we had been given the rules around going to the toilet and that these rules were very strict. I then proceeded to tell her that we had been told in no uncertain terms that the urinals were for doing wees in and the toilets were for doing poos in, and my mum was obviously confused by my issue.

'Well, yes, that's right, but what's the problem?' she asked.

'Don't you see?' I said. 'I can't go to the toilet for a poo, because whenever I do a poo a bit of wee comes out and we can only do a wee in the urinals . . .'

My mum tried to assure me that doing wees was absolutely fine in the toilet, and there would only really be an issue if I tried to do a poo in the urinals. I wouldn't budge on this at all, though. She hadn't been there and that was what we were told.

My mum actually had to go into the school and explain to my teacher what I thought the toilet rules were and ask her to set me straight on this issue before I had an accident on the way home. My teacher then had to sit me down and explain to me exactly what my mum had already tried to tell me, which was basically to do whatever feels right but just don't shit in the urinals.

This could probably be seen as a prime example of literal thinking that today might raise a few flags for a youngster, but back then it was just seen as being a little bit weird and quirky, and possibly cute – yeah, let's go with cute.

It's absolutely bananas to me that I have ended up as a performer for a living. It was never a dream of mine to be on the stage one day. If I'm honest, I hated performing when I was a kid.

I always disliked being part of school assemblies and end-of-term concerts, concerts being such a grand term for what were essentially ramshackle and tuneless events that seemed to fit no other purpose than to make parents regret ever having children in the first place. I never liked being up there with a roomful of people staring at me, and as I grew older I always just found it all a bit naff.

Performing was not something I ever sought out as I reached my teenage years. No drama clubs or auditions for me, no secret yearning to be lit under stage lights or thrust onto the TV screen: performing stand-up would come almost entirely out of the blue and would surprise me as well as everybody who knew me.

My first ever time in front of an audience was a bloody disaster, literally. I was approaching the end of my first term in school and was still a whole six months away from becoming five years old. I was an angel in the chorus of angels. Picture the scene, me, an incredibly cute – yes, we're sticking with cute – blond, freckly kid dressed in a little white frock. Back when I was in school, the chorus of angels was the bit for all the kids who didn't get a proper part so were just corralled together into one big ensemble of leftover kids.

There aren't too many proper parts in a school nativity, are there? Mary, Joseph, the three shepherds and the three wise men, the innkeeper, if you can call that a proper part with just the one line of dialogue.

'Sorry, we're completely full. You might want to try booking in advance next time.'

These days, it's a little different and there is often a part for every child. You are just as likely to see a kid dressed as a squirrel or a tree as you are one of the wise men.

'Ooh, you're the Christmas hedgehog,' you might find yourself reacting to your own child's exciting school nativity news, while hoping it's not going to be up to you to find them the costume.

I was stood there on one of those long wooden benches you get in every school hall up and down the land, one of those long benches with the two little nobbles on either end.

I wonder if those benches are all made by the same company or if there are several companies that are all sharing exactly the same design. I must remember to google that at some point, but not now: I'm being good, I'm writing a book.

I was stood there with all of the other leftover kids, a sad little row of angelic rejects just waiting for our moment when we would no doubt have praised the Lord as one through some kind of ritual chanting, or murdered a fairly miserable hymn that did much the same thing but was dragged out over several minutes and to piano accompaniment.

I don't know whether it was the pressure of the situation that got to me, it being my first time in front of an audience, or whether I'd just had my finger too far up my nose looking for lost treasure, but all of a sudden I experienced what can best be described, under the circumstances, as the 'holy mother' of all nosebleeds. Just as the baby Jesus was being introduced to the three wise men, there was an eruption that took place within me that seemed like it caused 20 per cent of my blood supply to burst out of my face in a single instant.

I immediately started screaming in the middle of this nativity and frantically shaking my head from side to side, spraying angels to the left of me, and angels to the right.

From the perspective of the audience it looked like there had been a drive-by shooting and that several of the angels had taken fatal hits. Maybe those three wise men had actually been three wise guys instead, capeesh?

One of the teachers came rushing in and grabbed me from that bench I'm resisting googling because I'm writing a book, and airlifted me out of Jerusalem, or Bethlehem, or Nazareth, or wherever we were meant to be, and carried me out of the hall under one arm before dumping me in an industrial-sized sink in the school kitchen until I was completely drained of the remaining 80 per cent of my blood.

As a comedian, I've been at plenty of shitty horrible gigs over the years – more on these later – where I would have loved somebody to come racing in, airlift me out of the room and dump me in a massive sink until it was all over.

Thankfully, though, that childhood nativity is the only time my nose has ever bled on stage. The mad thing is I've never even sneezed. Thousands of gigs over twenty-odd years and I have never once even had to stifle a sneeze on stage. I think there must be some subconscious process going on that shuts down a lot of my natural bodily functions while in performance mode. I don't know whether this is to do with focus, adrenaline, or just that I am so incapable of multi-tasking that my brain has to stick itself on 'Do not disturb' for the duration of any set. Never sneezed, never broken wind, never once even needed to hold one in while on stage, and that's remarkable, considering that if you ask my daughter she will tell you that 'Farty-pants' is my middle name.

My childhood was dotted with examples of on-stage disaster or humiliation. The holy mother of all nosebleeds was just one of many.

During one performance my only job was to crash two cymbals together at a specific point in one particular song. My contribution had been boiled down to this single moment so they could still say I was involved in some way, but so they could also keep that involvement down to an absolute minimum. This is risk management 101, but it didn't work.

Mr Wilson was my music teacher, a rotund man with what seemed like impossibly small feet for his level of rotundness. It seemed inconceivable that he was able to stand on his own without just toppling forward. If he were an ornament you would think that surely he must have come loose from a base that had once offered him stability, unless you were just meant to lean him up against a vase or something like that.

Whenever he talked to me, I would make sure that I was stood slightly off to one side, just in case the natural laws of physics were suddenly to kick back into gear and he was to come toppling down in front of me. I would then only need to calmly take a small step out of the way rather than leaping for my life.

Mr Wilson had tried to teach me to play the piano. He had spent the best part of a school year doing so before asking me to stop.

'I don't think this is for you,' he had said. 'After a year we really should be further on than just playing the very basic single notes of "Jingle Bells" with one hand.'

He had a point and, to this day, a very basic 'Jingle Bells' with one hand is still all I can play on a piano. He mightn't have been able to teach me much, but what he did teach me is still in there somewhere, because if I ever cross paths with a piano around Christmas time I can't help but have a festive tinkle. If I'm honest, the time of the year is irrelevant as I've done it in August. It's all I've got, after all.

Mr Wilson had so little faith in me to contribute anything musical to the performance, beyond a single crash of cymbals at one specific moment in one specific song. I mean, it's not like I could mess that up, is it? Do you see where this is going?

My main job was to wait quietly for my moment and not interfere with the rest of the 'concert'. The problem with this plan, though, was that just waiting quietly was so boring. So impossibly boring that I started to fidget and fiddle with the cymbals that I had strapped to my hands.

I would always fidget and fiddle. I had been a chronic nail-biter since as far back as I can remember and I still struggle with it today, but if there was any object to hand I would fidget and fiddle with that until I likely broke whatever it was I was fidgeting and fiddling with. I could never just sit still or wait quietly as the stillness would be unbearable. I would always have to see what happened if I poked or prodded. I would pry, peel, pinch and press, flex, flatten, fold and flick. I would stretch, squeeze, shake and spin whatever I could get my hands on, and I would generally do this until something went snap. Have you figured out where this is going yet?

I realised I could use my fingers on the outside of the cymbals to spin them really quite fast, as far as they would spin before the central pin holding them onto the hand straps would become wound tight with tension, and then I would spin them back the other way. I would do this until the tension in that central pin would again build to a point where all spinning would come to a halt, upon which I would fire the two cymbals spinning back the other way with great force. I repeated this spinning game over and over. Little did I know it, but each time weakened the integrity of those central pins that were holding the cymbals to those leather hand straps. I mean, surely you've figured it out by now.

My moment finally came closer, closer and closer. I stopped spinning and waited. I waited for the moment upon which I was going to smash those cymbals together like nobody had ever smashed two cymbals together in the whole history of cymbal-smashing. Closer and closer, the moment was here! I flung my arms apart to enable the biggest smash of cymbals that my tiny frame could manage. Immediately, the central holding pins broke free and the two cymbals went flying off in opposite directions into the roomful of parents and teachers. I was just left there on the stage with my arms still flung wide apart, but with two now vacant leather straps hanging limply from each of them.

One cymbal careered off to the right, over the top of the audience as everybody ducked for cover, and crashed into a side wall. The other took a similar route to the left of the hall with everybody over there also ducking for cover, everybody apart from one lady who rather bravely managed to stop the cymbal dead in its tracks with her head. The cymbal hit the lady right in the side of her head and both cymbals came crashing to the floor making a humungous smashing noise only slightly after when I should have made the noise myself. It was barely noticeable and, in terms of the timing, I almost got away with it.

There was nothing anybody could do to blame me, though. I was just the poor kid who had enthusiastically flung his arms apart to smash those cymbals together as he had been instructed. Nobody knew about my secret spinning game, and nobody would find out: that would be my little secret. If the unfortunate lady had a problem, then she could take it up with the cymbal manufacturer for what seemed like an obvious quality-control issue in their cymbal-making factory.

I think I'm safe now, as I believe that the statute of limitations has passed on cymbal-related head injuries from the 1980s. Plus, that lady is no longer with us: she died shortly afterwards from completely unrelated brain injuries, honest.

The legal team has asked me to make quite clear that this lady did not actually die from being hit in the head by a flying cymbal. Talk about sucking all the fun out of a joke.

On a brighter note, though, I can tell you that those school benches were commonly known as Balance Benches, and they were manufactured by multiple companies based on a standardised design that best suited the requirements of schools primarily for PE and assembly purposes. Right, it's done. I'll be able to sleep tonight.

Chapter Four

The first memories I have of my eyesight not exactly being as it should relate to the blackboard in school. I could see the blackboard, I could see that there was writing on the blackboard, but I often couldn't make out what that writing was. Sometimes it would look like white squiggles with no real rhyme or reason or definition to it, a chalky soup of mystery notations that no amount of squinting or craning my neck forward would bring into focus. After all, if my sight was just half of what it should have been and I was sat a few feet away from the thing, then craning forward a few extra inches wasn't going to make a lot of difference, was it?

I think conversations were had and I was moved to be sat at the front of the class, but this didn't entirely solve the problem. I was told that I could get up out of my seat as and when I felt I needed to, something that was forbidden to all of the other children without express permission from the teacher, so I could take a much closer look and investigate these squiggles from any distance I deemed fit.

Even at that young age, though, I remember feeling very self-conscious about it and embarrassed by this special concession to the normal rules. I would often rather remain in my seat and just guess what I thought the squiggles might say rather than finding out for certain.

It's remarkable how primitive eye tests and knowledge were about my eye condition back in the early eighties. My very first eye test at about the age of four consisted of the specialist dropping a handful of ball bearings on the floor and telling me to pick them up, like he was throwing a handful of grain down for a chicken to feed on. On my successful completion of this task he reported that there was absolutely nothing to worry about and that my eyesight was perfectly fine, and possibly that if I was a young chicken I would certainly not go hungry, although this last comment I can't be 100 per cent sure of.

Nobody in my family seems to know why, but when I was five years old I was given a pair of glasses. Now, the thing about glasses is that they correct problems with the lens of the eye by placing fully functional machine-engineered pre-scription lenses in front of your underperforming rubbish biological ones. My problem, however, was nothing to do with the lenses at the front of my eyes, but rather the retinas at the back of them, and glasses would have done nothing to help with this. Putting a pair of glasses on me was like giving a pair of orthopaedic shoes to somebody whose legs were broken and just hoping that these new prescription shoes might somehow help them walk better.

So why was I given glasses? Who the hell knows? But there I was at the age of five sporting a pair of brown plastic NHS ones that came in a hard leatherette clam-shell case that smelled stuffier on the inside than a shoe shop on a summer's day.

This was my second year of infant school, year two, as it was known back then because logic still meant something in the school-year numbering system. These days, that would be year one as the first year of infants is now just known as Reception, which I think is a little confusing when the school also has an actual reception.

As part of a post-Christmas assembly that our class was putting on for the rest of the school, each child needed to stand up and say something that was new in their life and that they were grateful for. For most kids this meant just standing up and saying something they had received for Christmas that they were especially happy about. I know, very materialistic, but this was a Church of England school, not Catholic, so I think there was a general acceptance that Jesus was nothing without Santa.

The must-have toys for boys when I was five years old were things like Star Wars figures and vehicles, Lego sets, Action Man and Matchbox cars, which were all the rage, not accounting for anything as awesome as a bike or any football paraphernalia whatsoever.

My teacher thought it would be a good idea for me to shun this convention and that I should stand up and tell everybody about my brand-new pair of glasses. Now let me be clear: I had not received these glasses for Christmas. Santa was not in the business of eye health back in 1982 and my parents had not pretended he was. These had obviously been prescribed at some point around the festive period by an overly optimistic eye doctor and my teacher thought it would be good for me to claim them as my most exciting of new acquisitions.

But wait, that's not all.

'I don't think you should call them glasses,' she said. 'I think you should call them spectacles. It would be far more special to call them spectacles.'

Even back then I remember thinking that 'spectacles' was a bit of an odd choice of word for a five-year-old kid from Liverpool to use, but she was fairly insistent and, to be honest, I probably thought that surely she must know best.

One child got up and told the school that he'd got Ker-Plunk for Christmas and everybody cheered. I had also got Ker-Plunk for Christmas, and Buckeroo. A girl in my class stood up and announced to everybody that she'd got a new Barbie doll, and everybody clapped like she'd made it herself.

The theme did deviate slightly from Christmas presents, with one child who had just moved house telling everybody how happy he was now he had his own bedroom, which brought a cheer, and another informing the school of a new baby sister, a younger sibling being something many of the kids in the school could relate to, so they all clapped this new arrival. Generally speaking, though, the work of Santa featured very heavily in this assembly, with kids taking turns to stand up and announce the exciting new toy they had just received, before it was my turn.

I stood up, and in the proudest clearest voice I could manage, I announced to the whole school that I had got a new pair of spectacles.

Rather than the cheer or the round of applause that had followed each of the other children's announcements, I received laughter, laughter from the entire school. Laughter from every child sat cross-legged on the floor, all of the children in my class who were up front alongside me and, to be honest, probably many of the teachers as well.

'I got a new pair of spectacles.'

Of course they laughed. Not only is it a weird thing to stand up and announce alongside toys and new houses and baby sisters, but it is a ridiculous way to say it, 'spectacles', like I'd used a word from an era gone by. It's not even like I was standing up and announcing I had received the gift of better sight because, as we've already established, the spectacles were a pointless addition to my face and did absolutely nothing to help in that regard.

Even back then I knew the difference between a room full of people laughing at me and a room full of people laughing with me. I knew that this was certainly the first of those two things, and in that moment, I wanted the world to open up and swallow me whole, or at least to be turned invisible for ever.

I might have felt too self-conscious and embarrassed to get up and investigate the blackboard more closely, but this is the first moment I can remember of feeling humiliation and shame related to my less-than-ideal eyesight. Nobody was laughing because I couldn't see very well, or even because I had glasses on my face, it was simply because I'd said 'spectacles', but for me in that moment the two things were inextricable.

It's actually quite mad that I can whisk myself back to that moment over forty years ago and still relive it to some extent. With our earliest memories it does seem to be those moments of relative trauma that bed themselves in deepest, and that moment has managed to retain a fairly prime piece of real estate in my noggin ever since.

Maybe it's no surprise that I would one day go on to actively seek out and command the laughter of rooms full of people purely to make them all laugh entirely on my terms. Maybe this brief moment of humiliation and shame when I was five years old is what has subconsciously driven my desire to be the one in control of that laughter for the last two decades and counting. Maybe it's also got absolutely nothing to do with any of it, but a psychologist would possibly have a field day with this nonetheless.

Imagine that, though, a stand-up comedian for the last twenty-two years because a teacher made me say 'spectacles' when I was five years old. I mean, it seems like a stretch but I wouldn't put it past me.

My poor teacher was mortified that she'd been the one who had created this situation with her hugely misjudged idea to make spectacles sound cool, and she apologised profusely to me in my red-faced, teary, snotty aftermath.

Just for the record, though, this was the only time during my five years at that school when I would encounter any negativity from my fellow classmates towards my less-than-perfect eyesight, and even in this instance I hardly blame them. I probably would have laughed as well if it hadn't been me.

My sight issues were always just something that had been accepted by my peers, I think because we had all started off together as young kids without any slant towards the meanness or judgement that would one day taint us all.

The fact that my eyesight was slowly deteriorating in their presence meant that, like me, they didn't really notice it happening either. It was just something that we were all acclimatising to at the same time.

I do remember, though, when I was about eight years old and had long since got rid of those pointless spectacles, another kid joined our class who had a pair on his face that looked like they were doing the job of five pairs in one. A really thick pair of bottle-top glasses that looked like they must have given his neck a good workout. He would look at things from a funny angle and squint at you through these glasses like they were causing more of an obstruction to his sight than solving any problems he may have had.

The children in the playground were not quite as accepting of this newcomer with his funny eyes as they were of me with mine. They would make fun of him and his hefty eyewear with a fair bit of name-calling, finger-pointing and mean chants, although I can't remember what any of those names or chants were. What I do remember was feeling awful for him and wondering why they were like that with him but not me. I would come to realise that it was just because, although a touch of meanness was blossoming in us all, I was part of the furniture and he was the new guy who was different in some way from everybody else . . . everybody else but not me. I knew that we had more in common than separated us.

I felt guilty for not standing up for him when the other kids would torment him out on the playground, guilty that he was being bullied and that I was not, guilty that, although

I felt sorry for him, I was scared to make friends with him in case I would bring the same fate upon myself.

I'm not sure if or how this experience of somebody else's torment may have affected me at that young age, but I still remember it now, don't I, so I'm sure that in some way it did. I think it likely made me wary and anxious of entering new environments in the future where I would be the newcomer with the funny eyes, not the piece of furniture that everybody was used to.

One day he did not come in to school and I never saw him again. I hope that, forty years on, everything worked out for that eight-year-old kid with the funny-looking glasses. Sorry, David.

Although I have plenty of memories of seeing things throughout my childhood, I've never really known what perfect regular eyesight is meant to be. I've always been operating on some form of reduced visual service, so 20/20 is something I can only try to imagine.

When I was about seven years old we had a school sports day that was held in the playing field at the back of the school, and this particular school sports day is memorable for two main reasons.

First, the sack race. If I was to ask you to picture in your mind what the sack race is, you would imagine children in sacks, clutching the top of the sack in front of them while leaping forwards over and over again as fast as they are able. That's it. There is no alternative. There aren't exactly other versions or techniques. The sack race is as standard as standard things come.

Well, that's what I thought anyway, but it just so happened that one of my dad's friends was around at our house a few days before the big event and, luckily for me, he was a bit of an expert when it came to the sack race. I was all ears.

'Listen,' he said. 'Instead of putting your legs in the sack and jumping, like everybody else, work your feet right into the corners and just run.'

'What? Just run?' I asked. This advice seemed both insane and revolutionary to me. How had nobody else ever thought of doing this?

'Yeah, you'll batter everybody,' he said, and then, leaning in and speaking in hushed tones as if sharing some top-secret information, 'Everybody thinks it's better to jump and that the rules say it's what you should do, but it's not better and you don't have to. It's better to put your feet in the corners and run. Trust me.'

This was incredible advice. I was so grateful that he had decided to share this top-secret winning strategy with me. I couldn't wait to try it out for myself and wipe the floor with the rest of the field as they tried to jump their way to second place while I was already claiming my prize.

The day rolled around and all of a sudden it was time, time for the sack race, time for me to go down in the history books for setting a new international global world record for the school sack race, seven-year-old classification obviously, let's not get carried away.

We all got into position at the start of the race and clambered into our sacks.

Losers, I thought, as I worked my feet into the corners,

like I had been told to do. These bozos aren't going to know what's hit them.

'On your marks . . .' called one of the teachers. 'Get set . . .'

I was poised and ready to –

'Go!' she shouted.

The rest of the field started to jump. I tried to do as I was told and just run, but there wasn't enough slack sack available down at feet level to facilitate anything even close to a running motion. Straight away my feet got caught up in the sack and I smacked down face first onto the ground.

The rest of the field were leaping away from me now, but I got up and I tried again. As soon as I attempted to run, my feet got caught up in the sack and I smacked right down onto my face again.

There is a really great saying that can be perfectly applied to the next few minutes of my life on that playing field: 'Insanity is doing the same thing over and over again and expecting different results.' Such a shame that I had never heard of this at the age of seven because it would have come in handy, and it couldn't have been proven to be more true, as I tried to run inside that sack over and over again, immediately smacking down onto my face every single time.

I might have struggled to see the blackboard in class, but I had no trouble seeing the ground rushing up and hitting me in the face over and over again.

And thus played out what can best be described as the worst last place there has ever been in a school sports-day sack race.

The Simpsons was still some years away from being created, but I swear that Matt Groening must have been present on that day and found his inspiration for little baby Maggie Simpson in my catastrophic sack-race strategy: her stumbling with every attempted step from inside her swaddle cloth and repeatedly and relentlessly smacking her own face into the ground without ever learning a single lesson. It would all feel a little too close to this sack-race experience when I saw it some years later.

The second reason that this sports day was so memorable was the egg-and-spoon race.

Still feeling quite bashed and bruised in both body and spirit, the egg-and-spoon race was an opportunity to turn the tables and try to claw back a little bit of dignity. My strategy here was not that dissimilar to what it had been for the sack race, to just run, run like the wind.

'On your marks . . .' said one of the teachers.

This time I was gonna take no prisoners.

'Get set . . .'

No mercy.

'Go!' she shouted.

Everybody set off quite precariously. Everybody except me, that was. I ran like nobody had ever run in an egg-and-spoon race before. Not just like the wind, but like the wind on a really windy day, like my life depended on it. I passed the finish line while the rest of the field were still teetering along some distance behind, like they were handling radioactive isotopes. Every so often one of them would have to stoop to pick up their downed egg and rebalance it on the spoon.

Smug doesn't come close to describing the expression on my still grass-stained face and how I felt inside.

Losers, I thought. They'll be talking about this race for years. They'll probably rename the playing field after me. They'll probably even ... What do you mean disqualified?

It seems that in order to enable my lightning quick never-before-seen speed in an egg-and-spoon race, I had maybe possibly used my thumb to hold the egg onto the spoon, maybe just a little bit.

The truth is, yes, I did do that, but the truth is also that I honestly didn't think anybody would be able to see me doing it, and surely it was okay to cheat if nobody could see that's what you were doing. Surely?

I'd had my thumb so subtly positioned on the very end of the egg so that only a hawk would have been able to spot my sneaky tactics, or so I'd thought anyway. As I was discovering, though, everybody's proper eyesight was actually a lot better than I had realised.

Damn them and their 20/20 vision, whatever that was anyway.

Chapter Five

Back at home, and my parents were evidently considering developing the family in some way, but money must have been a major factor when deciding in exactly which way this should be done.

'What would you rather?' my mum asked me. 'To have a baby brother or sister, that we get a car, or that we move house?'

I didn't hesitate. 'A baby brother or sister,' I said.

They must have got straight to work, because within the next year and shortly after my seventh birthday a baby sister arrived, closely followed by a car and a new house anyway.

Seven years it had taken my parents to get over the trauma of having me before they were able to even think about potentially putting themselves through anything like that again. Luckily for my parents, though, my sister Louise was the exact opposite of me in many ways and caused them both absolutely no trouble whatsoever for . . . well, for ever, really.

My sister was brilliant and still is today, and although I could be a bit of a nuisance and a torment to her over the coming years, and vice versa I might add, we have always been very close.

It turns out that the car, on the other hand, was shit,

although at the time I thought it was the coolest thing in the world. It was an Austin Allegro, and quite possibly its only redeeming feature aside from it being an incredibly efficient smoke machine, was that it once broke down directly outside a garage.

After the Allegro came a Ford Fiesta, which had its own problems for a child. It had two options when it came to the seat covers: naked or hairy. Naked meant those faux-leather vinyl seats that got hotter than a frying-pan if the car was left in the sun so would burn the skin off the back of your thighs if you had shorts on, which, of course, you did because the sun was out! Hairy, though, meant hideous elasticated yeti-like coverings that shed copious amounts of hair if an even slightly sticky hand was to come anywhere near them. The number of times I'd enjoyed some form of candy floss or other sticky confectionery while in that car, only to end up with car hair stuck all over my hands and then in my mouth for the entire journey, thinking I'd probably rather have the skin burned off the back of my thighs.

The house move was definitely a step up, although hardly the most adventurous, as you could still see the old one from the new one. Yes, even I could.

Opposite us had lived the Kellys in a similar two-bedroom terrace house. They had recently upped sticks and moved about three houses around the corner into a three-bedroom semi. I hope part of their reason for moving wasn't that they didn't like living opposite us, because we ended up doing exactly the same thing and moving around the corner to live opposite them again.

I loved growing up on those streets. From such a young age the neighbourhood kids would spend weekends and school holidays roaming free with that small network of streets and alleyways as our playground.

There were a lot of kids in the neighbourhood, but there were five of us, all the same age, who would play and hang out on those streets and at each other's houses.

Paul was the first to join Neil and me to make up a trio that was incredibly tight from a very young age, but a few years later Peter and Theo would join us to make up a quintet that would pretty much do everything together until we reached about fifteen years old.

Football was everything, to us kids and to the city as a whole. One of my favourite memories is of the houses, cars and taxis decorated in reds and blues in May of 1986 when Liverpool and Everton were to meet in the FA Cup Final for the very first time. I remember the day so vividly, of the sun being out, of the smiles in the streets, and of Liverpool winning, of course.

Street football existed in all of its forms, and for any number of kids who were available at any given time: from full matches with the whole neighbourhood out in force, to Headers and Volleys, which were the only two ways you were allowed to score, and Three and In, which was the number of goals you had to score before it was your turn in goal. Each of those last two could be played with three, but even just two of us could spend the whole day playing football against each other, each attacking an empty goal and having to dribble around parked cars to get there. It really didn't matter just so long as we were chasing and kicking a ball.

Even without a friend, I've probably spent days upon days of my childhood playing football alone, just kicking a football against a wall while providing radio-style commentary for the game I was playing inside my mind.

'McMahon, brings it down, plays it to Dalglish. Dalglish takes it past one, past two, through to Rush. Rush shoots . . . Goal!'

It makes me wonder what kids used to do before football was on the TV or the radio, before commentary was a thing. Did they just used to kick a ball around in silence?

We would play on the streets until we were individually called home for our tea, leaving just one child who would then decide whether to continue kicking a ball against a wall on his own or whether to call it quits as well.

Everybody's mum, it was always mums, would venture out into the street yelling the name of their child until they got some kind of feedback that either their call had reached its target or the message was being passed on.

For anybody reading this who isn't a British northerner, tea is probably what you call your dinner, or even your supper, if you're a bit posh like that. Your main evening meal. For us dinner was what we would call lunch, or your Sunday dinner, and supper was just a pre-bedtime snack, like some toast and jam with a glass of milk. Breakfast was always just breakfast, and nobody had ever heard of brunch.

My daughter corrects me on this all the time because I'm raising a bloody southerner, aren't I?

'Come and get your tea,' I'll say.

'It's dinner, Daddy, dinner.'

There were three parallel alleyways where we lived, or entries as they were known to us back then. 'The end entry' was L-shaped and started behind the house where we'd lived on Craigside, running behind the entire street before turning left at the far end. 'The middle entry' was a straight affair that was, you guessed it, the middle of the three and ran behind the houses on the other side of the street. The entry that was the furthest of the three was known as 'the dirty entry' and this one was absolutely filthy. It was full of rubbish and junk and all kinds of detritus that we would often end up trying to use for some kind of filthy play.

One game that the local neighbourhood kids would play when there were a lot of us was something we rather imaginatively called Dustbin Mange. This basically involved getting one kid and sticking them in a filthy bin so that they got the mange, basically a bit of bin juice or bin filth on them. Then that kid who had the dustbin mange would have to chase down the rest of us and try to rub their bin juice and/or filth onto one of us, therefore spreading the mange. Now there would be two of them chasing the rest of us down and trying to spread the dustbin mange. This would continue until the entire filthy mange-infested population of neighbourhood kids was chasing down just one child to rub their mange on him. It was glorious!

Underpants Mud Bombs was another classic. We would climb over the wall into an old folks' residential home, where there would inevitably be some rather large pairs of massive Y-fronts hanging on the washing line. We would drop a mud bomb down into the gusset of a pair, and then explode it by smacking our hands together either side of the pants so that the mud exploded out of the top of the pants. The game would be to see how many pairs of underpants we could explode before getting spotted and chased. Classic!

On one occasion Neil and I spent all day in the dirty entry, building a go-kart out of an old pram frame, some rusty bits of metal we'd found, and a shit load of this lovely soft dense fibrous material that had been perfect for making a padded seat. It turns out that what we'd actually done was build our go-kart out of asbestos insulation that had been dumped there rather than being disposed of in the much-preferred and legal manner.

One story that Neil will never let me forget is when two empty skips had been left at the end of my road, with one being stacked inside the other. We were taking it in turns to climb on top of the edge of these skips, and then we would try to walk around that edge without falling either into the skips or off them completely. Unfortunately for me I fell, but I wasn't lucky enough to fall into the skips. Nor was I lucky enough to fall off them completely. I did in fact just drop straight down, one of my legs slipping into the narrow gap between the walls of the two skips, causing me to land right on the solid metal rim, right on my knackers.

I imagine that you are wincing and crossing your legs as you read this, even the ladies. This wasn't the end of my predicament, though, was it? Because I couldn't even unseat myself from the unbearable saddle I was now straddling. My leg that was down the gap between the two skips was wedged tight. And Neil's attempts to work me loose were proving futile as my poor little knackers throbbed with every attempt. In the end he had no choice but to go and get my dad to come and lift me free. I mean, he was a fireman so if he couldn't do it I was really screwed.

Four decades have passed and Neil has never forgotten this, and he will likely tell this story at my funeral if I happen to go before him. I only hope that, by including it here, I've kind of stolen his thunder a little.

The thing that is truly remarkable from all of this is that it's a miracle my daughter even exists. I mean, I can't believe I didn't take my bollocks completely out of commission on that day before they'd even been brought fully online.

I do feel sorry for my daughter and the other kids around where we live. They just don't have the same freedom we had when I was a child. Even at the age of six or seven I had significantly more freedom and independence than my daughter has now at the age of twelve. To be able to play out in the local streets, to have significant time away from parents or guardians, to have a certain degree of autonomy and be in control of your own movement and play, and to come home when called for your tea. All of this was such a valuable and liberating part of my childhood and it's sad that it is denied to a huge number of kids today.

I understand that even back in the eighties there might have been a difference in what was allowed or even possible in the streets and neighbourhoods of Liverpool compared to where we live now, but I don't think time has been a friend to children in this regard: many streets that were once full of the sound of kids playing outside during the weekends and summer holidays are now very quiet indeed.

No children play out in the streets around where I live. All activities away from the home and playdates are facilitated by the parents. Yeah, kids today have got so many things a lot easier than the generations that came before them, but they are missing out on so much that we all took for granted. Of course I wouldn't want my twelve-year-old daughter to spend all day building an asbestos death trolley in an alleyway somewhere, but I do feel sad that she can't.

Chapter Six

My behaviour in school had continued to be a bit of a problem and I was getting myself into trouble on a fairly regular basis. It wasn't anything too serious, but I was a disruptive presence in the classroom and was still spending considerable amounts of time either stood up facing a wall or sat outside the headmaster's office. If I'm honest, I think I was what the teachers would technically have referred to behind closed doors as 'a little shit'.

My mum and dad used to dread going in for parents' evenings because there was never good news.

'Don't worry, Mr and Mrs McCausland. Chris is a model pupil at this school. He sits down, has impeccable focus, never gets into trouble and does all his work to a very high standard. He's gonna go far, I tell you, far!'

Cue the wavy dreamy effect as we realise that was all in my parents' shared imagination, as they sit on two tiny chairs, glassy-eyed, while a teacher rants about my behavioural issues, flecks of teacher-spit hitting them in the face as they pretend not to notice.

Every Wednesday our class would board a coach and head off to the Norris Green swimming baths for a lesson.

Well, most of them would. I would often not be on that coach due to some behavioural incident for which I was being punished.

Liverpool's Norris Green swimming baths was a fairly dated facility even back in the early 1980s. It consisted of three separate and very functional pools. There was a main pool that ran from a few feet deep to pretty damn deep; a smaller pool that ran from about a single foot deep to what still felt to me like pretty damn deep but was probably just a tiny bit more than I could reach with my toes at the age of seven or eight; and a tiny square pool that was apparently just for diving into from a high board, although I'd never actually seen anybody doing this.

That tiny pool had an unfathomable depth and I found it truly terrifying. I think it may have been a hundred feet deep, or at least twelve, but either way, on the rare occasions I would make it into the building, I would avoid walking anywhere even remotely within its vicinity just in case its sheer gravity dragged me in and I was never seen again.

I have never liked swimming. I have never liked swimming because I have never been any good at it. I honestly think I am just not biologically capable of staying afloat without some kind of inflatable or polystyrene buoyancy aid. Part of the reason I have never been any good at it probably stems from the fact that I didn't make it onto the coach very often with all of the other kids.

'No swimming for you this Wednesday, Christopher McCausland,' is a phrase I heard a lot.

'See what your parents have to say about that when you

get home and have to tell them why you were not allowed to go swimming.'

The idea was that not only was not going swimming a punishment, but also that returning home with an unused towel and trunks would let your parents know you hadn't been swimming, so you would then have no choice but to tell them what you had done to exclude yourself from that week's excursion.

Well, I wasn't having any of that, was I? On my way out of school I would run into the toilets under the pretence of needing a wee, and very quickly give my trunks a run under the tap before rolling them up in my dry unused towel to create the suitably damp illusion of a well-behaved child who had been swimming with the rest of his class. The only missing ingredient in my cunning plan was the smell of chlorine, but my mum never noticed this omission and I got away with this ridiculous charade for the remaining two years of my time at the school.

I have never taken to swimming, even later in life. All I ever managed to achieve before becoming a teenager was my twenty-five-metre swimming certificate for front crawl. This did come on the back of my ten-metre swimming certificate for front crawl, so I suppose it did demonstrate a rather impressive improvement of 150 per cent on my previous achievement, which is not to be sniffed at. The only reason I managed that twenty-five-metre distance, though, and no further, was that twenty-five metres was about as far as I could swim in one single breath.

Even to this day I'm no better. I have about the same

ability to float as that rubber brick they used to throw in for us to fetch out again. Nobody has ever been able to teach me how to tread water without it looking like I'm being electrocuted. Electrocuted for approximately twenty seconds or so, before running out of energy and slowly starting to sink to the bottom.

My daughter puts me to shame in the water, which I'm grateful for as the last thing we need is two rubber bricks in this family.

I think that a great deal of my discomfort in a pool comes from not being able to see where the nearest side is. Cue the tiny violin, the tiny waterlogged violin. That sense of disorientation likely just adds to my panic while I'm attempting to tread water, and that panic just speeds up my demise.

The panic is amplified significantly if I'm ever unlucky enough to find myself in the sea. I am not a fan of the sea. I mean, don't get me wrong, I'm glad it exists as it's somewhere to keep fish and without it sharks would probably have legs by now, and who wants that? I just don't belong in there and I would be fairly happy in life if I never entered its domain again.

Long before my daughter was born, when myself and my wife Patricia were still in the early phase of our relationship, Patricia took me to visit her homeland of Brazil. We were spending the day down on the beach, which, if I'm honest, I'm not a massive fan of either. It's just hot dirt, really, isn't it?

She wanted to take me out into the sea, a plan I was not really comfortable with at all. I should have stuck to my guns and remained either firmly planted back on all of that lovely hot dirt, or at the most just sploshing around in the shallow bits of cold wet dirt, like an oversized child, but I am weak and she is relentless, so in we went.

She dragged me out just ever so fractionally past my comfort zone, probably just a gnat's cock beyond the point where I could reach the bottom with my toes, but a gnat's cock might as well have been three miles. I was already blind and felt not in control of my own safety or movement, just entirely dependent on Patricia and at the mercy of the sea, with no real idea in which direction safety might be located if I should need it.

At least in a pool there is safety in all directions. Yeah, sure, there might be one side that is closer than the others but, generally speaking, I could probably make any of them in a single manic breath if need be. In the sea, though, safety lies in only one direction, and even after just a few seconds without the seabed under my feet, I had no idea in which direction that was. If a freak wave had separated the two of us in that moment I would have likely just used my single breath to swim twenty-five metres further out to sea before flailing about for a few moments and sinking slowly to the bottom.

I do wonder if I'd be more comfortable in the water now if I'd been better behaved at school and had more opportunity to learn how to swim, or at least had learned how not to drown quite so quickly.

I do know now that I was an ADHD kid, and although this affects me differently in adulthood, I can see how it fuelled a lot of my impulsive and disruptive behavioural problems back then.

The problem was that ADHD did not exist in the 1980s. I mean, it obviously did, but it didn't have a name and we were oblivious to it. Instead, there were just kids who were a pain in the arse and I was one of those kids.

I was diagnosed with ADHD about ten years ago when I was in my late thirties. It had actually never crossed my mind as being a possibility. I was just very aware that as an adult I would usually end up doing anything but the thing I should actually be doing, and thinking about anything else but the thing I should actually be thinking about. I was a procrastinator, an under-achiever, a useless piece of crap who couldn't control his own mind properly – and why couldn't I stop biting my nails? It had been nearly four decades now!

As an adult I would zone out of conversations, fidget and fiddle. My mind would wander. It did occur to me that maybe it was because I couldn't see who I was talking to – I was without the visual reminder that I was having a conversation and should probably keep paying attention to the person stood in front of me with their mouth flapping open and closed like that.

I thought that the fidgeting and fiddling and nail-biting might have been to do with stress, but stress would come and go, while these restless behaviours remained as a constant.

I suppose that losing my sight and living life in the dark has brought along its own anxiety that's always under the surface to some degree, like my own personal cosmic background radiation reminding me that something big and traumatic has happened in the past, and that I should always remain on my toes and be at least a little bit nervous about the world around me. I had spent a lifetime trying to ignore this background anxiety, but maybe it was this that was causing me to fidget and fiddle and chew my fingers as much as I did.

I did come to understand that my inability to focus on things was often not really a problem with my inability to focus, but rather the opposite: my inability to stop focusing on things I shouldn't be focusing on. It wasn't that I had no attention, but rather too much of it and for the wrong things.

How can I sit there and work on my taxes when I've just wondered when Liverpool are next playing, and now that's all I can think about? I'll have to check it first or I'll get nothing done.

How can I listen to everything Patricia is telling me about the food shopping and how there is barely anything left to eat, when the mere mention of apples made my mind wander to the new iPhone that is coming out soon and –

'Sorry, what was that about eggs?'

How can I write a book when for the last hour all I've been thinking about is what's the biggest rubber brick you can buy? It's exhausting being me sometimes.

The bottom line is that I was convinced that all of this was fixable, that I just needed to train myself to think better, to concentrate more, to procrastinate less, achieve more and stop being such a useless piece of – you get the point.

If you look through my audiobook library on my Audible account, you will see that it is absolutely swamped with self-help books until that diagnosis around 2015. I was a self-help-book junkie and was almost at the stage of needing a self-help book to help me stop reading self-help books. I would move from one to the next, finding them motivational while I was reading them, but being unable to retain or implement much of any use from any of them in the long run.

One day, though, I was crashed out at home in front of the telly, and a documentary happened to be on about adults who had been diagnosed with ADHD quite late in life. I had heard of ADHD, but only really in terms of explaining the disruptive and hyperactive nature of more recent generations of young children in school.

I had even joked with my parents that I'd probably had ADHD when I was a kid before it was even invented. Until I stumbled across that TV show, though, I didn't know that ADHD was something adults could have and, more importantly, that if you had it as a child you have it for life.

Watching those strangers on the TV and listening to their stories of all of the things they struggled with as adults, it was honestly like the programme was about me.

I did a bit of research – it's always nice when the thing I want to focus on and the thing I can't stop focusing on align as I can finally get stuff done. I made an appointment with my doctor and was referred for an NHS assessment before getting yourself diagnosed was anywhere near as popular as it is today. The assessment was very thorough and as part of it the psychologist even spoke at length to my mum about my childhood, my hyperactive and disruptive behaviour at home and at school, and about the shitload of awful school reports I had received over the years.

His conclusion was that I was certainly textbook ADHD as a child, and obviously still struggling with many of its symptoms today.

Now, it's worth pointing out here that ADHD within the world of comedy is as ridiculously abundant as entitlement and privilege are at Eton: it's everywhere, the place is literally dripping in it.

It's hardly unique, and there is probably a chapter on ADHD in every comedian's autobiography written in the past ten years.

There have been many steps taken to increase the visibility of under-represented and minority groups in comedy on TV over recent years, but the one aspect of the human condition that needs no help here is this particular corner of neuro-diversity: it's everywhere you look.

In fact, two places where you will find a far greater representation of people with ADHD than you would out in the wild are the world of stand-up comedy, and prison. The impulsivity, the risk-taking, the adrenaline and attention-seeking, the inability to conform and fit to a standard nine-to-five, the resistance to rules and constraints, these are all qualities that can lead somebody to try stand-up for the first time and can ultimately help to make a good comedian. The same traits, however, can also lead to robbing a bank or stealing a car. So, obviously, it was after getting away with the first of these but then crashing a few stolen cars that I thought maybe I'd best give comedy a go, I suppose.

My diagnosis didn't exactly solve anything, but it 100 per cent changed how I thought about myself. I knew now that it wasn't just me being useless. I knew I'd been trying to fix a problem in a way that just wasn't fixable.

It has also made me look back at that younger me with a lot more understanding and admiration. I was trying to function with ADHD as I also lost my sight. All of these ADHD traits were getting me into trouble on a fairly regular basis and would ultimately make anything greater than mediocre academic success a huge achievement.

I do think that idea of my sight loss playing some role in my attention and behavioural issues may have some merit, as it's probably the case that when I was a kid, unable to see and visually focus on the things my classmates were able to see and visually focus on, that boredom and distraction could kick in easily and the ADHD would love that. Also the anxiety and pent-up frustration I must have carried with me to some extent through childhood as I was losing my sight must have caused me to act even more impulsively than I would have done with the ADHD alone. Surely?

What I'm saying, I suppose, is that I am 100 per cent convinced now that the combination of ADHD and the experience of losing my sight corrupted an angel. I hope you're on board with that hypothesis?

Good, I'm glad we're in agreement.

But just one more thing before we move on. The biggest rubber brick you can buy seems to weigh just ten pounds – less than five kilogrammes! That's a bit disappointing, isn't it?

Chapter Seven

When I reached nine years old and my sight was fast approaching that level of roughly 25 per cent remaining, it was decided that it would be best for me to leave the mainstream school I had attended for the last five years and to enter specialist education.

My headmaster was probably delighted at this news as he would have so much of his time back and wouldn't have to see me sitting outside his office any more. It wouldn't surprise me if he threw a little party once I'd gone.

I was okay with this plan. In fact I was quite excited by the idea of attending a school that was better suited to my needs with other kids who would have similar issues to what I had. In truth, I had been struggling in school, hardly able to see the blackboard and my textbooks at all by now, and in 1986 my school just didn't have the facilities or equipment to make any of it more accessible for me.

There was a school in Liverpool that was specifically for kids with sight problems, and I would attend it now until I had completed my GCSEs. Well, kind of. I would go away to boarding school for a short spell when I was eleven, but I would return a couple of years later due to being homesick.

My new specialist school was Catholic and the head-mistress was a nun. I was not Catholic, my last school was Church of England and I wasn't really even that either. My parents did not attend church, I hadn't been christened, and they never said anything at home that even suggested the existence of a god. My only exposure to religion had come through school. Well, if I thought that the Church of England had been a lot, I would soon realise that I'd been drinking from the diet font all these years, because the Catholic beverage was full fat, made your teeth feel funny, and was likely to lead to diabetes if consumed with too much regularity or enthusiasm. This point cannot be scientifically verified, but neither can all the God stuff so I think they're all right with that.

The heavier religion got, the more I realised how nuts a lot of it was, and I think I actually reached this point while I was still quite happy to believe in Santa. The world in seven days? A massive boat with two of every animal on it? Parting the seas? Coming back from the dead? Nonsense. A big fat man in a red suit who delivers presents to every child on earth in a magic sleigh pulled by flying reindeer? Now that I can get on board with.

The nun who was headmistress at my new school was actually all right, to be honest. Yes, okay, she might have believed some absolute bananas and bored me close to death on several occasions during school services, and she may have had to reprimand me more times than I can remember, but in the grand scheme of things she was also fairly reasonable and decent, and probably about as normal a lady as a nun can be. I know this because the school shared grounds with a convent for elderly nuns so there were a lot of them around, and I think it's fair to say that most of them were horrible, mean-spirited, spiteful and physically vicious old ladies, who seemed to resent everything. There was no corporal punishment in schools any more, no hitting or caning allowed, but those old nuns were rough. They would grab hold of you and squeeze and pinch and try to leave a mark if they caught you having even the slightest amount of fun in their presence.

My disruptive behaviour in class had persisted throughout my time at this new school, and parents' evenings had not improved for my poor parents. My school reports were often hideous collections of scathing diatribes about my lack of attention, inability to sit still in class, and my tendency to interrupt and make jokes at inappropriate times.

'Thinks he's the class clown, no good will ever come of this' was a sentiment shared more than a few times over the years.

Well, this clown appreciates your feedback and is willing to accept that maybe you were part right but not entirely, as admittedly my desire to say the funny thing at the wrong time has definitely got me into trouble on a fair few occasions over the years, but it also pays the bills. So, let's call that one a score draw and say no more about it, eh?

Underneath all of the behavioural problems, I think my teachers could see that I was a clever kid, and so the most commonly used words that featured in my school reports were probably 'potential' and 'however'.

'Chris has got the potential to do anything he sets his mind to, however, he's a little shit.'

I'm paraphrasing – kind of.

As I was approaching the transition into secondary educa-tion it was suggested that I would likely benefit from attend-ing a different specialist school that was more academically focused. The only problem with this new school was that it was in Worcester and that was well over a hundred miles away from our house by car. A hundred miles is a long way for anybody, but to an eleven-year-old kid in the eighties it might as well have been the moon as the distance was already fairly inconceivable.

I know that my parents were very apprehensive about packing me off to attend a school that was over a hundred miles away, and I can only imagine how much they must have felt caught between the sadness of having to say goodbye so regularly and the desire to do what was best for me in the long run.

The truth was, I actually liked the school. It was a boarding school but not in the traditional sense of what a boarding school is. It wasn't something that was access-ible only to a certain demographic or wealth bracket, or to parents who thought their children would thrive and learn discipline better in a boarding environment. Nor was it single sex or antiquated in its traditions and ceremony. This was a boarding school for kids of both sexes, who were from all walks of life, and who simply shared a similar struggle of not being able to see either properly or at all.

When I arrived I was allocated to a house where I was going to be living under the supervision of a house mother. I know what images this conjures up in the mind, of houses being no more than collections of stuffy old dormitories overseen by an authoritarian figure who would teach independence through strict discipline and punishment. It could not have been further from that reality, though, with my house being an actual house, a brand-new massive house that had only just been built. This house had lots of bedrooms for kids aged from eleven through to sixteen, and our house mother was wonderful.

Sheila lived in this house with her own family, and the Cuddys were such a lovely caring family-away-from-family that they made this eleven-year-old feel like he fit right in straight away.

It was conker season when I first arrived in Worcester and, with a lot of free time on my hands outside the school days, I set about amassing what can best be described as a shit ton of conkers.

Although my sight was diminishing at a rate that hugely put me at a disadvantage in the general population, here in a school full of kids like me, I was actually one of the more capable at this stage of my sight loss. There were plenty of kids who were fully blind and had never been able to see a thing, and others whose sight was already significantly worse than mine was. I am ashamed to say, but also a little bit proud of the initiative in that young version of me, that I saw a market here and very quickly became the guy to go to if you wanted some conkers.

One conker for 10p or ten conkers for 50p was the going rate that I arbitrarily decided seemed quite reasonable. I'm not gonna lie, I made a killing selling conkers to blind kids. I saw a gap in the market and I cornered it. After all, it wasn't like they could get them themselves, was it? In the kingdom of the blind, the partially sighted kid with the conkers is king, or something like that.

This initiative, though, was seen as taking advantage of those less fortunate than myself, and I was straight up in front of the head before I'd even learned a thing.

This school was led by a reverend. I know, from a nun to a reverend. I was only ever going to end up either really, really religious or resistant to it in all of its forms. There was never likely to be any middle ground for me.

I'm not sure whether the reverend was genuinely outraged by my business sense, or just a little concerned that he now had a school full of blind kids trying to play conkers with each other. We've all read something in more recent years about how even regular mainstream schools have been banning conkers in the playground due to health and safety concerns. Well, imagine the carnage when those kids are blind or can hardly see a thing. I had only just arrived but had apparently become entirely responsible for the largest number of instances of personal injury that the school had ever seen. There were smashed-up knuckles, bruised faces, and even a couple of chipped teeth. One poor kid had his glasses smashed right off his face.

I'd like to think I defended my actions and every child's right to have conkers with some kind of catchy slogan that the National Rifle Association would have been proud of.

'Conkers don't kill people. It's people that kill people.'

But I suppose the reality was that blind kids with conkers were definitely more likely to kill other blind kids with conkers, and my business was therefore shut down with immediate effect. I was also banned from ever running a conker business in the future, and to the best of my knowledge that ban is still in place.

You might wonder what a boarding school for blind kids was actually like, well, the truth is that it was just like any regular school, really, but one where every day was odd-socks day.

Looking back, I can see how my two years at this school really did start to shape me. I learned to be practically and emotionally independent in ways that I probably wouldn't have become for quite some time if I was still living at home. When not actually in classes, I spent a lot of the time living among kids who were a lot older than me. I think this made me very comfortable in the company of my elders and in some ways more socially mature than I otherwise would have become at that age.

I was introduced to music and films that I likely wouldn't have heard or seen for a few years yet at least. A year or so earlier my favourite film by quite some distance had been *Beverly Hills Cop*, and I would watch it over and over and over again, often several times a week. I was completely captivated by Eddie Murphy as Axel Foley, and even now I can't really believe that he was only around twenty-two years old at the time of filming.

A few months back I rewatched *Beverly Hills Cop* and could not believe how utterly graphic and inappropriate the language was for a ten-year-old child. It's certainly not a kids' film, but my tape was recorded off the telly, so I can only imagine that my version had been highly edited by the BBC to make it far more suitable for an earlier broadcast slot. Well, either that or my parents just didn't give a goddamn shit motherfucker.

At the start of my second year in Worcester, the film *A Nightmare on Elm Street 5* was released in the cinema, and by then, at the age of twelve, I had already seen the first four, thanks to some of the older kids I was living with. These films had been Sunday-afternoon viewing, so to me at that age, Freddy Krueger was not this horrifically violent and sexually gratuitous, foul-mouthed and rated-18 icon of adult-only horror. He was more like a comic-book character, a wise-talking supervillain with badass one-liners and the coolest glove in the history of gloves.

By this point I was allowed to head off into Worcester town centre independently, and the cinema there had provided the children of the school with free passes to watch any film they liked for free, within reason obviously.

I wandered in and showed the guy my pass and said that I was there to watch the new *Nightmare on Elm Street* film.

'Err, yeah,' he said. 'That one is rated eighteen, I'm afraid, so I won't be able to let you in to see that, but we do have *Turner & Hooch* starting soon.'

'Yes,' I agreed, 'but *A Nightmare on Elm Street* is only rated eighteen because of how scary it looks, and I'm from the blind school and can't see the screen, so that doesn't really apply to me, does it?'

I know, what a load of bollocks. I was certainly full of shit when I was twelve years old.

'Oh, yeah,' said the guy. 'I never thought of that. Well, if you can't see the screen, in you go. Enjoy the film.'

Honestly, I think that one single moment in my life is the closest I've ever felt to being an actual Jedi.

'I'm not the twelve-year-old you're looking for.' Or something to that effect.

'Yes, you're not the twelve-year-old I'm looking for. In you go. Enjoy the film.'

My two years at Worcester didn't just kick my second decade of life off with a full exposure to the offerings of 1980s home cinema: they also provided me with a similar exposure to some of the older kids' kick-ass tastes in music that it would certainly have taken me longer to find on my own.

I had arrived at Worcester as a massive Michael Jackson fan, but this wouldn't last for too long. Hair metal was the genre that drew me in the most, and at the age of eleven I was mainly listening to leather-clad bands, like Poison, Def Leppard, W.A.S.P., and Whitesnake.

This is a point that I am very proud of, but the first album I ever bought on vinyl was Alice Cooper's *Trash* when I was twelve years old. This is the one that contains his track 'Poison', which was huge when it came out, and I am pleased to say that I still have this original record and it still plays through entirely without a single skip or audible scratch.

Mainly, though, cassette tapes were handed around and copies made, and I will never forget being handed a copy of the first albums by both Skid Row and Guns N' Roses and my tiny little mind being blown wide open. Those two bands had taken something that was very eighties in style, but were dragging it into a new era. It was bad, it was angry, it was so unbelievably awesome, and I bloody loved it!

I'm very aware that I'm painting a picture of a cool kid here, a kid who is so much cooler than his young years should suggest. Oh, my goodness, was I possibly the coolest eleven- to twelve-year-old that had ever existed?

Well, for balance and full disclosure, let me also just say that the first single I ever bought on cassette was 'Opposites Attract' by Paula Abdul, I think entirely because the music video had a cartoon cat in it that did a rap.

And for the final nail in my coffin of cool, when I was twelve years old I would also become the biggest Vanilla Ice fan for about eighteen months, but the less said about that the better.

Right, I think we should end this chapter now before I say anything else I regret.

Chapter Eight

During my time in Worcester I would sometimes get a little bored of a weekend if I was not able to return home, but I did have an entire school to explore so exploring is what I would do.

While on one of these weekend expeditions I stumbled across a fairly extensive library of homemade religious cassette tapes of hymns and sermons that the reverend and the school had obviously been compiling over quite some time. It is fairly well accepted that the Devil does make work for idle hands so, presented with this holy treasure trove, I started doing a little bit of work on the side for Lucifer himself.

Being a non-religious kid in a pretty damn religious school, I saw this as an opportunity to take a stand, albeit completely anonymously and without any actual bravery or accountability on my part whatsoever.

What I would do is I would randomly select tapes from that huge library of religious offerings, take them back to my bedroom and fast-forward them in a little bit. Then at the point of a hymn I would record a kick-ass hair-metal anthem over the top of it before returning the tapes to their place in the library.

I thought it was hilarious that one day somebody would be listening to one of these tapes, and just at the point where they were getting comfortable to enjoy a lovely little rendition of 'All Creatures Great and Small', they would be treated to the far superior 'Bed of Nails' by Alice Cooper.

I am aware that the irony here is that Alice Cooper is actually a very religious man and starts every morning off with prayer and by reading from the Bible, so Alice would likely not approve of this mischief at all. Neither do I, really, not now: it was a childish thing to do, but I was a child. I'm sure that maybe a much younger Alice might have found it just a little bit funny, though, and, okay, maybe I still do as well, or I wouldn't be writing it here, would I?

I did this for ages, weekend after weekend. It became a bit of a pet project of mine until one day when I was brought up in front of the reverend. I don't know if he was working his way through all of the kids in the school, or whether he just had a feeling about me, but I stood there and tried my best to look genuinely shocked that anybody would even imagine doing such an awful thing. I don't think he believed me, but without evidence he couldn't exactly take it any further and my pet project was well and truly shelved now anyway. I was a mischievous nuisance, not a suicidal maniac. I'm just glad he decided to confront me about it rather than laying a trap, because I likely would have walked right into that and been caught red-handed, and the professionally religious do usually seem to opt for punishment over forgiveness, don't they?

It wasn't long before I would find myself in front of the reverend a couple of times in close succession, but this time for physical altercations with a couple of kids for which my parents would receive a combined invoice for breakages to the sum of thirty-five pounds, and this was not a tiny amount to my family back in the 1980s.

I've been told I can't name these kids here in case the adult versions of them get upset about it, so rather than changing their names, I've just decided to describe them as best as I can.

Ahem . . .

The first of these altercations involved a lanky horrible bastard who was a bully and a grade-A knobhead in equal measure. There is always one bigger kid in any class who develops ahead of everybody else, and this was him. He had a clear foot height advantage on all of the other kids in the class, a lot more body hair, and he liked to throw his weight about the place.

We had history, and on a recent occasion he'd been such an arsehole to me and some of the other kids that I filled his pencil case with tomato ketchup. As all bullies usually do, he ran crying to the teacher when he unzipped it later that day and stuck his hand into the sweet sticky mess.

As per usual, I was the prime suspect, but again I played it like I was an angel sent down from heaven to do only good on this earth. The heat was quite a lot, though, so in a moment of absolute madness and in order to throw the scent off myself, I filled my own pencil case with tomato ketchup.

Surely now they would not suspect me, not now that I was also a victim of the Worcestershire Pencil Case Ketchup Squirter. Well, it turns out that this only made them suspect me even more. I couldn't believe it when they had the audacity to accuse me of squirting tomato ketchup into my own pencil case in an attempt to shift the suspicion to somebody else, which was exactly what I'd done but I couldn't believe they would have the gall to actually say it.

On this occasion, though, the horrible lanky bastard was getting quite physical and was shoving me about a bit. There was no way I could match him in terms of heft or strength so, backed into a corner, I picked up a coffee-table and flung it at him. He made quite a decent size target and the coffee-table hit him square on before landing on the floor, two of its legs snapping right off as he went running off crying.

The cost of that coffee-table? Twenty pounds, so fifteen quid more to account for on that invoice, and from a horrible lanky bastard we move to a snide chubby little prick.

This time it was me that was the physical aggressor, although in my defence I was reacting to verbal provocation and just thought he needed shutting up. This kid thought he was better than everybody else and that he could just get away with saying whatever he liked without any consideration or concern for come-back.

I was keeping to myself, just playing a game of pool alone when he turned up and started badmouthing things I cared about.

It was 1989 and Liverpool had just been through the tragedy of Hillsborough, the worst disaster in British sporting history. I had been back home at the time and had felt the raw emotion of the city up close. In the days after, I went to Anfield with my family and left my favourite Liverpool track top among the thousands upon thousands of shirts, scarves and floral tributes that others had left on the pitch. The stadium had been opened up to the people of the city and beyond: it was a place to find solace, a place to pay respects, and for many it was a place to just sit and shed tears. The entire pitch became a sea of red and white tributes in the days that followed, a sight that was born from so much sadness but was one of the most overwhelmingly beautiful things I ever saw.

Grief, anger, and a deep sense of injustice filled the city, as the police and some portions of the press spouted lies and anti-Liverpool rhetoric that blamed the fans for the loss of life and accused them of criminal and antisocial behaviours that simply weren't true.

Liverpool fans had been made a scapegoat, an easy target for blame by the police and the authorities. It would take decades of relentless and dignified campaigning by the families of those lost before it would be officially acknowledged as the despicable cover-up that it was, the police and authorities shifting blame onto the fans to hide their own gross negligence and failings.

In 1989, though, I was just a twelve-year-old kid who was away from home and who loved his family and his city, who was perhaps feeling extra protective of both, and who was a lot more homesick than I think he realised at the time. So when this snide chubby little prick with a big gob started getting in my face and banging on about how Liverpool was a shit-hole full of violent criminals and thugs, I couldn't be bothered arguing with him and just smacked him with the pool cue.

I admit there were probably more sophisticated and less ironic ways to shut him up, but smacking him with the pool cue just felt like the best and quickest way of doing it at the time. I will never forget the high-pitched shrill noise he made as that cue connected with his chubby back, or the glorious cracking sound the cue made as it snapped completely in two.

'They both deserved it,' I told the reverend. I wasn't wrong. One was a bully, and one of them needed to learn how to keep his mouth shut.

My parents were obviously disappointed and concerned by these two incidents taking place so close together, but I also think that they were maybe also just a little bit pleased that I had stood up for myself. Although they likely would have preferred it if it hadn't cost them thirty-five quid for me to do it.

Thirty-six years have passed and that was the last time I ever hit anybody, but unless Lanky and Chubby changed their ways, I can't imagine that was the last time either of them got hit. I reckon it might have been a fairly regular occurrence for the latter.

It was Christmas 1989 when my lovely nan suffered a stroke. She had to spend some considerable time in hospital while recovering, and it was during this time that my grandad died of liver failure, the drink finally taking its toll.

I was at home on school holidays when both of those things happened. I don't know to what extent they affected how I felt about having to say goodbye and leave my family for school so frequently, but I would imagine they contributed more than I realised at the time.

It was during those next summer holidays at the end of my second year when I started becoming quite overwhelmed with the thought of everything I missed at home when I was in Worcester, and how I would soon have to return for the new school year.

I would miss my nan, who was now living alone and trying to rehabilitate, and obviously I always missed my parents, but I hugely missed my little sister. She had been just four years old when I left for Worcester that first time, but she was six now, and being at home during the long summer break made me realise just how much I loved being a big brother. I also missed my friends, and just being able to have a normal life playing football in the streets and computer games at each other's houses.

The pursuit of what I saw as 'normal' consumed me at times throughout my sight loss and the early years of blindness. For some time to come it would be a barrier between me and acceptance, but also I think probably the thing that would drive me on most to achieve success in comedy.

Although Worcester had not been a bad experience for me and I had enjoyed much of my time while I was there, there was no ignoring the fact that the thought of leaving home again was filling me with a huge amount of sadness.

'I don't want to go back to Worcester,' I said to my parents, expecting a bit of pushback or at least some sort of attempt to persuade me that it was all in my best interests. After all, I believe it had taken a lot of effort to get funding for me to attend that school in the first place. It turned out, though, that this was music to their ears and they were delighted with my sudden change of heart. It was also something they wanted, but I think something they felt they couldn't really be the ones to push for, if going away for school really had been in my best interests in the long run. After double-checking with me that it really was what I wanted, they immediately set about putting everything in place for me to start the new school year back in Liverpool.

Filled with the excitement of this return to family and normality, I doubled down on making life as 'normal' as possible, even though I would be returning to the same specialist school I had left just two years earlier.

My school was on the same road as both the girls' and the boys' mainstream comprehensives, and I had decided that I would forgo the local-authority-funded taxi to and from school, which all specialist-education kids were entitled to, in order to get the bus with Neil and the other kids who went to those schools on the same road. This all felt very normal until the point every morning when I would have to say goodbye to all of the boys outside their school, then be the only boy walking among pockets of girls until I had passed their school as well, after which I would complete the remainder of the walk alone.

As a teenager now, image and identity were becoming important, and I would often feel quite self-conscious during this walk, aware that I was going alone to somewhere different. I would feel embarrassed at having to turn into my 'specialist' school if there happened to be anybody walking behind me when I had to do so. My desire to regain what I thought of as a normal life had only made me more conscious of those parts of my life that were different from what I saw as normal, and as I entered my teenage years I would start trying to hide these differences.

On one occasion I became very aware that there were two teenage girls walking behind me as I approached the entrance for my own school. I didn't want the girls to see me entering a school for blind and partially sighted kids, so I decided to turn up the side-street that ran alongside our sports field and jump over the wall to enter the school that way. Unfortunately for me, the wall had been coated with a thick layer of anti-vandal grease and I ended up coated from head to toe in the gunky stuff before I managed to come clattering down on the other side. My covert entrance certainly didn't go unnoticed when I wandered into the building looking like I'd gone ten rounds with a deep-fat fryer.

Okay, little side note here – I wanted to write that it looked like I'd been jizzed on by Megatron, but I was told that it was not tonally appropriate for the book. So I'm hoping by including it in this way I still get credit for the joke while accepting absolutely no responsibility for it ruining the mood. It's only a side note after all.

We hear the term 'masking' often used to describe the coping strategies of, mainly, young girls with autism, as they attempt to fit in with the environment around them and not stand out as being different. Well, I think that this term also perfectly explains my own strategy, as I would mask my sight issues so that others wouldn't be aware of my differences in this regard.

On my return to home life and normality, I also wanted

a paper round – after all, what could be more normal for a teenage boy than having a paper round? Delivering the *Liverpool Echo* and other paid-for newspapers was definitely the most lucrative paper round for the amount of work required: just twenty or so papers a day to specific addresses that were pretty local to the newsagent's at the end of our road, although back then we called it a sweet shop or, more specifically, Tony's.

As I couldn't see the numbers on a lot of the houses, especially without having to walk up sometimes quite long garden pathways to check them out, delivering to specific addresses was not going to be very practical for me. It would have resulted in a lot of people complaining that they had not received the paper they had paid for, while an equal number of other people would have been delighted at getting one for free.

To avoid this inevitability, I got a round delivering the *Merseymart*, the free local paper that got delivered to everybody. This meant it was a lot more work and covered a far more expansive area from my house, but it was also less dependent on me being able to see properly because house numbers didn't matter.

I still remember the fee: 1.2p per paper, which meant about seven quid a week for delivering six hundred newspapers. I loved the bright orange news bag I would cram with copies of the paper, I loved wandering around the neighbourhood and just waltzing into people's gardens, and most of all I loved the automatic permission it gave me to wander into a few of the local pubs at the age of thirteen so I could hand a copy over the bar.

It would be a lovely symmetry, when I had doubled in age to twenty-six, that the *Merseymart* would be the very first newspaper I would find myself featured in as I took my initial steps into comedy. It was after I'd been performing stand-up for less than a year and had won one of the many new-act comedy competitions that I'd entered in that first year. I knew that the *Merseymart* was thinking of running a news story about my victory in the competition, and I kind of expected that if they did, it would be featured somewhere deep within its pages.

I spoke to my mum on the phone.

'You're in the paper,' she said.

This was exciting: they had done the story after all. Probably page seventeen or eighteen, I thought, something like that. Somewhere between the classified ads and the obituaries, I would imagine, but that didn't matter. The main thing here was that they had run the story.

'You're on the front page,' she continued.

Bloody hell, the front page! That was a bit of a surprise. I couldn't believe it, the front page of the *Merseymart!*

'You're the second story,' she added excitedly.

'I'm the second ... What?'

Immediately I went from being amazed I was in the paper at all, to being gobsmacked that I was on the front page, to being slightly miffed that I was only the second story in that week's edition. What had happened in Liverpool that week that was more interesting than me winning a new-act comedy competition? Well, I'll tell you what the main headline was . . .

WHEELIE-BIN BARRICADE
ON ALLERFORD ROAD

A wheelie-bin barricade? I was beaten by a wheelie-bin barricade?

Residents annoyed at traffic diversions causing congestion on their road had dragged their wheelie-bins out into the street and created a barricade, and judging by the relative space allotted to each story it seemed that this wheelie-bin barricade was thought of as being about five times more interesting than me taking my first steps into comedy.

Coincidentally, Allerford Road was the road my nan had lived on throughout my childhood and I had many happy memories there. But now it would be for ever tainted in my mind by its residents and their improvised blockade. If only they'd put up with those traffic diversions and left the bloody wheelie-bins where they were, I could have been the lead story on the front page of that week's *Merseymart*. How utterly selfish of them!

Chapter Nine

I have loved watching comedy for almost as long as I can remember. Throughout my childhood, our home was very much a TV household, where comedy and sitcoms were staples of family viewing. As a younger child I just tended to watch and enjoy the same comedy as my parents did, family entertainment of the time.

All of the big game shows on TV were hosted by comedians and stage entertainers, such as Ted Rogers on *3-2-1*, a game show in which the connection between clues and prizes was so bafflingly tenuous that if you watch any of it today it barely makes any sense at all. The mascot of *3-2-1* was a bin called Dusty Bin, and I had a large Dusty Bin that took pride of place in that bedroom of the house on Craigside Avenue that we moved from when I was eight years old. Poor old Dusty never did make the move around the corner as he was not in a good state by then, which tells you how young I must have been when I got him.

Les Dawson was a brilliant comedian who simply mesmerised me as the host of *Blankety Blank*. It was incredible to me how funny he was, and how he could often be so cutting and mean to his contestants and the celebrity guests while still managing to remain so completely charming and likeable.

Blankety Blank would also introduce me to a whole raft of funny people in those celebrity seats, from the theatrically camp Duncan Norvelle and legendary Barry Cryer, to Scouse comedy icon Stan Boardman and the funny, captivating Faith Brown.

Faith Brown was a comedian and impressionist who . . . Well, let's just say she had a cleavage she could have kept a cricket bat in. I'm ashamed to say that, as a young child, if left in the living room alone while she was on the TV, I would move closer and closer to the screen, to see if elevating my viewing angle would enable me to see further down into that ample bosom. I think there is a good chance that Faith Brown might have been my very first ever celebrity crush before I even knew what one of them was.

At the point of writing I have been lucky enough to make four appearances on the recently revamped *Blankety Blank*, which is brilliantly hosted by Bradley Walsh. I love how I've been able to be part of a whole new generation of young kids seeing comedians at play for the first time on the very same show I watched as a child. My daughter loves the show, and I love being able to take part in something she can enjoy and that is so universal in its appeal.

The game involves writing answers down on large pieces of card for all to see, but when I did the show for the very first time, I hadn't actually written anything by hand for decades and was quite nervous about having to do so on the telly. My daughter was about eight years old at the time and sat at the table with me and helped me practise my handwriting with a felt pen on blank pieces of A4 paper. She would give me words to write down, then grade my efforts based on their neatness and how nicely they were centred on the page.

The one thing she couldn't help me with was my spelling. As somebody who hadn't visually absorbed words written down for more than four times longer than she'd been alive, my spelling was awful, and in that first episode I had a complete brain fart when trying to write the word 'TRACTOR' and in a panic, I wrote down 'TRAKTER'. Yep, that went out on the telly for everybody to see.

Blankety Blank is one of those shows that really does make me pinch myself when I'm on it, as it makes me feel like I'm actually inside the TV. It also pays well and requires absolutely no prep whatsoever, so 'winner winner chicken BLANK!'

Jim Bowen, Bruce Forsyth and Bob Monkhouse also brought laughter into our living rooms as truly brilliant hosts of some of the nation's favourite game shows. There is a debate to be had about how professional footballers of the seventies and eighties might fare against modern elite footballers, and whether their comparative lack of physical fitness and tactical intelligence might be plain for all to see in today's game. Well, when it comes to hosting game shows, I think the opposite might just be true.

It can be argued that what was once labelled 'alternative comedy', but is simply known now as stand-up, is artistically better and more original than the forms of gag-based comedy that preceded it. There was just something about that more traditional form of comedy, though, which just lent itself so well to being a truly brilliant game-show host who would certainly not be out of place today.

Sitcoms were very much part of my young comedy experience, from *Only Fools and Horses*, which has more than stood the test of time, to seemingly long-forgotten shows, like *Fresh Fields*, *Only When I Laugh*, *Sorry*, *Watching* and *Bread*, comedies that were all very much of their time. Enjoying all of this wonderful entertainment in the 1980s was the norm for a lot of the country. Often there was just one screen per household and families would gather to enjoy and laugh at whatever was on the TV that night.

It was at about the age of thirteen when I would start to find my own comedy, things that felt like they were written for me and my friends, and not for my parents. I had missed out on the impact of *The Young Ones*, but *Bottom* was an absolute revelation. The chaos, the anarchy, the violence and the filth. I mean it's one of the most quotable shows from the last thirty-five years. I still don't think I've laughed harder at anything than I did when my friend Paul brought that very first *Bottom Live* video around for us to watch, in which Richie and Eddie were no longer constrained by the broadcast rules of the BBC and could dial it up to eleven.

I was lucky enough to get to do a TV show with Ade Edmondson a couple of years back. We appeared alongside each other on *Between the Covers*, a book-club show for the BBC, which doesn't sound too exciting on the face of it. I couldn't wipe the smile off my face, though, just getting to share the screen with such a comedy hero of mine. I absolutely hated one of the books we had to review, but so did Ade, which just made me love the experience even more.

I'm not really a fan of those talking-head shows that you get on the telly and have tended to say no to most of them along the way.

A top-fifty countdown of the best British adverts? 'No, thanks.'

A look back at the best TV clangers of the last decade? 'Err, I'm washing my hair, I'm afraid.'

When I was asked to take part in one that would be a celebration of everything *Bottom*, though, there was no way I was turning that one down. Not only did I get to talk about *Bottom* for money, but I got to rewatch all of it beforehand and actually count that as me doing work. I was crashed out on the couch laughing my arse off at Rich and Eddie playing a game of chess with random items they'd found around the flat, when Patricia came into the living room.

'Are you just gonna lie about watching telly all day?' she asked. 'If you haven't got any work to do, maybe you could tidy up and do the hoovering.'

'Actually, this is work,' I shot back. 'I'm doing a TV show all about *Bottom*. This is *Bottom*. I'm watching *Bottom*. This is work. It's not my fault I have a great job!'

Thankfully, her dirty looks are wasted on me.

Shortly afterwards, I got asked to be a part of a similar retrospective on *Blackadder*, and there was no way I could turn that one down either.

Blackadder was one that my dad got me into. It never

appealed to my mum, who liked the more traditional family and workplace sitcoms, but *Blackadder* was a work of genius. I only really tuned in during the final series as I think those that came before had been a little over my head for my young age at the time, but I would go back and enjoy them later.

The end of *Blackadder Goes Forth* was something I had never experienced in a studio sitcom before, such emotion and sadness for something that, up to that point, had been so utterly daft and hilarious. I still find it quite remarkable that one of the greatest moments in British comedy is one that has no laughs in it whatsoever.

The *Blackadder* retrospective was happening because a lost pilot episode that was never broadcast had been found in a BBC cupboard covered with dust, and it was to get its first airing. I was invited along to a viewing and will never forget arriving in that cinema room to watch this unearthed pilot episode, and Baldrick, I mean Sir Tony Robinson, coming over to introduce himself to me. Yes, I wrote that right: he came over to introduce himself to me!

'Bloody hell, Chris, you're never off the telly, are you? Every time I turn it on, there you are.'

I honestly couldn't believe that Baldrick, I mean Sir Tony Robinson, knew who I was. I'd like to say I played it cool in that moment, but I doubt I was able to hide the sheer glee on my face. It wasn't only that I was meeting Baldrick, I mean Sir Tony Robinson, and it also wasn't just because he had come over to introduce himself to me, but that this comedy legend and hero of mine was actually aware of my own existence within his world.

The cherry on the cake was when, after chatting, we discovered we both had the same favourite *Blackadder* episode as well. I'll give you a clue.

'Sausage!'

If you know, you know.

There would be other incredible British comedy shows that would come along and really strike a chord with this teenager who was fast becoming a comedy nerd, from *Harry Enfield's Television Programme*, which would soon become *Harry Enfield and Chums* as Paul Whitehouse and Kathy Burke would prove to be just as key to its success as Harry himself, to *Father Ted*, *Coupling* and my favourite of all the US sitcoms, *Frasier*.

My all-time undisputed favourite of the lot, though, has to be *Red Dwarf*. It has played such a huge part throughout my life that I could probably devote half of this book to it, although I think that might put a few of you off, so I will try to be brief.

Red Dwarf is basically all the things I love in comedy. It is wall-to-wall funny, clever while also being totally daft and not taking itself too seriously, and it is creative and out there in a way that the vast majority of other sitcoms just aren't. Among a huge number of family-based and workplace sitcoms, *Red Dwarf* is definitely one of the more bonkers offerings, and it just works.

I've done a few gigs over the years with Norman Lovett, who plays Holly, *Red Dwarf*'s senile ship's computer, in a few of the series, and these have been such incredibly exciting highlights for me within my club career.

I've also crossed paths with Craig Charles a few times

over recent years and been interviewed by him as part of his radio show. Moments like these where I've got to work with comedy heroes from my youth have been such huge treats for me as I have tried to carve my own path through comedy.

My first introduction to a new generation of stand-up comedians would come via a show called *Friday Night Live* on Channel 4. This was during the very late eighties and super-early nineties as I was becoming a teenager. *Friday Night Live* wasn't just a name, it was on a Friday night and it was actually live.

This is a thought that fills my stomach with pure liquid anxiety, even just thinking about it, as the only stand-up I've ever done on the telly has always been pre-recorded before being edited for public consumption. I'm sure that thirteen weeks of dancing live on *Strictly* have likely toughened me up to the point at which simply performing stand-up on live TV wouldn't be as daunting to me now as it otherwise would have been but, still, the idea of performing raw stand-up for what would have been millions back then in the glory days of Channel 4, well, it makes me need to run to the loo for a sit-down visit. I'll be back in a minute.

Phew, that was close. A poo with a bit of wee thrown in as well. Don't worry, it's allowed. Right, where was I?

Friday Night Live had introduced me to comedians like Harry Enfield, Lee Evans, Jack Dee, Jo Brand and, of course, Ben Elton.

This new generation of comedians was just so vastly different from the traditional stand-ups I'd grown up watching on shows like *The Comedians, Live from the Palladium* and the annual *Royal Variety Performance.*

When I had first started at school in Worcester, the legendary and timeless Billy Connolly had received a lot of play time from some of the older kids around me, and although I was drawn into his shaggy-dog stories and his hypnotic Glaswegian drawl, a lot of it had gone right over my young head, even though I had laughed along anyway to fit in with everybody else.

Billy and Albert was the album of the time, recorded at Billy's show at the Royal Albert Hall, and there was a gag in it that I always laughed at but never really understood.

'Have you ever seen a dachshund try to go upstairs with an erection?' Billy would say.

A dachshund is a sausage dog, of course. A sausage dog trying to go upstairs with an erection? Hilarious!

Back at that young age, I had never heard the word 'dachshund' before. I knew from the story that it was a dog, just not that it was a sausage dog. Even though I didn't get the joke, the sentence still made me laugh because it contained the words 'dachshund' and 'erection'.

Specificity in comedy is always funnier. 'Sprite' is funnier than 'fizzy drink'; 'Shreddies' is funnier than 'breakfast cereal'; and 'dachshund' is funnier than 'dog'. Even back then, at the age of eleven, I think I appreciated this mechanism of comedy and enjoyed the inclusion of that strange new word I had never heard before.

It seems that I then continued throughout my life without ever learning what a dachshund actually was. That line had remained stuck in my head, though, as a funny thing I'd heard when I was a child, but not something I'd ever really understood.

It would be more than three decades later, during the second lockdown of the coronavirus epidemic in late 2020, when my wife, daughter and I were out walking the dog in the park. We crossed paths with another dog that was enjoying a bit of fresh air but had no consideration for social-distancing rules whatsoever, and as that dog ran towards us to be fussed over, my wife and daughter both squealed with delight.

'Wow, a dachshund!' shouted Patricia.

Ha, I thought. That's the dog trying to go upstairs with an erection from the old Billy Connolly bit that I never really understood.

'A sausage dog!' shouted my daughter.

Oh. I lifted my hand to my face and finally understood why it was so funny.

I reckon I might hold some sort of unofficial world record for the longest amount of time it has taken anybody to get a joke. I heard that joke when I was eleven, but I only got it when I was forty-three years old. That's thirty-two years, which is quite embarrassing for a stand-up comedian to admit, isn't it?

I think this is a good example of how we often just passively learn through what we see. I'm sure that if I'd had my sight into adulthood, then probably at some point along the way I would at least have seen a picture of a sausage dog labelled 'dachshund', or maybe seen one out in the wild that was referred to as such, but without that visual awareness

I've had to wait for the actual fact to be spoken out loud in my presence.

On a brighter note, though, I am very confident that this part of the book has been quite funny due to it containing the word 'erection' four times. Well, five now.

Erection. Six.

Friday Night Live was revolutionary to me: Lee Evans trying to manically reach the centre of the stage with a microphone lead that was way too short for the job, Jack Dee with his incredibly downbeat and miserable persona, and Jo Brand with her even more downbeat and even more miserable persona.

My love affair with stand-up had begun and my parents would buy me my first two live comedy videos for Christmas in 1992, beginning a tradition that would continue for some years to come. Those first two videos that I would own were Jack Dee's debut release, *Live at the Duke of York's Theatre*, and *Rowan Atkinson Live*, which although not exactly stand-up comedy was near as damn it, with Rowan performing a series of comedy sketches and situations live, and with Angus Deayton as his sidekick and straight man. I played the absolute hell out of both of those videos, and from then on live comedy videos always featured heavily on my Christmas list.

Christmas must have been so much easier for parents back then. Nothing was digital and everything existed in a physical form that could be wrapped up as an actual present. I reckon that for about five years from when I was thirteen, you could have done my entire Christmas shop under one single roof: HMV.

Between comedy videos, music CDs and computer games, what else was left? These days, my daughter streams everything; games exist in the cloud; TV is Netflix and YouTube; the whole of humanity's entire collected output of music is just there to be summoned with a single finger. What the hell are parents, or even Santa, meant to do, these days?

'Happy Christmas, sweetheart. Yes, it's a small piece of card with a handy forty-character code on it. Enjoy tapping that in to redeem your download. Somebody's been good this year!'

Wow, I really am pining for those simpler times of my childhood, aren't I? Sorry if I've brought the mood down.

Erection. Seven.

Chapter Ten

Computer games played a big part in my childhood. From the Sinclair ZX Spectrum I received for Christmas when I was maybe ten years old, to the significant improvement of the Atari ST when I was becoming a teenager, and then there was the truly Super Nintendo console when I was around fifteen.

The Spectrum was basic but the games were cheap, ranging from a couple of quid to an absolute maximum of a tenner. This meant that you could get a cheap game fairly regularly for good behaviour, and a couple of quid was a level of good behaviour that even I found it possible to reach from time to time.

The Atari ST was a significant bump in graphics and play-ability compared to the Spectrum, but that bump also hit the price of the games, with them now costing anything from a tenner to as much as twenty-five quid, and that was a level of good behaviour I found very difficult to attain.

The Super Nintendo was the absolute business, though. I think this was the machine that I spent my happiest gaming years on, but the games had jumped up to an eye-watering forty-five pounds, and I don't think I've ever behaved that well in my life.

I did, however, manage to get my hands on a strange but wonderful little machine called a Pro Fighter, a device that facilitated the copying, ahem, I mean the backing up for personal usage, of Super Nintendo games onto floppy disks.

It meant that you could place a cartridge into the top of the machine, pop a floppy disk into the drive, and copy, I mean back up, the actual game from the cartridge onto the disk. Then in the future you could just load the game straight from the disk rather than having to use that expensive cartridge that you definitely owned but had just put safely away somewhere.

It also meant that you could back up games straight from floppy disk to floppy disk, which lent itself to the almost limitless amount of games you could play without the machine ever having had a sniff of the originating cartridge.

I have no idea how, but somehow through this suburban underworld of dodgy games copying, I mean backing up, I had crossed paths with a guy called Damien. Now, Damien was an adult, a grown man somewhere in his late twenties, who would always have the latest games and would do the rounds selling copies of them on floppy disk.

'Oh, no, what a personal disaster,' was kind of his catch-phrase.

I would say, 'Oh, that Street Fighter game you gave me last week didn't load properly.'

Upon which he would reply, 'Oh, no, what a personal disaster.'

'I'd like to buy six games off you but I haven't got enough money on me.'

99

'Oh, no, what a personal disaster.'

'I'm going blind.'

'Oh, no, what a personal disaster.'

The weird thing here, though, was that the fully grown adult man Damien would knock at our front door and my mum would answer.

'Hello, is Chris in?' he would ask, like this adult man was knocking for me to come out and play.

'Yes,' my mum would reply, 'he's upstairs in his bedroom,' and then she would just open the front door nice and wide and let that fully grown adult man up the stairs to her young teenage son's bedroom without any real understanding of the transactions that were taking place.

For the record it was one pound fifty for a game, unless it was an extra special one in which case I had to stroke his penis. Only joking, I had to let him stroke mine.

While writing this book I did remind my mum about this, that she used to let this grown man up to my bedroom without ever questioning it, and just like with that dead wasp, she thought it was hilarious and laughed so hard that she could barely catch her breath.

She then asked me if the penis thing was true.

There was another grown-up bloke we used to buy dodgy games off, but this time we would go to his house or, rather, his mum's house. This time two teenage children would knock at her door and she would send us through to her grown-up adult man-child's bedroom. What the hell was wrong with mums back then?

This particular guy was the thinnest, scrawniest bloke you

can imagine so we used to call him 'Pan o' Scouse' on the basis that he needed a good meal, or fifty.

'Scouse', as well as being the tag given to those of us born and raised within the city of Liverpool, is also the name of a local dish. It's basically a thin beef and vegetable stew, or a really chunky beef and veg soup if you'd prefer to think of it that way, and Pan o' Scouse? Well, because he could have done with pans of the stuff.

Just as a side note, but a scouse without any meat in it is called a blind scouse. Bit offensive.

Computer games were among the areas of life where my declining eyesight was proving to be a humungous pain in the arse. When watching comedy on my own I could get as close to the TV as I needed, and if I was watching with anybody else, I would have to move back a bit so that they weren't just having to stare at the back of my big fat head in front of the telly. This wasn't too much of an issue as I'd probably seen whatever we were watching ten times anyway and I could kind of get the gist.

Computer games were different, though, as getting the gist wasn't good enough. I needed to be able to see what was going on to play any game properly. I was probably approaching that phase of just 12 per cent vision remaining, and when playing alone I could get as close to the screen as I needed, but when playing with my friends I could often find it a real struggle.

This was probably the first experience I had of something social being removed from me completely because of my failing sight. Computer games are fun if played alone, but they are even more fun if played with friends. Gaming was a huge part of hanging out together, a shared interest and the mechanism that facilitated countless hours of conversation, banter and laughter with mates. As gaming became more and more difficult for me to participate in, the effort required to try to see, plus the mistakes I made along the way, would often leave me feeling incredibly exhausted and frustrated.

Think of it like a set of scales: when the weight of frustration or the strain of the effort required starts to tip the balance away from enjoyment, then maybe it's just time to find something else to do instead.

One of the things that Neil and I would do was to get the phone book out, pick a name at random, then phone that random name pretending we were calling from one of our major local radio stations and that there was money to be won. Neil would get a pop song lined up on his tape player and hold it next to the phone. I would ring the number, and as the person answered and I started talking, Neil would slowly fade the song down just like a real radio station might.

'Mr D. Higgins?' I would say, in my best cheesy radio voice. 'This is DJ Davey Stewart calling from Radio City FM, with a chance for you to scoop one thousand pounds in the top of the charts tiptop cash grab.'

By this point Neil would be leaning in so he could hear the other end of the call while the music still played quietly in the background.

'All I need to know from you,' I would continue, 'is what tiptop tune is tiptop of the network charts right now and one thousand pounds is yours!'

Sometimes we would honestly create delirium at the other

end of the phone as household members would be shouted in from other rooms to help answer the question.

'It's Radio City,' they would shout. 'Quick, quick, what's number one in the charts right now to win a grand?'

If they didn't have a clue what was number one in the charts we would usually give up the pretence, and hang up in fits of laughter as they shouted obscenities at us. If they got the question right, the pretence would remain in full swing as I congratulated them and gave them instructions to turn up at the Radio City studio the following day to collect their prize.

'Just bring ID,' I would instruct, 'and tell us that you're here to collect your tiptop prize!'

And DJ Davey Stewart would then say goodbye as the music was turned back up again and the phone was placed back down. I know, very immature, but I couldn't play Street Fighter any more so give me a break.

I did love playing computer games and would imagine that if I hadn't lost my sight I likely would have continued playing them until, well, let's be honest, I'd probably be playing them now instead of writing this book.

What I do wish, though, is that I could enjoy gaming with my daughter. I would love to be able to sit on the couch and play Mario Kart with her for a whole Sunday afternoon. I would love to be able to pass a puzzle game back and forth on the iPad as we try to complete a tricky level together or beat each other's scores. I would love to be able to enter into her Roblox world and spend some time with her in there and actually see what this thing is that is sucking money out of my bank account with such alarming regularity.

When it comes to gaming with my daughter, I am primitive. I have Ker-Plunk, Connect 4 and Uno. You might think Ker-Plunk is visual, and it is, but try it with your eyes shut and just work from the tension in each of the straws. It works, kind of. Our Connect 4 has holes drilled through the centre of each of the red pieces so I can tell the difference between the two colours.

I also bought a pack of Uno cards that have braille on them, and although I don't read braille I have figured out enough to be able to read the brief notations that tell me the value and colour of each card. As a result, we have probably played more Uno together than most people ever come close to playing in a lifetime.

As she's got older, though, it has been getting more and more difficult to make a game of Ker-Plunk, Connect 4 or Uno with her old dad sound exciting when she's got a shiny iPad in front of her.

It's a bit like saying, 'Hey, why don't you stop eating that big delicious chocolate fudge cake with ice-cream and come over here and lick this sprout instead?'

At some point along the way to becoming a teenager, I had replaced *Beverly Hills Cop* with a brand-new all-time favourite film, and it's probably quite sad to admit that this has never changed since. For nearly the past forty years my one true cinematic love has been *Back to the Future*, and soon afterwards the trilogy as a whole.

I never did see the original in the cinema when it was first released, but was certainly there for the second and third instalments alongside my dad.

Back to the Future Part II was a real step up for my dad when it came to his parental cinema obligations: the last film he'd had to take me to see was Michael Jackson's *Moonwalker*. Sorry, Dad.

When I got married back in 2012 I hired a DeLorean for the day and didn't tell my wife. In fairness, I was surprising her with a traditional wedding car, but then thought, Why should she have all the fun? A little google found a man with a DeLorean who was happy to drop it off and collect it the next day for five hundred quid all in. To this day I still consider that to be one of the best five hundred quids I've ever spent, despite it being an absolute death trap and almost killing me several times along the way.

The thing about the DeLorean is that it was a huge flop and terrible to drive, and it is only really its iconic starring role in one of the biggest movie trilogies of the last forty years that has made it desirable or looked upon with any fondness.

It's incredibly cramped inside, which made my best man, Neil, of course, at six foot seven, a ridiculous sight trying to fold himself into it as there was no way he was letting anybody else drive it.

The DeLorean also seems to have a braking speed of friction plus gravity, and that is to say that the brakes do sod all and it only really seems to be the incline of the road and the physics of the natural universe – or collision – that are able to slow it down. We had so many near misses on the way to the wedding venue that it's a miracle I'm here at all.

'Bloody hell, where did that come from?' asked Patricia, when she saw the car for the first time after we'd tied the knot.

'Err, I hired it,' I said.

'How much was that?' she asked.

'Not too much,' I said, 'and it's all right because we went halves.'

My dad loves films, whereas my mum has probably seen five in her life. One of those films is *The Rocketeer*, which had a cinema release in 1991 and which the four of us attended together on one big family day out. I think we'd received promotional tickets via some means or my mum wouldn't have been there. As I said, she has no interest in films and certainly wouldn't have paid to see one, but also loves a freebie and would likely sit through any old crap if she felt she was getting something for nothing.

She was so bored during the film that she would sneakily hold her index finger up to the side of my face, right next to my cheek, and then wait. Wait until I'd turn my head towards her so that I'd poke myself in the face with her finger. She thought that this was hysterical, and repeating this over and over again entertained her much more than the film did.

My dad was always getting films from the local rental store, and I would connect my video recorder up to the main one in the living room and copy every single one of them. I basically had my very own bootlegging operation running, but entirely for personal use, honest, guv.

I created a numbered catalogue system for them all and had at least a couple of hundred titles by the age of about fifteen. To this day I have a nostalgic affection for so many big hitters and truly obscure titles from the late eighties and early nineties golden age of cinema, golden age for me at least.

Three O'Clock High? A forgotten gem of the high-school comedy genre that starred Casey Siemaszko, who also played one of Biff's gang in *Back to the Future*. This was a great film that was completely overshadowed by *Ferris Bueller's Day Off* and some big releases of the time.

UHF? A spoof comedy film made by and starring internationally famous musical parodist 'Weird Al' Yankovic, and probably my favourite spoof movie ever made. It contains a trailer for a film called *Conan the Librarian*. I'll say no more.

The Final Sanction? A 1990 straight-to-video B-movie action flick starring Robert Z'Dar, a guy I have always remembered entirely for having a ridiculously humungous jaw line. Googling him now informs me that he actually had a condition called cherubism, which causes abnormal bone growth in the lower face, so don't I feel like the arsehole. At least he made it work for him, I suppose.

I became such a regular at the video store that the guy who owned it would let me have his time-coded preview copies of the latest films before they were even due for release. I basically consumed films faster than they were able to make it to the market. I bloody loved them.

I'm very aware that a great deal of my consumption of entertainment during my childhood in some way involved me sidestepping UK copyright laws in order to have way more of a thing than your regular Joe Bloggs would ordinarily have. Rest assured that I've long since grown out of all that nonsense, and now I just counterfeit hard cash. If you wanna buy any fifties, get in touch.

At some point around this time pop-up bootleg stalls

would start appearing on shopping thoroughfares and in markets around Liverpool. There was one at the Heritage Market that operated as a place to buy the latest films while they were still out in the cinema, but on the urgent say-so of a lookout would instantly transform into a stall that sold quilts and pillows, the nefarious products being hidden underneath a mountain of budget bedroom apparel.

The picture quality on those bootleg videos was extremely hit and miss. Occasionally you'd get one that was pretty decent, but usually they'd be a bit crap, or sometimes even just filmed with a video camera at the back of a cinema somewhere in a far-flung part of the world. You'd be watching at home, but then occasionally would see somebody standing up in front of the camera to go to the toilet or to get more popcorn.

My copy of the 1992 horror film *Candy Man* was so bad I decided to take it back the following week, and ended up having an insane argument with a dodgy geezer about what was an acceptable standard of quality for something that was not actually legal in the first place, and why Charlie Chaplin wasn't in *Candy Man*.

'I want a refund,' I said. 'The quality is so bad, it looks like an old Charlie Chaplin film.'

The guy stuck the video into a machine and hit play.

'Where's Charlie Chaplin in that?' he asked.

'Sorry?' I said.

'Charlie Chaplin. Where is he?' he asked again.

'He's dead,' I said. 'I think he died years ago.'

'So he's not in this film, then, is he?' argued the dodgy geezer.

'Of course he's not,' I agreed. 'But I didn't say he was in it. I just said that the picture quality is so bad that –'

'Point Charlie Chaplin out to me now and I'll give you your money back,' he demanded.

This guy was nuts.

'This is *Candy Man*,' I explained. 'Charlie Chaplin is not in *Candy Man*, but the picture quality –'

He ejected the video and thrust it back at me. 'No Charlie Chaplin, no money back!' he said.

This guy was taking the whole Charlie Chaplin thing a bit too literally, and he didn't seem to be concerned in the slightest about honouring the same twenty-eight-day returns policy that other retailers might have felt obligated to abide by.

The irony was that the film *Chaplin*, starring Robert Downey Junior, was out at exactly the same time, so part of me was tempted to buy that and then return with it the following week to have exactly the same argument regardless of its picture quality.

'Where's Charlie Chaplin in that?' he would ask.

'There,' I would say, pointing out Charlie Chaplin.

'Shit,' he would have to concede. 'Well played, sir.'

What I did instead was to return each week and purchase just one new video from him, but then, while he wasn't looking, I would sneak a few others into my bag. Yes, I was shoplifting, but I'm not really sure how illegal that is when you're shoplifting from a shop that isn't legal. I might actually have been working for the law by this point.

One day I decided to not even buy a video. I just sneaked

several into my bag and brazenly strolled away from the stall without a care in the world.

'Hey!' shouted the guy from the store. 'Stop that lad!'

I ran like the wind. I ran like I was holding an egg down on a spoon with my thumb and hoping nobody would notice. That kind of speed was fairly brave in a populated environment such as this, especially considering that I was operating on less than 12 per cent by now. People would only appear in my vision a few metres or so in front of me – and I was moving like the clappers. The guy was in pursuit, though, so I wasn't slowing down, especially not for something as innocuous as insufficient vision. I'd take my chances.

Invigorating doesn't come close to describing how I felt as I ran and he chased. The wind rushing through my hair, the surge of adrenaline, the sound of the guy's footsteps pounding behind me, I'd never felt so alive.

I wove around people, past people, over boxes. I was lightning fast but I knew I didn't have the luck to keep this pace up for too long. The market was both indoors and outdoors and I was currently sprinting through its outdoor area, but an opening was coming up on my left. I ran inside and immediately flattened myself against the wall to the side of the entrance I'd just burst through.

The guy arrived, stopped in the open doorway and scanned ahead for any sign of me. I could see his blurry form stood there in the opening to my right and can imagine his first-person perspective in the movie scene of that moment, as it flips from the left-hand avenue of market stalls, to the right avenue, and then back to the left.

I stayed pressed up tight against the wall, expecting him to just look over and see me there at any moment, but he didn't. He called me something that was probably quite mean, I couldn't exactly hear as my heartbeat was in my ears, before he spat on the floor and retreated empty-handed.

Needless to say, that was the last time I went to that particular market looking for dodgy vids.

I was a mischievous nuisance, remember, not a suicidal maniac.

Chapter Eleven

It was during my time at school in Worcester when I discovered music, but it was as a teenager that I fell head over heels in love with it, and there I remain in a goofy heap on the floor to this day.

In terms of an obsession, I had dabbled with Michael Jackson during his *Bad* era, and Vanilla Ice during his, well, bad era, but these phases had been relatively short-lived even though they had felt long and intense at the time.

Among the mass of eighties rock and hair metal I had been immersed in, one of its newer additions to the genre had truly stood out and would survive with me and millions of others into the nineties and beyond: Guns N' Roses. At the age of fourteen I was completely captivated by Axl Rose and the rest of the band, although mainly Axl, of course.

What made Guns N' Roses different was their genuine bad-boy attitude, their rebellious antics both on stage and off and, of course, all the bad language.

Unlike a lot of other hair-metal bands that came across like they were trying to fit a manufactured image, Guns N' Roses seemed to be living the life they portrayed. It felt so completely authentic and I loved it. They also had a ton of kick-ass tunes and were innovating musically within what was fast becoming a fairly dated genre, dragging it kicking and screaming into a new decade as many of their contemporaries were about to become yesterday's news.

This is because throughout the late 1980s a musical revolution had been brewing, one that was beginning to take America by storm and that would soon smack the rest of the world in the face. A new type of rock music was emerging, challenging the old guard and gaining widespread airplay at its expense.

Grunge, a term coined for this new wave of rock bands originating from Seattle, would encompass such a diverse range of sounds and influences that labelling all those bands with one umbrella term would seem absurd. It was more about a time and a place, their shared geographic location, liberal politics and casual authenticity, with jeans, board shorts, T-shirts, sneakers, flannel shirts and cardigans in place of the leather trousers, metal-studded vests, and extravagant stage outfits of many of the popular bands that came before them.

Fronted by its reluctant poster child Kurt Cobain and his low-fi garage rock band Nirvana, grunge and America's wider alternative rock movement of the 1990s would soon become everything good about music to me, and I've never really grown out of it.

Neil had been on a family holiday to America and had returned from his travels with a few cassettes and tales of many of these new bands that were dominating the radio waves across the Pond. Bands like Soundgarden, Alice in

Chains, Mudhoney, and the band that would very quickly become our all-time favourite and remains so to this day, Pearl Jam. This new generation of bands was finding mainstream success playing rock music in their everyday attire, blurring the lines between everyday normal life and performance, and shunning the masculine bravado and ego of mainstream rock to bring with it a new epitome of musical authenticity.

Authenticity means a lot on stage and this is so true in comedy: an audience can often see right through a comedian who is pretending to be something they're not, and they don't buy it. I'm not talking about character acts or comedians who are exaggerating a trait or aspect of their persona for comedy value, but rather a comedian who is pretending to be something they're not and attempting to sell that fiction as their genuine self. Usually this is because they're portraying themselves as being cooler, or quirkier, or edgier than they actually are, or because they're trying to mimic another comedian's unique persona or stagecraft because they haven't yet found their own. It comes from inexperience, insecurity and lack of confidence to just be yourself, and I was certainly guilty of this early on in my career.

You have probably heard it said that it takes a while to find your voice on stage. It is strange how true this is when finding your voice often means just learning how to be yourself, or at least a more confident, funnier version of yourself. It took me many years to learn how to be comfortable in my own skin on stage, and off stage, to stop trying to be the comedian I thought I probably should be, or that I thought audiences would appreciate more, but to just be me. It took a while for me to become comfortable and confident with my own authenticity and, in truth, I had to find it off stage before I was able to find it on stage.

There is always room for those with bravado and ego in performance, and if you can wear it well, then good for you. I had explored moments of it in my early years of comedy, trying at times to come across as being a bit cooler, moodier or edgier than I actually was, and it fitted me like a sumo wrestler's underpants.

Guns N' Roses wore bravado and ego well, but grunge brought vulnerability and acceptance into mainstream rock. This musical revolution was not being solely driven by grunge, although grunge would often be the flag that was planted in its name. A new wave of alternative rock bands from across America was also contributing to this new musical landscape, the Smashing Pumpkins, Stone Temple Pilots, and Red Hot Chili Peppers to name just a few.

When Britpop exploded in the UK a year or two later, my ears and my heart would be elsewhere. I appreciate the impact that these British bands had on the culture over here, the music scene they created and how much they mattered to so many, but back at the time I just didn't give a shit about any of it: I was grunge all the way!

At the age of fifteen Neil and I received guitars for Christmas, and we would spend hours thrashing through anything we could even remotely figure out how to play from our American idols.

On one occasion we were in Neil's bedroom ploughing

through a lesser-known Nirvana track called 'D7' complete with all the screamed vocals.

'Dimension seven, defect, defect!' we screamed, thrashing away on our Fender Stratocaster Squires.

A bit more 'Defect! Defect!' we wailed.

I thought it sounded pretty good, or at least half decent, but suddenly we were interrupted by a knock at the front door. It was Neil's next-door neighbour.

'Sorry, boys,' said the neighbour, 'but do you think you can keep your "defect, defect" down, please? I'm trying to have my tea and watch the news in there and you sound bloody awful.'

A bit harsh maybe, but perhaps we didn't sound as good as I'd thought.

Despite enjoying picking up a guitar for the last thirty-plus years, I can still only really play half of a handful of songs. I still love guitars, though, and probably own just as many now as I can play proper chords, and that's five. I just like to pick one up from time to time, hang it around my neck and close my eyes, not like that makes much difference, and play my extremely limited repertoire to fifty thousand screaming fans in my head. I think that a lot of stand-up comedians are probably just wannabe rock stars with not enough cool and no real musical talent, and so telling jokes on stage is the closest we can get to that feeling. Rock star is certainly the cooler job – well, put it this way: how many rock stars do you think close their eyes in their bedroom and pretend they're on stage telling jokes for a living? I rest my case.

Underage drinking is a rite of passage, and it was at the

age of sixteen that Neil and I would start trying to get into various establishments with mixed success. Our problem was that when we tried to dress up for the night, I think it actually made us look even younger than we were so we just had to hope that whoever was on the door didn't care about such an arbitrary concept as age.

The first time I had ever got drunk was at a family event. It was my auntie and uncle's anniversary and I was fifteen years old. I had been allowed to have a drink, or a few, and I don't think I had that much, but what I did have went straight to my head.

A little like when a child will protest that they aren't tired despite the fact that their head is lolling all over the place, I tried to make out that I was absolutely fine and dandy and handling the drink like a man, despite the fact that my head was lolling all over the place.

At one point I threw my head back to laugh at a joke one of my older cousins had made and smacked my head into the brick wall behind me so hard that you could have heard it from three tables away. My cousin thought this was hilarious because it was pretty damn obvious that I couldn't handle my drink. Obviously I had to pretend it was absolutely nothing and didn't hurt at all, even though I could now feel my pulse in the back of my head.

On the way home I got into the taxi with my parents, my sister Louise, who was eight years old by this point, and my nan, who had been recovering well but would soon start to show the first signs of cognitive decline that would see her moving into a residential home.

I pulled down one of the folding seats you get in all black cabs and sat down, but as the taxi set off and took a sharp corner I just slid right off that seat and into a heap on the floor. I tried to pass this off as being entirely the taxi's fault and quickly went to regain my seat behind me, like nothing had happened. However, the seat had flipped back up so I basically sat on thin air and ended up in another heap on the floor as my nan tutted her disapproval at my state.

If my parents wanted any more evidence that maybe I'd drunk a bit too much, I think the *Exorcist*-style projectile-vomiting later on would have been the final nail in my coffin. I threw up all over my bed, the floor, my TV and video recorder, and the electrical plug board that was supplying their power. I didn't just throw up; I was oscillating while doing so, like I was trying to achieve maximum coverage as my dad walked into my room.

'Oh, shit!' he shouted to my mum, 'He's thrown up everywhere. This is the last time he's being allowed to drink anything!'

The first time Neil and I would venture out together would be to the Sefton Arms in the village. I was only on my first bottle of K cider when I started to feel incredibly strange. To this day I have no idea what came over me or if somebody had put something in my drink, but all of a sudden I started to get hotter and hotter and could feel myself going extremely faint and woozy. It was winter at the time and had been snowing, so I rushed out of the pub to get some of that lovely cold air and leaned myself up against a car. The next thing I knew I was face down in a puddle of icy slush. I had passed out and dropped like a sack of spuds, smacking my face into the car park so hard that I ended up with cuts and grazes all down one side of it. It hadn't been the best start to pretending to be an adult, but surely I could only get better at it from there.

To the people of Liverpool the city centre is known as 'town', and once my face no longer looked like it had been in a fight with a car park, which it had, of course, our initial attempts to go out into town were to big dance clubs that played horrific music neither of us liked. It was more about pretending we were older than we were and doing the things we thought we should be doing, rather than actually enjoying any of it.

On one particular night out during those winter months, we headed into town on the bus in absolutely Baltic conditions. We didn't take coats with us so that we wouldn't have to wear them inside the club or pay to put them in the cloakroom. We had enough money to get into the club, and for two drinks each and the taxi home, but when it came time to leave we decided to spend that taxi money on one more drink each because, even though the music was shit, there were girls, tons and tons of girls. We then drank our third drink in the nearby proximity of some girls before having to walk several miles home in sub-zero temperatures without a coat. I arrived home verging on hypothermia and my dad had to stick me in front of the fire to thaw me out until I'd stopped being quite so blue.

What a price to pay for a shit night out. What were we doing? We hated the clubs and the music they played and, to be honest, we didn't really feel like we fit in with a lot of the people in those places anyway – it just wasn't us. Simply getting to stand in the nearby proximity of girls we had no business standing in the nearby proximity of, well, it just wasn't worth the effort.

Soon, though, we would find it, our salvation, our Mecca, our place where we could just be us and actually get to listen to some proper banging tunes.

Chapter Twelve

The KrazyHouse was a rock and metal club on Wood Street in Liverpool and I spent so many of the best nights of my youth inside that lovely, dingy, sticky, glorious place.

The KrazyHouse was somewhere we could go without having to pretend we were somebody else. No more dressing up and trying to look like we fit in with the dance-club scene, this was a place for boots and jeans and combats, for flannel shirts left open over band T-shirts, for shirts tied around the waist, and for short sleeves worn over long, which was all the rage back then. It was also the place for those leather trousers and studded vests of the previous decade, if that was your preference, because the rock and metal was varied and plentiful.

Drinks were two-for-one every single night, which meant that a night out wasn't that expensive at all. This was the very beginning of the alcopop market and there was a range of drinks called 'Mad Dog 20:20'. I know, how ironic I should be drinking something with '20:20' in its name. Mad Dog Blurry Shit would have been far more appropriate.

Mad Dog 20:20 came in a hip-flask-style flat bottle, and in a range of flavours that all tasted like some variation on nail-varnish remover. Basically, they were alcopops before anybody had really figured out how to add the pop to the alco.

We would make drinks called Blastaways from a bottle of Diamond White cider and a bottle of some sugary alcoholic pineapple drink called Castaway, both poured into a pint glass to create a kind of tropical version of a snakebite that would go straight to your head and ruin your guts for two days afterwards.

We would start with lager but switch to these concoctions halfway through the evening, and would spend all night either on the dance-floor or making new friends with like-minded souls.

When I started on *Strictly* I commented that I had no dance experience whatsoever aside from head-banging and mosh pits, and the dance-floor of The KrazyHouse was where I first gained this experience.

The moshing was violent but friendly, sweaty bodies colliding and shoving each other around, often with cigarettes in hand. The next day my clothes would stink and would often have several burns from impacts with lit ends.

I grew my hair long, which my parents weren't quite so keen on. They obviously knew how much I loved comedy and films and football and music, so they tried to play on this side of me when it came to offering me a bribe to get it all cut off.

'We've got a proposal for you,' they said. 'If you get your hair cut short again, we'll get cable TV installed.'

To this point we had just been enjoying the limited

selection of four channels provided on the terrestrial service, but cable TV would mean access to tons of US comedy, almost unlimited movies, all of the football and MTV, which at that time was a purveyor of the best in American rock music.

The problem for them, though, was that I knew my dad would love cable TV just as much as I would, and if they were offering it now as a bribe it was obviously something they had already decided they would get, and something that my dad had likely already got his own heart set on.

'Nah, you're all right,' I said. 'I'll keep the hair and just stick to the regular channels.'

And two months later we got cable anyway – told ya.

I loved having long hair. Head-banging with short hair just wasn't the same: you needed something up there to flick all over the place, and I would do just that while bouncing around to whatever beautiful chunky heavy riff was filling the floor.

Because of all the head-banging, I would often wake up the following morning without any functioning muscles in my neck. I was like a bobble-head version of myself, and my mum would give my neck a massage as I lay whimpering on the floor in front of the fire, questioning my life choices. The one thing you could be sure of, though, is that I would do exactly the same thing the following week and then be whimpering in front of the fire again the morning after.

Being underage meant that I would occasionally encounter issues getting through the door, depending on which jacked-up massive bloke was guarding it on that particular night. I'm not implying that some of them knowingly let underage kids inside, but others definitely would scrutinise us a bit more.

On one night out when I was sixteen, I remember leaving at 2 a.m. as one of the bouncers pointed right at me as he let out a laugh of disbelief and gestured to his bouncer mate. 'Fucking hell, Tony, how young is he?'

The guy who was evidently Tony, and who had been manning the door when I arrived, just played it dumb, like it was the first time he'd ever laid eyes on me.

'I dunno, eighteen?' he said, trying to sell the idea like it might have been a possibility.

Maybe his eyesight was worse than mine. Who knows? Either way, nice one, big massive short-sighted Tony.

In order to help me get into places while I was still underage, my dad actually doctored my passport so that I wouldn't have any bother. Back before 9/11 happened and international security measures were changed for ever, it was possible in the nineties to get a short-term passport from the Post Office that came on a folded piece of cardboard. It wasn't laminated or printed by machine: rather, personal details were just filled in by hand by the Post Office clerk.

I had one of these for a school trip I'd been on to Sweden at the end of the summer term, which was the first time I'd ever been abroad. That trip was also the first time I ever saw a band perform live as the Swedish school we were visiting had arranged for us to see U2's Zooropa tour in Stockholm. As school trips go, that's not bad, is it? So U2 were the first band I ever saw live, except they weren't because they were supported by the Stereo MCs, so really it was them, but who wants to admit to that?

My short-term cardboard passport had a standard tiny photograph of my beaming happy face on it, because before 9/11 we were still allowed to smile, and there was a rubber seal of authority partially stamped across this so that it couldn't be swapped for another. The date of birth, however . . . Well, it was just sat there begging to be changed, wasn't it?

As I didn't need the passport any more, I wasn't going anywhere any time soon, my dad used a safety pin to meticulously and delicately scratch away the last digit of my birth year, and then he found a pen that perfectly matched the one that had been used and wrote me in a brand-new one that instantly and legally made me older – what a dad, eh!

Despite my sight being pretty damn poor by my mid to late teens, I could just about see enough to navigate Liverpool of a night and inside the darkness of a club. This ability would leave me over the next few years and instead be replaced by dependence on others.

I think my parents were very aware of this, and rather than over-protecting, they wanted me to get out there and enjoy my youth and my independence while I was still able to see something at least.

Throughout my childhood and my youth, my parents had never once tried to restrict me out of concern for injury or incident. They always just encouraged me to engage with the world as any other child or teenager might. It is natural for parents to worry about their children, especially if a disability or obstacle makes life more challenging or dangerous for them, but I think that over-protection can end up being more damaging in the long run. I was very lucky that my parents were able to not let their own fears restrict my engagement with the world and ultimately limit my experiences, because thirty-plus years on, those experiences mean the world to me. Yeah, even getting mugged at knifepoint.

Neil and I had arrived in town for a night out at The KrazyHouse and I had just visited the cash machine to drain my bank account of its last remaining funds for the evening's fun and frivolities.

We were walking down Church Street, the main pedestrian thoroughfare in Liverpool city centre when, with a casual glance across the way, out of the corner of my vision, I clocked the blurry forms of two guys walking suspiciously right behind us. Church Street is wide, and for those blurry guys to be walking so perfectly behind us, well, it just raised a few alarm bells.

With a few further casual glances from left to right I was able to keep a bit of an eye on them when I saw them split up and pick up the pace, one heading to Neil's right and one to my left. Even though I'd never been mugged before, I knew what was about to happen and I only had a moment to process the best course of action.

I decided that the best thing to do was to wait until they were either side of us, stop dead on the spot and let them overshoot, because they were moving fast. Once they had passed us there was no way they would then double back in order to blatantly mug us in a busy area like this.

They doubled back. Shit. I wasn't expecting that: the plan

was that they would realise they'd been rumbled and compliment me on my brilliant awareness of my surroundings and imminent threat perception, doff their caps and just carry on their merry way to find another unfortunate victim.

They came a little more into focus as one of them grabbed me in a headlock and dragged me into the doorway of the Littlewoods department store, a shop whose catalogue was the first access to even remotely sexy pictures that I or any child of my generation could look at. A whole section of stocking-clad legs and lacy bras on real actual ladies' chests, often without heads, but that didn't matter. Anyway, now's not the time to be thinking about these things. I'm in the middle of getting mugged here.

Both of them pressed flick knives into my stomach as a threat that didn't really need much in the way of explanation.

'Money,' one of the under-achieving bastards said.

'Okay, okay,' I said, and then, in a stroke of spontaneous genius, surprising bravery or complete idiocy, I tried to fob them off with just loose change that I had in my pocket.

I don't really know what I was thinking. I scooped out a small handful of change that must have totalled no more than a couple of quid. 'Here,' I said, offering it upwards to the two hefty losers.

'Nice try. We just followed you from the cash machine,' one of them said, as they pressed the knives a little harder.

Shit. I needed to come up with something quick as I didn't want them thinking I was taking the piss.

'I know, I know,' I said back. 'I, err, I was getting to that. I just wanted to make sure that you got everything.'

I pulled out the two folded notes from that little ticket pocket in my jeans and handed them over.

'Hey!' shouted a lady from behind. 'That lad's getting mugged!'

And with that the two pathetic scumbags ran off down towards the backstreets of Liverpool with a whole thirty quid between them. Saddoes.

Those guys weren't mugging me because they were skint and desperate and needed a fix, or to eat or to support their families. They were mugging me because they wanted a night out and, judging by the way they were dressed, they did it for a shitty night out in one of those trendy clubs I hated so much. I was shaken, but also flooded with adrenaline.

'Do you want to go home?' asked Neil.

'No,' I said. 'Why should they ruin our night?'

The adrenaline had more than papered over any cracks in that specific moment and fuelled a defiance that made me still want my night out.

We headed to the club with just Neil's money between us and ended up having one of our typical great nights out, with the generosity of friends we had made in there bringing us a few beers and Blastaways to compensate for our earlier experience.

It was afterwards, though, that it affected me. For a while it would make me nervous of other people when out at night. It would have me on edge when there was anybody walking behind me, and all for what? Thirty quid. Thankfully, I suppose, they just took my money and headed off to spend it. If that had been twenty years later in any city centre up and down the country, they probably would have stuck the knives in anyway, just for shits and giggles.

I don't think I ever did tell my parents about it, because I didn't want them to worry about me being out any more than they probably already did. Reading this might be the first they learn of it. I know being mugged at knifepoint had nothing to do with my poor eyesight, but I think my concern was that telling my parents might change things. It might allow their natural worries about me heading out into town with limited sight to become an obstacle to me doing just that, and I didn't want to lose their encouragement to live as normal a life as I was able.

It is far more valuable to release the reins whenever possible than wrap a child up in cotton wool out of caution. As I've said, this is something I think we could probably apply to all kids, these days. We could likely do with releasing those reins a little more than we do, but I can't overstate its value and importance to a child growing up with a disability who can already be at a social disadvantage without further barriers being put in place.

I saw at first hand the results of this over-protective cotton-wool approach in many of the blind and visually impaired kids I went to school with. It only really leads to social immaturity and naivety about the world, which I would imagine only ended up being a bigger obstacle to success and fulfilment in later life than their disability was.

I am also very aware of how lucky I was to have such a good close friend as Neil to navigate my youth with. I know a lot of my parents' comfort likely came from the fact that Neil and I were as thick as thieves and that Neil would always be looking out for me. That was the case then and it remains so to this day.

Neil is very proud of everything I've been able to accomplish in comedy and in my wider career, but I wouldn't have squeezed anything like the amount of fun and enjoyment out of life if it wasn't for his friendship throughout it all.

Neil supports Everton, though, so he's had a much harder life than me anyway.

Chapter Thirteen

By this point in my life I'd finished with school. My exams had gone all right, not outrageously good across the board but I'd done decent at the things I liked and rubbish at the things I didn't, which is pretty typical for a smart kid with ADHD, I think.

I got top grades for computers and maths because I was a geek and I enjoyed them, so those subjects would therefore become the focus of any future studies. Stick to what you're good at and bollocks to the rest!

I surprised myself and everybody else with a B in English literature, but that was mainly because I cheated in my exam. I was meant to have read *To Kill a Mockingbird*, but I hadn't bothered. Reading had become such a chore and so incredibly frustrating. It was just not enjoyable to me on any level whatsoever. By now I required a special version of the book to be reproduced in such large print that it would weigh about three kilos. I'd still have to hold it up close to my face, so my arms would feel like they were going to fall off after about five minutes. The other option was to leave the book flat on the desk and lean right over it, repeatedly swiping my head from left to right with each line, like John Belushi in his prime.

The final method was to read it on a CCTV, which was a mega pain in the arse. In this context, a CCTV was a machine that was basically a large TV monitor on a stand, with a camera underneath it facing downwards and a roller board some distance under that. The book would be placed on the roller board and you would hold it open while the camera above would magnify a small portion of the page to a preposterous size on the TV. Reading would then involve having to roll that bloody board from side to side as I tried to track each line one after another. It was entirely functional and out of necessity, but it wasn't reading with any enjoyment at all.

Because I also couldn't see my handwriting well enough, I was allowed to use a laptop to type my answers in my exams. So I got a hold of the electronic copy of the book that had been used to produce my supersized hefty arm-killer version, and I secretly hid that file on the laptop. When a question asked me about something in the book, I would then just 'Alt F' and try and find that bit in it. I would then read a couple of paragraphs and promptly write out an answer about whatever I'd just read.

If anybody from the UK exam board would like to take my GCSE in English literature away from me I won't put up a fight. I haven't used it since and I doubt I'll need it in the future.

I did pretty average in geography, history, English and art. I thought a C in art was pretty decent, considering I couldn't really see what I was drawing. I couldn't do detail and any faces I drew looked like they had at least a couple of disabilities of their own.

I never really got the point of geography, which primarily seemed concerned with taking us to a river to measure some rocks, and mainly writing as much as we could about those rocks.

I enjoyed history but only got the same grade as I did in my rock-measuring studies, but this is probably because I couldn't write essays for toffee.

I got a D in biology, but I was never going to be a doctor, was I? So what was the point in putting the effort in? It would have done me as much good as studying for my driving theory test.

French was my all-time worst. I've never been good at languages and despised the lessons so much. My French teacher tried to organise an exchange trip for me without consulting either me or my family first.

'I've got it all arranged,' she said. 'You can go over there for two weeks and stay with a French family and immerse yourself in the culture and the language, and there's a French boy who can come over here and stay with your family and do the same.'

'Err, you're all right,' I said. 'I've got no interest in going.'

'But you'll never get any better at French,' she protested.

'That's all right,' I said. 'I just won't go to France.'

Also, I know my family, and they wouldn't have wanted some smelly French kid staying with them for two weeks, and that isn't me saying he would have smelled bad because he was French by the way. I was a teenage boy so would probably have smelled a bit iffy a lot of the time as well. He just would have smelled worse, because he was French.

I knew such a ridiculously small amount of French and did warn them that there wasn't much point in putting me through the exams, but they insisted, so for my French oral I pretty much entirely spoke English with a French accent. Honestly, hand on heart, for about twenty-five minutes she would say things to me in English and I would just repeat them back to her in an Eric Cantona voice.

I've always struggled with languages. Programming languages and the language of mathematics I could learn, but spoken languages have always been a hill I could never climb. During those two years at Worcester I learned German, for the whole two years, and when I left at the age of thirteen the only German sentence I was able to put together pretty much translated into English as 'I am a town hall.' Two years of weekly lessons to be able to announce to anybody German that I am in fact a municipal building generally designated for administrative purposes.

Because Patricia is from Brazil, I thought I would make the effort and try to learn her language. I thought I was doing all right. I had phrases and I was progressing, slowly, but progressing nonetheless. The difference here was that I wanted to learn her language, plus I thought I could speak it with her at home all the time, which would no doubt allow me to improve so much quicker. After two months, though, she ordered me to stop.

'Please!' she said. 'I'm coming home from work after a long day and this is the last thing I need.'

'I have bought a hat,' I said, in Portuguese obviously.

'It's like talking to a toddler!' she wailed.

'I am a businessman from São Paulo,' I said, with a smile.

'You're not. You're English. Stick to that. For the love of God, please just stick to that!'

After collecting my mixed bag of GCSEs and attending specialist schools for eight years, my plan had been to double down on my pursuit of a normal life and attend a regular mainstream college in Liverpool to study A-level computers, maths and French. One of those is not true.

I attended a Liverpool college for the not-blind, and in fact did so for approximately three weeks before it became apparent that I was unfortunately not not-blind enough. It very quickly transpired that the college did not have the ability or even the faintest idea as to how it would teach these subjects to somebody who couldn't see the projected slides and whiteboard at the front of the classroom. The obligations and desire for inclusion thirty years ago were hugely different from what they are today, but so were the means.

My lecturers just didn't have a clue how they would relate some of this visual content to me during class in a way that would make much sense. They were also unable to get the course materials to me in advance of the classes in a format that I could access, and not exactly confident that they would be able to get them to me afterwards either. I do have some sympathy for them, as nowadays there would be policies and infrastructure in place, or you would hope so at least, but back in 1994 they didn't even have the internet to google the problem.

The sticking-plaster solution was that the local authority would pay for a personal assistant, somebody who would come with me to each and every lecture, sit with me and be my eyes for the entire day.

That wasn't the idea of normal I had in mind, sat there among my peers with somebody significantly older than all of us who was being paid to continuously mumble and mutter the contents of slides and whiteboard jottings at me while everybody else tried to ignore us and pretend it wasn't happening. The poor guy had no background in maths or computers and didn't really have the faintest clue what he was meant to be describing to me.

'Okay, there's a letter A, then a bracket,' he would mumble. 'Then I don't know what that is but it looks like an angry letter E. Do you know what an angry letter E does?'

This arrangement wasn't really working for anybody. I hated every moment of it, I wasn't really taking anything in, and I could tell that the poor guy sat next to me was losing the will to live with every angry letter E that he encountered.

So for his sake and mine, and in a move that surprised everybody, I moved to Hereford to join the SAS. Unfortunately the SAS wouldn't have me, but Hereford has also got a college for the blind so I decided to go there instead.

It seemed that my pursuit of normal was going to have to be put on hold for a couple more years yet, although my time in Hereford would surprise me by being a lot more normal than I'd thought it would be. If I'm honest, I absolutely loved the place, and being there did me the world of good by making me think differently about whatever the hell normal was anyway.

Sight loss and blindness had always felt very normal within the context of family and school, but among friends I had always been the one who was different. From hide and seek and football in the streets, to computer games and movies at each other's houses, to encountering new pockets of kids as we grew older and ventured further and further afield on the hunt for something to do and trouble to get into, to making new acquaintances and friends on nights out at The Krazy-House, I was always the only one who couldn't see properly.

My friends on those neighbourhood streets in Liverpool had never once made an issue of my deteriorating sight. They were all great kids and good friends to have. Normal for me in these social contexts, though, often meant straining or pretending to see more than I could so that I could try to fit in better with those around me, or at least not stand out too much.

Here I was now, though, living in Hereford and socialising with others who all had similar sight issues to what I had, so suddenly poor eyesight became my new normal in a social context as well.

One of the friends I would become very close to during my time in Hereford was Kev. He is also from Liverpool and had attended the same school I had, although he had been in the year ahead of me. We knew each other well already, but in Hereford we became good friends and over thirty years on we remain so to this day.

Kev is brilliant, but he creates and attracts chaos like no other person I've ever known. You could write a sitcom about Kev and people would think that a lot of it was just over the top and not really likely to happen to anybody in real life.

Just a few years back, a gang of us went to watch our

favourite grunge rockers Pearl Jam at Hyde Park. We met Kev at London Victoria – he'd struggled to get a cab from his house to his local train station so had walked three miles in his trainers with no socks on, which meant that by the time we found him his feet had blistered so much he could barely walk.

We got him some blister plasters from the Boots on the station concourse and helped him patch himself up so that he could enjoy the rest of the day. We then left the station to begin the walk to the concert, and as soon as we stepped out into the open air a bird shit all over him. It was so much and so loud that I heard it splatter off his head and down his back. It might sound a bit mean to say, but in that moment it was so unbelievably funny that I could barely breathe, and even now writing about it is making me laugh at the memory. Sorry, Kev, but if a bird shitting on you is meant to be good luck, then you must be okay for a while yet because it was a lot.

I think this story sums Kev up perfectly, because often it is both himself and something much grander that seem to conspire against him. The blisters were all himself, but the bird shitting on him, well, that was the universe.

In Hereford I studied A-level computing, maths and added further maths to the mix, because I was good at maths and I liked it. I didn't see the point in trying to add something different on top when I could just do more of the thing I was all right at.

I was seventeen and living in halls during my first year, when a group of second-year guys I had become close with had a bedroom become free in the house where they were living and wanted me to move in with them.

Being under eighteen meant that I had a curfew of 10 p.m. every night and wouldn't be eligible to live off campus until I was eighteen. I did my best puppy-dog face, though, and asked nicely, and the college agreed that if my parents signed a form they would cut the cord prematurely and I could go and live there.

Again, never ones to stop me doing anything they thought would probably be a good experience for me, my parents agreed, and at the age of seventeen I was off to live with three other guys. The freedom I had was remarkable and I have such good memories of living in that house, the nights out, the parties, the carnage and the friendships.

Colm, one of my new housemates, was from Northern Ireland.

He introduced me to vodka, in fact vodka mixed with Taboo. This was in essence taking a very strong alcohol and mixing it with a fairly strong alcohol. The result was a drink that was not as mental as drinking straight vodka, but much more mental than vodka and Coke would have been. A bottle of each between us before heading out into the town would mean we were more than ready for whatever Hereford would throw at us without having to spend much extra money at all, really, and I still had my trusty passport, so my age was never an issue.

Chapter Fourteen

I spent a great deal of my time in Hereford but would still try to get home during each term and, of course, had all of the holidays to spend in Liverpool.

Each time I returned home, Neil and I would pick up exactly where we had left off and usually head straight into town for a noisy night out. I was likely into that final 10 per cent by now, and was starting to get the first signs of my sight becoming more problematic of a night time and in dark environments, but for now I would just blunder through as best as I could.

On one night out during my first summer return from Hereford, we had popped into McDonald's for a bit of pre-drinking stodge. It was 22 July 1995, and I know this because the incident that was about to occur would be, in some part, googleable, as I have just found out when I did, in fact, google it. Now, don't get excited, this doesn't mean I ended up in the papers or anything like that. I did nothing that would get me arrested or barred from McDonald's for life, but there was a specific event happening in Liverpool on that night that would come to haunt me and it is this event that I was able to google.

I was eighteen years old, just about, in McDonald's, and I needed a wee.

'Wait here,' I said to Neil, as we were leaving the place. 'I'll be back in a mo,' and with that I ran back inside to find a loo.

Straight up the stairs I went to the first-floor eating area. It couldn't have been a very busy night in the town centre as the upstairs had been closed for business. There was a rope stretched across the top of the stairs and the lights were all off. Well, at least that meant the toilets would be free and I'd come all the way up, so a measly rope wasn't going to stop me. Besides, if they didn't want anybody coming up the stairs then they really should have roped off the bottom, not the top. It was completely unreasonable to expect people to come all the way up the stairs to find their path blocked by a rope, although maybe anybody else would have been able to spot it and the darkness from the bottom rather than having to climb the stairs first.

Anyway, I was there now so what did any of that matter? I climbed over the rope into the gloom to try and find the toilet, but I found it a lot darker up there than I'd thought I would. I clattered into tables and chairs, into a bin that appeared to leap out of the shadows at me, and I totally demolished a cardboard cutout of something although I'll never know what.

I ricocheted around the place like a ball-bearing in a pinball machine until I found a door. I felt the front and could work out from the sign that it was a toilet, but that the simple figure on this sign was wearing a skirt, not trousers. Oh, well, it wouldn't hurt if I just nipped in there, would it?

It's not like there was anybody else about – I was the only one up there.

So there I was, in the middle cubicle of three in the ladies' toilets in the closed-down upstairs of the McDonald's in Liverpool city centre when everything changed.

The door burst open and a girl entered, maybe around my age if I had to guess. I could tell by her voice, because she was talking. Hang on, talking? That means she's not alone. Two of them? Yes, the other one sounds the same age, damn!

Hang on, who's that voice? That's not one of the two of them. That's a different teenage girl. Three of them? Shit, this isn't good.

Three of them and only two cubicles, but don't girls all just share the same one? Didn't I hear that somewhere?

Okay, just stay quiet, let them do their business and get out of here.

They did their business either side of me and were just washing their hands when more of them turned up. More teenage girls. What was going on here? Some kind of teenage-girl convention?

It turned out that there had been some kind of teenage-girl convention: I was able to decipher from their coded chit-chat that just down the road at Liverpool's Royal Court Theatre PJ and Duncan had been performing a concert. PJ and Duncan were the *Byker Grove* and short-lived pop-star names of those who would soon become known to us all as Ant and Dec. They have obviously gone on to have an incredible TV career, but as PJ and Duncan they only had one big hit that I can remember, and that was 'Let's Get Ready to Rhumble'!

Well, now it was me who was about to be rhumbled, as there was a stream of them, a stream of teenage girls that sounded like it ran out of the door and God knows how far. There were too many voices to count. It sounded like a crowd.

The time ticked on but the flow of girls didn't show any signs of subsiding. The best thing I could do was to stay quiet and hope that none of them would notice that there was somebody in the –

'Is anybody in that middle one?' one of the girls asked. 'Nobody's gone in or out of it in ages.'

Shit. Stupid observant busybody. Why couldn't she just wait her turn and go into one of the cubicles either side of me, like all of the other girls had done?

'Hello?' she shouted, as she thumped on the door. 'Who's in there?'

I was going to have to make my move, but how? It's not like I could just walk out now and pretend everything was hunky-dory: I'd been hiding in there for a good fifteen minutes by then.

'Sorry, girls, I was just in the cubicle when you all started coming in so I just thought I'd stay in there and listen to you all pee.'

I needed a plan. I needed a story. I needed to pretend I'd been asleep. Perfect, well, not perfect, but it was the best I could do. I would pretend I was drunk and had been unconscious in the middle cubicle and that was why I was only just leaving now. Their thumping on the door had awoken me from my unconscious state and now I was quite disorientated and couldn't really understand where everybody had come from.

I messed my hair up more messy than it was already and I made my head a bit floppy, like I wasn't quite able to support its weight on my neck due to it having been all crooked at a weird angle while I had been slumped in Dreamyland on the loo. I then flushed the toilet to let them know that something was about to happen.

I opened the door and staggered out slightly pitched to one side, as somebody recently awoken from a deep slumber might, and I can still hear the uniform noise of disgust that all those teenage girls made as I fake-stumbled from that cubicle. Probably partly because there was a boy in their midst, but also probably more partly because, as PJ and Duncan fans, this long-haired greasy, grungy boy was as far from their type of boy as it was possible to get.

I continued the stumble past the girls with just three words muttered to them as the only form of explanation I could think of. 'Sorry,' I said, 'fell asleep,' as I left their toilets.

The previously gloomy upstairs was now brilliantly lit as I did a walk of shame like no other along the seemingly endless queue of teenage girls, which continued all the way to the top of the stairs and down them, the noise of surprise and disgust passing along the line like an electrical current.

'Where the hell have you been?' said Neil, as I met him at the front. 'I've been waiting for ages.'

'We've got to get out of here,' I said. 'Toilet. Girls. PJ and Duncan. Absolute nightmare!'

144

During that summer I attended the first of many music festivals that would become a regular feature of years to come, Reading '95, which would turn out to be one of the best and craziest sober weekends of my life back then.

Before the internet made event tickets so much easier to acquire, and then often so much harder to acquire, it was possible to buy tickets from actual shops and outlets in a casual and healthy manner. Hey, young people, imagine this. You could actually see that tickets were on sale for a popular event, go home, have a think about it, save some money and then return to buy the tickets when you felt good and ready. You didn't need to have a load of you operating across multiple screens and accounts, like a team of stock-market brokers to try and secure your tickets within a ninety-second window, or before the robots could get them all.

We bought a coach package to Reading from Liverpool for sixty-five quid including our festival and camping tickets. God bless 1995 prices! The line-up was ridiculous and my idea of heaven. Tons of American rock bands, like Soundgarden, the Smashing Pumpkins, Green Day, Mudhoney and, making their first ever appearance on these shores, Foo Fighters.

I went with Neil and my cousin Colin, who is only a couple of months younger than me and with whom I have always been very close. That Foo Fighters gig was insane as the festival organisers had completely underestimated their draw and scheduled them for the second stage, in a tent, when the main stage probably would have been a lot more sensible. Their appearance was halted so many times due to overcrowding, as bodies climbed the tent's supports to get out of the crush. It was so tightly packed in there that at one point I pulled a leg up to make sure my shoe was tied properly, but then couldn't get it back down again and had to hop around on one leg for a while with the motion of the crowd. I found Colin afterwards and he hadn't been so lucky, losing half of his clothes as he'd tried to escape over the top of the crowd.

It is remarkable how unbelievably clueless we were about how to attend a festival. We turned up with my eleven-year-old sister's single-skin garden tent, one sleeping bag between the three of us and not even enough cash for a decent night out, hence the sobriety. I have attended many festivals over the years that have been an absolute washout, but luckily this one was not one of those or I think that particular tent would have washed away entirely with us inside it.

Each night we would lie next to each other, the three of us in a tight little row, like sardines in a tin, and we would throw this one sleeping bag across us all and try not to move too much until the morning.

We had no idea how to camp. Of an evening when we needed some heat, we didn't have a clue how to make a campfire so we got an empty box that had once contained somebody else's cans of beer, stuffed it with bits of wood and paper that we found around the place, and just torched it with a can of Lynx and a cigarette lighter until it caught fire. There was a charity tent selling small paper cups of soup with a bread roll for 50p, so that was what we lived on for the duration. Our lack of suitable equipment, sufficient funds and relevant knowhow was both comical and ridiculous, but the financially enforced sobriety made every moment of it memorable.

The baking hot sunshine and warm evenings on that August bank holiday weekend in 1995 were a friend to our tiny child's tent and single-sleeping-bag arrangement, but the sun wasn't a friend to me. It blazed down for three days, and as we spent every single moment right out in the thick of it, I ended up with sunstroke pretty bad on the third night and finished the weekend as a shivering wreck.

I had no idea how to find our pathetic tiny child's tent in the dark, so I just sat there shivering uncontrollably at the place where we had arranged to meet. Music legend Neil Young was headlining on the Sunday and he had none other than Pearl Jam as his backing band, which should have been incredible and probably was, but I spent his whole set trying to stop my teeth chattering and silently begging them to stop playing so that it could all be over. None of us had one of these new-fangled mobile-phone things yet, so we just had to make our plans and stick to them.

If you thought that a coach of long-haired teenaged rock and metal fans might smell bad at the best of times, you can only imagine what the return coach journey was like after three days camped out in a heatwave. I'm just gobsmacked the driver didn't pass out amid the overwhelming funk and drive us all into a motorway bridge.

My experience of festivals would change significantly over the coming years, as friends and family would become experts in navigating me around and over all of the bodies, bags and beers strewn on the ground.

It is common for those in the midst of sight loss to want to travel the world and visually experience as much as they can while they are able to soak up wondrous places and landmarks, and to fill their visual memory with those sights that will soon be taken beyond their grasp.

I get it. I can understand the overwhelming awe that people must feel in standing at the foot of a pyramid, gazing up at its enormity and feeling the Egyptian sun beating down while wondering how they were able to build this colossal structure long before even the Romans were a thing. It's not something I've ever done, but I'm good with that, because what I have done is crowd-surf across the top of a sea of bodies as hundreds of hands kept me aloft, as the sun set and the stage lights blared, as grunge legends Soundgarden played and fifty thousand fans held their arms in the air. This is my Egyptian pyramid, a real-life cover of a Queen album that I was up there to see and feel, and to experience its overwhelming awe.

Chapter Fifteen

I had continued playing football during my teenage years and through into my time at college in Hereford. Five-a-side was a weekly treat, but even just taking a ball to smack into a goal over and over for half an hour on my own had been great for blowing away the cobwebs.

When you're losing your sight so slowly that you can't really notice it happening, it takes an incident, an injury, or a close shave to make you realise that maybe you should stop doing a particular thing you have always enjoyed and been able to do in the past. Anything involving running had started to become a problem for me. I was now unable to see far enough in front of me to allow for moving much faster than a slow jog.

One year earlier, on 1 November 1994, yes, that exact date, I had sprinted as fast as I was able from my maths lecture, which finished at 5 p.m., through the streets of Hereford to the tiny Our Price music store in its city centre before it was due to close in just half an hour's time. This was the date that Nirvana's *MTV Unplugged in New York* album was released and I had set my heart and my mind on having it in my hands as soon as I was able.

I ran as fast as I could and I ran without fear, but a couple of near misses with some street furniture and a cyclist gave me a bit of a wake-up call. Running straight into a sandwich board would have done nobody but me any harm, but my close shave with the cyclist could have ended up pretty bad for both of us. Still determined to get my hands on my prize, though, and for the safety of myself and everybody around me, I ended my self-imposed race against time in no more than a fairly careful jog. I did leave that little music store with a copy of that wonderful album in my hands, but also with an understanding that I now had some new limitations to take into consideration in the future.

The fact that this sprint through the streets of Hereford hadn't ended in disaster was probably a little more down to luck than anything else. I was running with the confidence of somebody who hadn't yet grasped that he probably shouldn't be running any more, racing into space that I hadn't really been able to process in advance, and charging into the unknown based mainly on what I thought should probably be there, rather than what was.

There is an exhilaration in running, a freedom and a refreshing sense of solitude. There is something about pro-pelling yourself through air and feeling that movement against your face, which is invigorating and humbling. Running is free. Running is freeing, but running to get this Nirvana album from Our Price before it closed at 5.30 p.m. on 1 November 1994 was the last time I ever ran anywhere on my own, just for the hell of it and just because I could.

I had continued to run for football: the lighting was better and by its very nature we were all a lot more aware of each other's movements. During one game, though, an eleven-a-side match on a grass pitch, I lasted about twenty minutes before putting myself in hospital. Our team was made up of people like myself, who had lost some amount of their sight but could still play regular football, and we were playing against a team of guys from a local college in Hereford who had nothing wrong with their sight at all. This was just a game for fun – it wasn't like we were the only semi-blind team in a fully sighted league. That would have been taking the piss a bit, wouldn't it?

I was chasing the ball down the right wing when suddenly a body appeared in front of me from absolutely nowhere. I was running at full speed so, rather than just smashing into him, on instinct and maybe a bit of self-preservation I dropped and slid studs first right at him. The guy in front of me leaped into the air to avoid the crazy bastard that was flying full pelt and studs up at his legs, and as I went sliding underneath him and he went flying over the top of me, his knees smacked me right under the chin and I was out for the count before I'd even come to a halt.

I came around to the splashing of water and the gentle tapping of a hand on my face. I'd been out for a while and it seemed that every man and his dog were gathered around me. My teeth had punctured my bottom lip and I had blood dribbling out of lacerations in my face. An incident had occurred. I wasn't being knowingly reckless, I just had no idea that another player was anywhere near that close to the space I was charging into. I injured myself and got packed off to hospital, but I could have broken that poor guy's legs.

I have never been massively precious about my own safety or self-preservation in the context of my blindness, but when my limitations have meant I've become a danger to others around me I have always had to take stock.

I was eighteen years old and that was the last game of football I ever played. I do miss it, or at least I did for a while. Playing football was a good way to keep fit, it was a healthy way to indulge in competition but, above all, it was social and it was fun. Just like when I was no longer able to play computer games with friends, I felt like a big part of my social life was being taken away from me. Of all the frustrations and difficulties that I would encounter throughout sight loss and those early years of blindness, I think the hardest thing to come to terms with was the loss of these social facets of myself, and the loss of having fun with friends.

No, leave that tiny violin alone this time, obviously not all fun. I've had a lot of fun in my life. It did feel, though, like I had to spend much of my teenage years and early adulthood relinquishing some quite significant parts of myself when it became impossible to indulge them any more.

I stopped being able to run freely at a different time from when I stopped being able to play football. I would no longer be able to walk safely after sunset at a different time from when I would stop being able to see anything on a computer monitor or a TV screen. It was a different time when I stopped being able to walk independently, even in daylight, and this was different still from when I was no longer able to make out even the blurry form of another person and be able to tell if they were still present in a drawn-out moment of silence.

All of these things would happen between my starting college in Hereford at the age of seventeen and around eight years later, when trying to see anything at all was more futile than attempting to peer through a bathroom window in the rain. From the inside obviously. I'm not a pervert. Any more.

If you lose your sight in an instant, there is one single moment that you have to deal with, the loss of everything happening at the same time. I can only imagine that this would be incredibly difficult and painful, but the flip side here is that you do just have two distinct identities: the sighted you that is lost in that moment, and the new blind you, which you must try to come to terms with. My loss was drip-fed to me over such a long period of time that my identity was constantly being forced to change and I lost many different versions of me along the way. I would find that I was always playing catch-up and never really allowed to settle. The loss was a constant, and as a result I think I developed coping strategies to protect myself against its relentless intrusion and probably against any sadness that all of that loss might have caused me to feel. I wouldn't let sadness be an option in case it ate me alive. Instead I developed the strategy of just taking a deep breath, shoving all that negative shit to one side, of pulling up my big-boy pants and of just getting on with it as best I could. I think that this attitude, strategy, lifetime of denial, call it what you will, has probably contributed hugely to me being able to find success as a comedian over the past two decades, but I think it has also likely numbed me to a significant part of the human experience. I look at sadness so logically in my mind. I process it rather than feel it, like I'm working in a mail sorting office, shoving it off into different tubes based on its label and without ever really opening any of it to see what is inside.

It is worth mentioning here that I wouldn't have it any other way. Obviously it would have been nice if I'd never lost my sight at all, but shit happens. I'm glad I lost my sight the way I did, constantly and continuously over twenty-five years, rather than being born with no sight or losing it in an instant.

I was lucky enough to see and do so much while I was young and able, and I had a lifetime to become accustomed to the loss. From my position now, these are all the same pathways I would take if I had to live it again and was given those choices along the way – although maybe I'd spend a little longer looking for the gents' toilet in McDonald's next time around.

My time in Hereford was my favourite two years of education, once I'd narrowed the focus down to things I actually liked and got rid of all the other crap, and before university would drill it down to such a level of tedium while reintroducing the stresses of a mainstream learning environment. Hereford is also where I had the teacher who would have the biggest impact on the rest of my life.

Tim Ashmore was a brilliant maths lecturer who, for my first year, sported the long grey hair of a crazy scientist, but who returned after that first summer break with his head as polished as a cue ball. Tim was brilliant and engaging. He made it feel exciting to learn, and he is probably solely responsible for me not just pouring the rest of my life down the plughole. Tim had been asking me what my plans were once I'd finished my A levels, and I didn't have an answer.

'I don't know,' I told him, 'but I'm not going to university.'

The thought of university had been terrifying me. I had spent ten years in specialist education and had wanted a mainstream education just a couple of years earlier when I'd tried regular old college in Liverpool, but that hadn't worked out well. University felt to me like it would probably just be the same as that but times a hundred. My plan, if you can call it that, was to return to Liverpool and just see what happened. Who knows? Maybe I would have focused on the guitar, formed a band and been a mega rockstar by the time I hit thirty, in which case – thanks for nothing, Tim!

Tim asked me, just as a favour to him, to complete the UCAS forms and apply to six universities. He applied no pressure whatsoever. He just wanted me to have options that were open to me for as long as possible, and he just wanted me to think about them.

As Kev had been a year ahead of me, he had headed off to university in Kingston-upon-Thames as I was starting that second year of college, so I put the name of his university on the form. We had remained very close throughout that second year and I just figured that the one thing that made the idea all seem a little less terrifying would be knowing somebody who was already there if I did decide to go.

Tim arranged for somebody to drive me to a few of these universities to have a look around and to attend any interviews that were offered to me but, again, with the aim of keeping those options open to me for as long as possible. I was offered several places, and Tim laid down a suggestion that was difficult to argue against.

'Why not just give it a go?' he said. 'Loads of people drop out of uni because it's not for them, so what have you got to lose? At least you'll never wonder what it might have been like if you try it and don't like it.'

He was right, of course. I didn't really have anything to lose as I was lucky enough to have caught the tail end of free university courses. I was one of the lucky ones who wouldn't be expected to begin the rest of my life with more debt than a decent-sized house deposit if I decided to take a punt on university life.

'I think Kingston is a good shout,' he said. 'Kev will show you the ropes, and Kingston is a nice place to be.'

After I'd decided to give university a go I told Neil about my plans.

'I'm going to uni in Kingston,' I said to Neil one day.

'Okay, where's that?' said Neil.

'Somewhere down south near that London. Why don't you phone them and see if you can get in as well?' I suggested.

'Yeah, all right,' said Neil. 'I'll give them a call,' and that was that.

So now the two of us were heading down to Kingston, and although, these days, Neil has moved a little further out to Hampshire for a bit of extra square footage, it's almost thirty years later and Kingston-upon-Thames is where I still live. I think it's fair to say that everything else that happens in this book is probably because of Tim, and his very kind and gentle encouragement to keep my options open and to do something that scared me. So, to the best teacher I ever had, cheers, Tim.

I have such fondness for the city of Hereford. I have been lucky enough to play some of the biggest theatres around the country, but getting to play Hereford's wonderful 400-seat Courtyard Theatre is one of the absolute highlights of touring for me and it's a huge source of pleasure. I have played there several times over the last two tours, and returning as a touring comedian to the place that helped to prepare me for life really does feel like one of those full-circle moments, because a lot had to happen between leaving Hereford in the summer of 1996 and getting to this point now, where this has all been possible.

Chapter Sixteen

My nan passed away as I was preparing to head off to university. It was heartbreaking, but it had been expected and we all got the chance to say our goodbyes. She taught me so much about making humour your superpower throughout blindness, and how to laugh in the face of frustration rather than letting it overwhelm you. She passed this on to my mum, my sister and me throughout all of the wonderful time we each had with her. My nan was capable, independent, and loved to joke and laugh. She just got on with life and never took herself too seriously. She taught us all to keep laughing, no matter what life may throw at you. Towards the end of her life, further strokes and dementia had left her in significant cognitive decline, but still some small signs of herself and her humour would manage to shine through.

My cousin Colin and I would go to visit her in the residential home, and towards the end we weren't sure sometimes whether she knew who we were, or even if she knew that anybody was with her at all. Dementia brings with it a hideous decline, but I can't imagine how scary or confusing experiencing dementia through blindness must have been.

At times like these when she would be sat in silence, Colin

and I would sit with her and just talk for the entire time we were there. We would tell her everything we had been up to since our last visit, and we would ask her a multitude of questions without expecting any response. In fact, often we would just answer these questions on her behalf to create the illusion of conversation.

'What have you done this morning, Nan? You've probably had a cup of tea and a biscuit, haven't you? I bet you've had a visitor as well, yeah?'

'What did you have for your tea last night, Nan? Probably cottage pie, was it? Or was it soup day yesterday?'

'That's a nice jumper you're wearing, Nan. Where did you get that from? Probably from one of our mums, was it? Yeah, it probably was, wasn't it, Nan?'

One day my mum had been visiting her and was getting herself ready to head home. 'Just to let you know,' said my mum, 'Chris and Colin are coming to see you later this afternoon.'

The way my mum tells it is that my nan then let out a low sigh of exasperation. 'Oh, tell them not to bother,' she said. 'They've been getting on my bloody nerves. They don't shut up. They just ask questions, questions, questions. I could do with a bit of peace and quiet today.'

This makes me laugh so much. Yeah, sure, sometimes towards the end my nan didn't know who any of us were, or that she had company at all, but sometimes we got on her bloody nerves and she didn't have the heart to tell us to put a sock in it.

My nan's funeral was to take place during my first week

of university, Fresher's Week. My mum said she thought I should head down to uni as planned instead of remaining in Liverpool for the funeral, because she didn't want me to miss out on those important first few days of making new friends, as even arriving just a bit later might mean that cliques and friendship groups had already been established without me.

I didn't go to my nan's funeral, but I felt like I'd already been able to say goodbye. Her passing had been imminent, so I had been able to give her a kiss on the forehead as she slept so peacefully and had been able to tell her how much I loved her before she slipped away. That for me was nice, it felt good. We have never been a religious family, and although my nan's funeral would have been another chance to say goodbye, it was never going to serve a spiritual purpose or be anything beyond a collective farewell.

Despite thinking that this was how I felt and that I had dealt with this trade-off in my mind, on the night of her funeral I had been out in Kingston with Kev and some of my new uni friends. I was walking back to halls with Kev and his girlfriend of the time, and I was several metres behind them while they chatted.

My sight in the dark was really very patchy by this point and I'd also drunk whatever the amount of alcohol is that a student on Fresher's Week would usually drink, when I walked straight into a metal post. I can still hear the *dong* of my forehead smacking into it with the precision and technique of a Glaswegian bell-ringer.

I have smacked my head into so many immovable objects

in my life: lampposts, door frames, and the bastard edges of open kitchen-cabinet doors to name but a few. Bathroom sinks and low-standing items of solid furniture are a particularly nasty surprise if you forget that one is present and bend down quickly to pick something up off the floor.

I once walked full pelt into a parking meter and took the entire impact on a single bottom tooth. Although it managed to stay rooted in my mouth, it was numb for months afterwards and has been a bit wonky ever since.

Every time I experience one of these brutal impacts out of the blue, I will either let out a primal yell of frustration at the universe, or I will swear profusely at the offending object. Honestly, I've called a bedside cabinet a cunt so many times it's bordering on insanity. After that, though, I'll usually take some deep breaths while applying an open palm to the impact area, and maybe even have a sit-down if possible until I stop seeing stars. It doesn't matter how blind you get, you'll always see those stars.

On this occasion, though, as soon as my head connected with that lamppost I just burst out crying in the middle of the street. It was like I had bottled up every emotion about my nan's passing. Not being at her funeral and the sudden impact of that lamppost had completely shattered that bottle to smithereens. It all came flooding out of me and I just sobbed and sobbed, like a very drunk student who was far away from home on the day that his nan's funeral had taken place.

My nan was called Violet Prout and she died on 19 September 1996 at the age of seventy-four. We love you, Nan! X

My mum has very much continued where my nan left off, making sure that we always try to find the funny in frustration or misfortune rather than being tempted to wallow in its depths. Her desire for me to experience that first week of university and make new friends might have been incredibly rational, but it would also prove to reward me in ways that I am still grateful for to this day. That's because in my very first week I met Gary, Steve and Haydn, three wonderful arseholes, who would join Neil and Kev to become my very closest friends over the next three decades and counting.

Would I still have met these guys if I hadn't been there during that very first week? Who the hell knows? Maybe I would. Maybe I would have met just two of them. Maybe if I'd turned up a week later, Gary would already have fallen in with a different group of guys rather than becoming one of my closest friends in the world. Life is just a series of sliding-doors moments, isn't it? And none of us can really be sure about how any of it might have played out under slightly different circumstances. The butterfly flaps its wings and big shit happens, or something like that.

All of these guys would be present throughout my eventual slip into blindness, and all of them would be incredibly supportive of my hare-brained venture into comedy when it happened, and have continued to be of the career that followed. When you have a disability, you don't get by in life without accepting practical help and support from others from time to time and these guys were always unwavering in this regard. I very much doubt I would have been able to carve out a career in comedy and make it off the open-mic circuit at all if it wasn't for their support. In those early years they would give up their time to accompany me to countless shitty rooms above pubs all over London. Haydn is probably the person I have the most to thank for during those first years in comedy. His companionship and support while I was doing stand-up for pretty much nothing but the stage time was more than anybody could reasonably expect from any single person. I think it's fairly safe to say that without him, that hare-brained venture into comedy would likely have been a fairly brief dalliance and everything that followed would never have happened at all.

As well as being best man at Neil's wedding, obviously, I was also best man at Haydn's and would even officiate at Gary's wedding, ending up as a blubbering mess as I tried to pronounce that they were now husband and wife through the relentless onslaught of snot and tears. Gary asked me to be a part of his day because I am one of his closest friends, but also I would imagine because I have experience of speaking publicly, because I've built up a certain confidence, because I've acquired a stage presence. How many weddings have you been at where the newly married couple have had to console their officiator in a three-way hug, because he's crying too much to get his words out and struggling to finish the ceremony?

We had a good time in that first year of uni – in fact so good that I barely made it to any lectures and memories are at best a little foggy. I'm especially short on mornings to recall as many of my days would involve waking up for the second teatime edition of *Neighbours* before embarking on a brand-new evening.

We smoked a fair bit of weed back then, but our metabolisms could cope with the frequent junk-food binges and munchie runs to the twenty-four-hour garage that this would inevitably lead to. Conversations through bullet-proof glass were a regular occurrence, and I would say we walked away with what we actually wanted less than half the time, often just agreeing to whatever items were held up and waved in our direction by the shop's only occupant so that we could end this futile escapade and get back to a safe haven.

This might be hard to believe, but it was only during my first year of uni that I tried pizza for the first time. Growing up I had never liked cheese, and had just assumed that I wouldn't like pizza either – after all, it was covered in the stuff. What I didn't realise, though, was that melted cheese tastes a damn sight different from just cold hard blocks of it. One day in halls Haydn offered me a slice.

'No, thanks,' I said. 'I don't like cheese.'

'Okay,' said Haydn, 'fair enough, but you're missing out.'

'Oh, go on, then,' I relented immediately, 'give us a go.'

I was a hungry malnourished student who had the munchies, and I probably needed to be less picky if I wanted to stay alive. I took a small slice from Haydn's plate and bit into it and, Jesus Christ, my world was changed for ever. The crazy thing was that it wasn't even a good pizza. It was a bottom-of-the-range supermarket 99p cook-in-the-oven job, with no more than eight pieces of pepperoni spread over a thin smear of cheap-ass mozzarella on top of a plate-sized, slightly burned bread base – although that's not how it was described on the box.

That slice of budget pizza honestly still goes down as being one of the greatest culinary revelations of my life: it blew my mind, it opened my eyes, and it changed my life for ever. The following day I went straight down to the supermarket to buy a stack of ten of the exact same pizzas with which to fill my drawer in the freezer. No matter what happened now, I knew I could eat like a king for at least ten more days and with minimal effort.

Looking back, I'm glad that my introduction to pizza was at that low-budget level: if my first taste had been a Domino's, a Papa Johns, or something like that, then I think my head might actually just have exploded clean off my shoulders there and then.

Pretty early on in that first year we were reported for smoking weed by security, who had been on patrol past my open ground-floor window while a few of us were in there creating a bit of a haze. As it was my room, it was me that was called up in front of the hall warden, buttocks clenched to take whatever punishment was thrown at me.

'You're the first one I've had up in front of me for this so far this year,' she said, 'so I'm going to cut you some slack.'

I couldn't believe it. My buttocks immediately unclenched as she continued.

'I understand what it's like when you first get here, but you need to know that I won't stand for this in the future and I want you to pass this message on to all of your friends. Do you understand me?'

'Yes, of course,' I replied. 'Thank you. Thank you very much.'

'Okay, good. So, what have you learned from this?' she asked.

I've spent a lifetime saying the wrong things in serious conversations and that's because the wrong thing is often the funniest. 'Thinks he's the class clown. No good will ever come of this.' Remember that? I've always been drawn to funny, especially in moments of pressure or discomfort, and it has got me into trouble from time to time.

'Next time keep the window closed,' I said, with a big grin.

'What the hell is wrong with you?' she said. 'I'm giving you a bloody pass here and you're making jokes.'

'Shit, sorry,' I said, backpedalling as fast as I could. 'Understood, I'll be on my best behaviour from now on and I'll pass that message on.'

I was indeed very lucky as it wouldn't be long before a couple of mates were kicked out of halls for exactly the same thing. Did I get a pass because I was the first one caught? Or did I get a pass because she didn't fancy kicking the almost-blind kid out in his first month? I'm not sure but I'll take either. After all, there have to be some perks to this blind thing, don't there?

Obviously we continued to smoke, but we would just try to be a little more careful about it moving forward. On a few occasions, though, we would forget to cover the smoke detectors and end up setting off the fire alarm. This would automatically trigger the arrival of the hall warden and the fire brigade, creating a level of panic among us that was so sudden and urgent that even when stoned we would move like lightning.

On one of those occasions we were in my bedroom when the fire alarm went off. The place stank like Bob Marley's dressing-gown and so, while everybody else frantically gathered up the various paraphernalia and accoutrements of the night's activities and made for the door, I tried to air the room as best I could. I opened the window and emptied the entire remainder of a can of Lynx in a desperate attempt to mask the unmistakable aroma with the scent of Africa.

The fire brigade arrived as we were all waiting outside, and part of me was hoping that an entirely separate incident had triggered the alarm for the whole building and that it was nothing to do with our activities at all. After a little investigation into the cause of the alarm, a fireman emerged and headed straight towards us.

'Which one of you lot is in W1E?' he asked.

I was in the shit, I knew that, so I shuffled forward to hear whatever judgement was about to be passed as the same hall warden emerged from the crowd and drew up alongside him.

'That's me,' I sheepishly replied, my head slightly lowered. 'W1E. What's happened?'

'Don't spray quite so much deodorant next time,' he said. 'It plays havoc with the smoke alarms. Maybe try a shower instead.'

I couldn't believe it. Saved by a can of Lynx Africa, and possibly a fireman who didn't know what weed smelled like, but either way – what a result. I was more than happy for him to proclaim that I must be a proper smelly bastard who needed a good wash than have to face possible eviction – or maybe he saw the face on our hall warden as she approached and thought he'd throw me a bone.

Either way, from the bottom of my heart, thank you, Mr Fireman.

Chapter Seventeen

Moving to London opened up access to so much live music for me. The number of concerts I went to watch throughout my first ten years in the capital is beyond a figure that I could even begin to estimate.

I wish I'd kept ticket stubs from every concert and gig that I'd been to so that I have a record of joyous and noisy nights out in sweaty mosh pits throughout my youth. It would be a lovely way to keep a firm hold of those memories in the absence of a diary. The truth is that most of the tickets would likely have been destroyed by sweat or beer or probably a combination of the two, as I would often emerge from these musical escapades absolutely dripping in both.

I have only ever been able to keep hold of one single ticket for the memories, and that is because it was never actually used and remains in pristine condition. It is for Nirvana's Manchester GMEX show in 1994. The original date had been rescheduled due to Kurt Cobain's health issues, but he took his own life just a few weeks before the rescheduled show was to take place. I never did see Nirvana perform live, but I kept hold of that ticket, I suppose, as a memory of the memories never made.

If I could pay five hundred quid for a DeLorean that actually worked, and go back in time to any concert that took place during my lifetime that I wasn't at, then set those time circuits to 30 August 1992 and I'd head straight for Nirvana's headlining show at the Reading Festival. They had pretty much been written off due to Kurt's addiction and conflicts within the band, and the swirling rumours were that Nirvana was over and they were probably not even going to make it onto the stage. What materialised, though, was one of the rawest and finest and loudest middle fingers held up in rock history, and to have been there in that familiar field to experience it as the sun went down, well, it would be my idea of musical heaven.

You can stream the whole show from all of the usual places, go on, I'll wait . . .

I've had to purposely narrow this wistful time-travel fantasy down to concerts that took place during my lifetime, as if we start stretching back the possibilities further, beyond 1977, we start opening up options such as Jimi or the Doors, and then it all starts getting very complicated, doesn't it?

Also, if anybody does have a DeLorean with fully working time circuits, I'd be happy to pay more than five hundred quid for the day. After all, time would be irrelevant, wouldn't it?

In just our second month in the capital Pearl Jam played two nights at Wembley Arena and it was just fourteen quid for a ticket, so we went to both, of course. Their last tour was £165 by comparison, that's well over a thousand per cent increase in the last thirty years, and this isn't just a Pearl Jam thing. I don't think anything has experienced inflation quite like concert tickets. I understand that this is in part due to the changing landscape of the music industry and how bands mainly make their money in the streaming age, but if the price of a standard Mars Bar had increased by the same rate, that simple delight would cost nearly four quid in today's money, while a Pot Noodle would set us back about seven of our earth pounds.

It's sad that so much live music is simply cost prohibitive to young kids, these days, when really it's Mars Bars and Pot Noodles that they could do with a few less of. When I was a student I used to have a Mars Bar and a can of Coke for my breakfast, and I would make white-bread sandwiches with a Pot Noodle filling. How the hell am I still alive?

Moving to London didn't just open the doors to being able to see countless American bands on tour, but it also opened the doors to a whole new world of brilliant live comedy.

I can't remember how, but I very quickly became aware that the Comedy Store was the place to go in London if you wanted to watch some top-level stand-up. Obviously there were famous comedians who would tour and play theatres, but the Comedy Store was somewhere you could just turn up for a night out without much planning involved. The Comedy Store would very quickly become a regular destination for us, the often unknown comedians performing there being just as funny as the household names I knew from the television. The standard at the Comedy Store was so ridiculously high, and now that I was able to watch it happening right in front of me, my love of stand-up was becoming ever deeper.

If you had asked me then, though, whether I thought I could do what any of those guys could do, I would have laughed in your face. This was a world of sublimely confident individuals who were obviously born with something special about them, an X factor that was present in only a tiny, tiny sub-percentage of the population. The idea that a normal regular person like me could get up on a stage and do what they could do was an absolutely preposterous suggestion. They were on that stage for a reason: they were special.

If I needed any more evidence that performing stand-up was beyond the attainment of us mere mortals, it would come in the form of Eddie Izzard. I was in my first year of university when I first stumbled across Eddie's comedy. It would have been some time between the latter part of October and mid-December of 1996 when I was having a potter about in a local branch of the smorgasbord of high-street enterprises that was known as Woolworths. For any younger readers who might not be aware of Woolworths, it was a glorious establishment that, although it specialised in nothing, did enough of lots . . . Everything from homeware and cleaning products to clothes and toys, through chocolates, cards, batteries and biscuits, to the latest and most popular music and video releases. Its non-specificity was both its brilliance and its eventual downfall, and its presence is truly missed from the fabric of our towns.

I've narrowed it down to the timeframe above, as this is when all of the stand-up video releases for Christmas 1996 would have been out on display. And while as a kid I'd had to wait until the day itself to get my mitts on any of them, as an adult all of those Christmas stand-up offerings just became a delicious buffet I could dip into as and when I saw fit.

Eddie Izzard's *Definite Article* caught my attention more than any of the other titles that were out on display. First, it wasn't in a typical plastic video case like the rest of them, but in a cardboard clam-shell box, which weirdly made it feel so much more premium. It also had a bit of velvety texture on the cover, so you could actually feel Eddie's clothes. I had never come across any little touch of detail like that on a video before. The other thing I found interesting about it was that I had never heard of Eddie Izzard. Here I was, holding this video, which had such a unique and premium feel to it compared to the rest that were out on display, and I had no idea who this person even was.

I was intrigued, but if I'm honest, I also thought I knew exactly what Eddie's comedy would be. From the way he was dressed on the cover, fairly flamboyant and in feminine attire, I made a judgement. I assumed that Eddie must be gay, and that this would almost certainly be fairly camp comedy, stand-up very much in the same vein as somebody like Julian Clary, but of course I couldn't have been more wrong.

I loved Julian Clary, and still do, so this was not a disparaging judgement in any way – after all, I bought Eddie's video assuming it would probably be similar to Julian's brand of stand-up. I was certainly guilty of judging the book entirely by its cover, though, and this video in its peculiar cardboard box would end up blowing my tiny little mind even more than that pizza had. It felt like an entirely new style of stand-up, one that I had never seen before, one that was so unbelievably original and hilarious, and one that was so infinitely quotable without seeming to have set out to establish any catchphrases whatsoever.

This video had taken every judgement and expectation of what I thought it would be and smashed them all to smithereens to become the best piece of stand-up I had ever seen. Not only did I instantly have a new favourite comedian, but I think that Eddie ultimately ended up being a huge influence on my own approach to performing stand-up some years later, particularly when it came to talking about my blindness on stage while also managing to remain true to myself.

The way I saw it was that there was one very obvious feature about Eddie that I had assumed would define so much about his comedy.

Eddie would talk about having a preference for wearing women's clothes, but would keep it down to just a relatively small proportion of his time on stage. He would talk about it in a way that was not only funny and interesting, but also in a way that normalised it and would leave the audience wanting to hear more.

I knew that when I was guided out on to a stage in a comedy club, audiences could probably be forgiven for assuming I would probably just do twenty minutes or so of jokes about being blind. The truth is that there is so much more about us and so much more going on in our heads than just the one obvious thing that people might assume will probably define everything about us. Eddie made me realise that it's fine to ignore the elephant in the room and to truly be yourself, to use stand-up as a way of normalising the one obvious thing that is a part of you, to let people in on your own terms and, more importantly, to make them forget about it, which I believe normalises it so much more.

The following year a few of us headed into London without tickets to see if we could get into Eddie's 'Glorious' tour at the Docklands Arena. We arrived to find that it was sold out, but the gentleman in the box office told us to wait off to one side and he would see what he could do.

A few minutes before the show was due to start he came and fetched us and told us we were in luck. What we didn't know, and what you mightn't, is that shows often hold prime seats back for press and industry so it's always worth turning up or checking on the day of a performance to see if any further tickets have become available. We were ushered through to the auditorium where we were given premium seats right in the centre of the stalls. This was the first of many times I would get to see Eddie performing live and he was incredible.

We left the show that night on such a high, and with several packs of 'Glorious Size Izzla' between us, Eddie's take on 'King Size Rizla', which are still the best branded tour merch I've ever come across. We were desperate for the night not to end and decided on a whim to head into central London for the midnight show at the Comedy Store. All combined, this remains the best full night of comedy I have ever experienced. The compère at the Comedy Store that night was a comedian called Tim Clark, and he was so insanely brilliant and spent much of the night ripping into a friend of mine that he cemented himself firmly into my memory. Throughout my career I would get to work with Tim many times, some of those at the Comedy Store, and I always loved doing so because of the incredibly vivid memory I have of sitting there as a comedy fan while he absolutely destroyed the room.

I have never worked with Eddie over the past twenty years, but I did have an encounter some years ago while in New York City. In 2013 I was over there for a holiday with Patricia, Neil and Neil's wife, Fiona. We happened upon a small theatre where Eddie was advertised as performing warm-up shows for an upcoming world tour. Tickets had sold out, but there was a show that night and the next. Having performed stand-up for ten years by then, I wondered what the point was of being a comedian if I couldn't at least try and wangle a few tickets via other avenues. I knew a comic who had the same agent as Eddie, so I dropped him a text to see if he could pull a few strings and arrange for us to get four tickets on the door for the show the following night.

Later that evening we were in a restaurant waiting for our food when my phone rang.

'Is that Chris?' said the voice on the other end of the phone. 'It's Eddie Izzard here. I believe you want to come to the show tonight.'

I had always been fairly relaxed around any famous comedians I had encountered along the way, but this was my comedy hero Eddie Izzard phoning me, on my phone, and completely out of the blue. I've always found the idea of asking, 'Are you sitting down?' before delivering shocking or surprising news to be an unnecessary piece of theatre – after all, it's not like you're just going to hit the deck if you're not, is it? Well, it's a good job I was sitting down because I think I might have hit the deck if I wasn't.

'Err, yes, yes, err, yes,' I think I said a few times, 'yes, yes, err, yes,' having to shake myself out of the loop within which I'd become a bit stuck.

I had asked for tickets the following night, though, not on that night, so I suddenly found I was correcting Eddie Izzard, who was somehow speaking to me on my phone.

'Not today, it was for tomorrow,' I explained.

'Ah, I'm not doing tomorrow any more,' said Eddie. 'I've got to go to Canada for filming.'

What the hell was happening? Eddie Izzard was on my phone telling me about the changes to his schedule due to filming commitments.

'I'm on in half an hour, though, if you want to come along,' he added.

'Err, yes,' I said, 'but we're in a restaurant right over the other side of town and I'm not sure we can make it in time.'

'That's all right,' said Eddie. 'It won't take you much longer. Jump in a cab and I'll wait for you to arrive before I start.'

I hung up as the others stared at me, waiting to hear what had made me stutter so much and turn such a peculiar shade of pale.

'That was Eddie Izzard,' I said, and the three of them replied in chorus with exactly the same response.

'Fuck off!' they said.

'There is no show tomorrow,' I explained, 'but he's waiting for us right now.'

The four of us all jumped up from the table just as the

waiter was bringing out our meals. He didn't have a clue what was happening as we flung dollars on the table to cover the food we were leaving behind, except for three pork chops that Neil grabbed and started to munch as we bolted for the door to hail a cab.

After the show Eddie invited us all backstage to say hi, but I think I was still a bit shell-shocked by the path the evening had taken so I probably came across as a little bit weird. I've often heard the adage 'Never meet your heroes: they'll only disappoint you.' Well, in this specific case, Eddie could not have been more hospitable and generous, so I think a more appropriate adage might have been 'Never meet your heroes: you'll only disappoint yourself.'

Between all the concerts and comedy, missed mornings and other indulgences of student life, I ended up so borderline in terms of passing my first year of university that I was required to attend an interview to determine my knowledge of what had been taught. I was informed that pass or fail would be decided from this face-to-face chat and that it would be entirely at the discretion of Professor Ling.

'Okay, I think I see the problem,' said the man who walked into the room where I was waiting. 'I am one of your course lecturers, and I don't recognise you. In fact, I don't think I've ever seen you before in my life.'

He had a point. He hadn't, unless he'd been drinking in some of the same hangouts that I had, or possibly sold us some weed.

I am told that for legal reasons I have to make it clear that that's a joke and he never once sold us weed.

He sold us it twice.

Okay, I am now told that I have to make it clear that's a joke and that he never sold us weed ever.

We sold it to him.

Right, I am now informed that I also have to make it absolutely clear that that's a joke as well and that we never sold him weed either, and to please stop mentioning it. Jesus, writing a book that keeps the legal team happy is boring, isn't it?

If I'm honest, Professor Ling wasn't exactly what I was expecting either, as from his surname alone I had assumed he would be Chinese. But even I was still able to see enough to tell that this bloke was a white British bloke who was quite clearly not Chinese. I had been fully expecting to have to pretend that I knew who this Chinese man was, because I'd been to all of his lectures, obviously, and that it wasn't my fault that this Chinese man just hadn't noticed me sat there in his class.

As he sat down in front of me, though, I think the momentary look of surprise on my face at his distinct lack of Chineseness let him know that I didn't know who he was either, and my game was up.

After a long chat, that lovely man decided to give me a pass to the second year. He understood that a lot of the first year of studies was just a regurgitation of stuff I'd done in my A levels and that it wasn't massively important in the grand scheme of things. The grades didn't even count towards your final degree. It would all start properly in the second year and so, with a few words of valuable advice about knuckling down from here onward, this lovely man, who I'd now at least met for the first time and who definitely wasn't Chinese, was off and away into the night.

Having Neil and me arrive at university had not been the best for poor Kev's academic success. He'd done really well in his first year, but having us degenerates turn up meant that his second year had been a total disaster and he was going to have to resit it. Oh, well, it wasn't all bad. At least now we would all be in the same classes and could try and knuckle down together, I suppose.

Chapter Eighteen

During that second year I ended up living with Kev in a two-bedroom flat. I know, two guys with shit eyesight living together, what could possibly go wrong?

My music tastes had been stretching to yet heavier and heavier sounds while I'd been at university, and I had been growing my hair to greater lengths in support of this development. I played really noisy albums from super-heavy bands that Kev would complain made him feel physically sick, actually physically sick – those are the words that he actually said, but this was a guy who had Hanson's Christmas album on CD so I don't think he gets to have an opinion.

Sorry that piece of information is out there in the world now, Kev, but this is my book and the people need to know.

I dyed my hair jet black and wore it approaching my belly-button, which with my almost translucent complexion and light eyebrows provided a harsh contrast that likely made me look pretty damn ill, regardless of those Pot Noodle sandwiches.

I was entering that final phase of vision now, which would have me well into that last 10 per cent, on the cusp of that 6 per cent mark, if my calculations are correct. I mean, they almost certainly aren't correct, but you get the point. Either way, it wasn't a great deal and the bottom line was that I was unable to see what I looked like in the mirror anyway.

I wore boots, combats and a long black coat, and I reckon it was only the failing sight that stopped me applying the face makeup, black eyeliner and matching lipstick, I would imagine, maybe even a Gothic design drawn on one cheek. Yes, I think it's safe to say that this was definitely the one area of my youth where my disability did me a favour.

Despite the hair and the fashion, or lack of, I had knuckled down when it came to the work, but even just knowing which of my lecturers weren't Chinese was a huge improvement on that first year.

As we approached our final term of the second year, I had to allow my hair to return to its natural hue and get it cut – well, just a little bit – and this was because I needed to find a job. As part of our degree we were required to spend the entirety of our third year out on work placement, so a significant part of that final term involved having to secure this placement. I was absolutely dreading it. The idea of having to integrate into a vast new environment full of new people, and to have to do all of this with the little sight I had remaining while trying to pretend I could see more than I could . . . Well, it felt both terrifying and exhausting before I'd even started.

If they could have just allocated me a placement and told me that this was my job for the year, I think it would have made the prospect far less daunting, but it was also the thought of having to go to God knows how many interviews in completely unknown areas of London to even reach the starting line that was making me feel sick to my stomach. I had such a high level of anxiety around having to go to those job interviews, and that was due to the practical logistics of navigating myself around new environments and finding the places when I couldn't read signs, street names or even the company names written on buildings and their intercom systems. I also really struggled with transitioning between outdoors and indoors, as the change from bright sunlight to the relative darkness of indoors could take me quite a while to adjust to. I would often enter buildings unable to see anything at all, and once inside I would have to stand and wait until my eyes had adjusted sufficiently or just blunder through as best as I could.

I didn't carry with me any symbols of blindness or limited sight, so I would imagine that my behaviour was often observed as more than a little bit strange. The irony is that in not accepting blindness and by trying to create the illusion of somebody who could see absolutely fine, I was likely coming across as a bit of a weirdo. If I'd carried a white stick with me I would have presented myself as a perfectly normal blind guy and people would probably have been willing to help to a far greater extent than just pointing out directions to me that often didn't help much at all.

You may think it would be impossible to get around with just 6 per cent vision, but I suppose it means that if you could see obstacles and objects from a hundred feet away, I could see them from six feet away. It's not impossible, but it's also hardly a stroll in the park. People engaged in one-to-one conversations with me wouldn't have a clue that anything was different, but observing my behaviour from a distance would reveal a multitude of clues.

The anxiety I had around finding these places and not looking like a prat while doing so, well it far outweighed any of the nerves I had around actually doing the interview itself. Whereas somebody else might have felt sick about being sat in an interview, I was far too anxious about everything I had to do to get there for the interview to even make a dent.

I would find that this would also be the case when I was performing stand-up in those early years, that the nerves I had around the practical logistics of getting up onto the stage would far outweigh any nerves I might have had about the gig itself. Think of it this way: the prospect of sitting in a field of rats might fill anybody with dread and terror, but if you've had to cross a river of crocodiles to get there then, all of a sudden, the rats don't seem so bad, do they? If anything, you're just relieved that the crocs didn't get you and bollocks to the rats.

If you're looking for a job under any normal circum-stances, then you look in the geographic areas where you think you might like to work. You are under no obligation to go anywhere you don't want to, and if a job is located in a shit-hole or is too much of a daily mission from wherever you live, you don't have to apply for it.

The process of finding a placement was different, as all of the vacancies came in via the university and we had to put our names down next to the ones that we liked the look of. I had been sluggish in this regard, taking my usual approach of ignoring the problem I had some control over, until it became an even bigger problem that was no longer within my control. This ultimately resulted in the university getting me three interviews that I had no choice but to attend.

The first of these was for a company that had a grotty little unit in the back end of an industrial estate deep in north-west London. It would take a considerable word count to fully express how much I didn't want this job. It was bloody miles away and the thought of having to make the journey every day into the back end of nowhere was not something I wanted to become a reality.

I had no choice about attending the interview, but I certainly had just one goal when I was there, and that was to make 100 per cent sure that I did not get the job.

It's easy to not get a job. Pick your nose, fart in front of the interviewer, swear a lot, or just take a dump in Reception and smear it on the walls. It's a little more difficult to not get a job while you're still trying to remain professional and respectful, and to not bring the wrath of your university down upon you for staging a dirty protest at an interview they have arranged for you. I therefore decided that the best course of action would be to act like the model university student and prospective employee, but to hugely underplay the knowledge and experience I had.

'So, all of our systems here run on Windows 95,' said the guy who was interviewing me. 'Tell me what experience you have with Windows 95.'

I'd been using Windows 95 since its release in, well, 1995,

so by 1998 I had a good three years of experience under my belt. With that in mind I cleared my throat, looked him straight in the eye, or as best as I could manage, and I conjured up as much confidence as I could muster.

'Windows 95?' I pondered out loud, as I sucked air through my teeth. 'Well, I've heard of it.'

The guy just sat there in silence for a few moments. 'Right,' he finally said, in such a long-drawn-out way as to fill as much time as possible while he wondered what the hell to ask next.

I worried slightly that I might be coming across like I definitely didn't want the job even though I definitely didn't want the job, so I thought I'd better say something else to show a little enthusiasm for the opportunity.

'I mean I've never used it myself,' I continued, 'but I'm really good at picking things up.'

I then beamed an enthusiastic smile at him through the silence while he leafed through some pages in front of him, suddenly realising that all of his next questions were now redundant. The first was 'Tell me what experience you have,' not 'Tell me if you have any experience at all.' We both realised that the interview was over, but as we were both too polite to end it so soon, we bumbled our way through the next five minutes or so while he tried to explain what Windows 95 was to a guy who knew all about Windows 95 but who had to pretend that he didn't.

The second interview I had to attend was for a mortgage company in Richmond upon Thames, which doesn't sound like the basis for a good story, but this particular interview has acquired somewhat legendary status among my friends and has been retold countless times by so many over the years.

Variable interest rates and endowment policies didn't float my boat in any way whatsoever, but Richmond was just a couple of miles away and appealed to me infinitely more than the prospect of a daily trek into the industrial badlands of north-west London.

It turned out that I had some local competition for the vacancy, as local as you could get, really: just the other side of my bedroom wall Kev was also preparing to interview for the exact same job.

Kev's eyesight condition is different from mine. His vision is poor but stable, and he can get about the place good enough. Oh, and he's also colour-blind. There would have been a point in the past when my sight was better than his, but the tables had been turned in that regard some years ago.

As this was a job I actually wanted, I had been out to buy a new suit for the occasion. Having no real money or fashion sense meant that I'd ended up buying a cheap, nasty, ill-fitting suit from C&A. I'd been showing Kev my new suit and joking about what an idiot I probably looked in it, when Kev showed me the suit he'd bought from M&S. Still cheap and nasty in the grand scheme of things but it had cost him more than twice what I'd paid for mine.

Both of our interviews were on the same day, but mine was up first before lunch and Kev's was to be straight afterwards. My interview was fairly unremarkable. However, I felt very self-conscious because the cheap, nasty, ill-fitting suit I'd bought from C&A was clearly a lot more ill-fitting than I'd realised. The trousers were massive and I'd had to gather the waistline up so much under my belt that I had big wavy folds in them and flappy legs, and I was glad to get out of there and go home.

The two-bedroom flat we were renting was above a tattoo shop, and that tattoo shop was within a larger parade of shops. Right next door to the tattoo shop was a dry cleaner's, and I was so embarrassed by how big and flappy my trousers were that as soon as I'd taken them off, I went straight down and dropped them in to be adjusted.

Later that night Kev and I were eating pizza at home while having a bit of a debrief on our respective interviews, and it turned out that Kev's interview had been just as unremarkable as mine.

'I'll tell you what, though,' he said. 'I think I need to stop eating so much pizza as those trousers were killing me today. I could hardly fit into them and couldn't get the top button fastened at all.'

'Ha, that's funny,' I said, 'because mine were so big on me, way bigger than I remember them being in the shop when I bought them, they were flapping all over the place like a pair of clown's trousers.'

We stopped chewing for a few moments while we mulled over this information in our heads.

'You don't think we had the wrong suits on, do you?' asked Kev.

'No, we couldn't have,' I said. 'There's no way because

your jacket would have been way too big on me, and you wouldn't have even got into mine, you fat bastard.'

'What about just the trousers?' he said, before jumping up and running off to his room to check his suit.

'Fucking hell,' murmured Kev, as he came back into the living room squinting closely at the labels in his suit. 'My jacket says M&S but the trousers say C&A.'

The realisation hit us both. We had worn our own suit jackets but each other's trousers to the same job interview. We had arrived for an interview at the same company, to be interviewed by the same person for the same job, wearing half of each other's suit.

This was a mix-up that might have gone unnoticed if both suits had been the same colour but, of course, they weren't.

Kev's suit was black and mine was blue. I had arrived at my interview that morning unknowingly wearing a blue suit jacket and a pair of humungous flappy black trousers. This is a combo that, although not ideal, could maybe have been overlooked or at least forgotten by my interviewer by the time he'd had his lunch. Until, that is, somebody else, who also had an eyesight condition, arrived for an interview wearing the never-before-seen and exact polar opposite combo of the traditional black suit jacket and a pair of ultra-tight blue trousers.

Kev threw my trousers back at me and told me to go and get his.

'Err, yeah. That might be a bit of a problem,' I said.

I held on to my trousers tightly as I informed Kev about

the fate of his. I told him they would be ready for collection from the dry cleaner's in the morning, but that he probably wasn't going to fit into those now either.

I don't think I can say that I came out of this one on top, but I think that poor Kev definitely came out of it worse. Oh, and, surprise, surprise, neither of us got the job.

Chapter Nineteen

It wasn't long before Kev and I would move on with our lives and decide that two almost blind guys living together just wasn't worth the stress. Kev moved into a lovely three-bedroom flat with two very clean and tidy female friends from uni: winner! I, on the other hand, moved into a six-bedroom abomination of a house with Neil, Steve and three other student mates and, yes, it was much worse than you could ever imagine.

This shoddy Frankenstein's monster of a house had been forged out of the office space that was above and below an accountant's business, and it was the accountant who owned it. The place was an absolute disgrace and the guy was a slumlord who took advantage of us students and knew how to play the game. It had been botched together in such a shoddy way as to be almost comical in retrospect but quite depressing and even dangerous when in the moment. This piece-of-shit landlord accountant would take me to court for my last two months of rent as I decided to move out early and withhold the payments due to the place being uninhabitable. He managed to take me to court without me knowing about it and as a result I ended up with a county court judgement against me causing havoc on my credit file for six years. It felt like a lot at the time, but I've since had bad reviews that have lingered on the internet for much longer than that so six years wasn't that bad in retrospect.

The place was horrific. There were two bedrooms in the basement, but if it ever rained heavily the drains would back up and the basement toilet would explode. A guy called Dave Knightrider was the unfortunate inhabitant of one of those basement rooms. You may be surprised to learn that Dave Knightrider wasn't actually his birth name: he had acquired this nickname on the very first day of arriving in halls because his name was Dave and when we first met him he was riding on a skateboard and it was at night. I know, clever, isn't it? Dave and I were very close during our time at uni but drifted apart some years afterwards, as is often the way of life. I have such fond and appreciative memories of our friendship, and I hope life has been kind to him since those crazy days.

It certainly wasn't kind to him in that house: I remember poor Dave waking up one morning in his subterranean lair after there had been a particularly heavy downpour to find local neighbourhood poos floating around in half a foot of drain water on his bedroom floor.

There was a second toilet on a half-landing, which I suppose you would have to call the main bathroom, although this was only big enough to contain the loo and a tiny sink. There was a hole in the wall in that tiny bathroom near the floor, which meant that if you slipped on the wet lino – and, let's be honest, with six guys it could often be slippy – your leg could go straight through that hole and stick out the other side. Anybody outside might then be able to see a building with a leg stuck halfway up the side of it, like there was a glitch in the matrix.

So, with only a tiny bathroom containing a toilet and a sink, 'Where was the shower?' you might ask. Well, I think that's fairly obvious, isn't it? It was in the kitchen, of course.

The shower had been built into a space in the kitchen like it was an integrated fridge-freezer. I suppose the benefit was that you could make some breakfast while getting yourself ready in the morning, but this was not designed out of any intention to build a house of the future, but rather to cram the basic amenities of life into whatever spaces they would fit.

The kitchen shower would leak through the floor and into the bedroom of, yes, you guessed it, poor Dave, who had the occasional floating-neighbourhood-poo problem. As the place was all repurposed office space, every single bedroom had fluorescent lighting, so in Dave's basement poo room, the kitchen shower water would leak through his ceiling and run along the electric fluorescent light in both directions, creating what an estate agent might describe as a bespoke interior dual waterfall feature.

I would imagine that it was also probably a fairly substantial fire risk, but that didn't really matter, did it? We were only student fodder, so just there to satisfy the relentless financial hunger of Mr Shit Face & Co.

The living room was on the top floor and had a fire door with one of those lever-closing mechanisms attached to it. You know the things, where one end of the pointy metal lever is attached to the door and the other end to the wall. As the door is opened, the lever uses the immovable nature of the wall to pull the door closed again. Well, this particular lever mechanism wasn't attached to the wall, but instead to the door frame, and regular usage over time had caused the door frame to become completely detached from the wall. This meant that whenever the door was pushed open with any real momentum, instead of the lever using the wall to pull the heavy door closed again, it would actually use the heavy door to pull the entire door frame right off the wall.

Granted, this could have been thought of as quite an ingenious burglar immobilisation system. A poor unsuspecting burglar breaks in and is momentarily confused to find a shower in the kitchen. They manage to shake off this incongruity and head upstairs past the little half bathroom without stepping inside and slipping into the weird little wall hole. Up they go into the living room. They push open the heavy fire door and take a couple of steps inside, upon which the door frame leaps off the wall and clobbers them over the back of the head.

The dividing walls between bedrooms were made of either cardboard or Ryvita crispbread, so if somebody got lucky that night everybody knew about it. Nothing puts the dampeners on sexy time like Ryvita walls and fluorescent lighting, though, so this tended to be not so much of a problem.

Take all of these horrific features and add six student blokes into the mix, who had absolutely no respect for either Mr Scrotum Neck or his premises, and it was the worst place I've ever lived in. There were probably more unique strains of bacteria and virus breeding within those walls than you'd find in a Wuhan animal market, and I can't believe we all made it out alive.

I think even *Bottom*'s Richie and Eddie might have moved out of that place due to safety concerns.

I ended up working that placement year doing web development for a software company in Guildford. I got the job for two main reasons. First, Guildford was pretty easy to get to and its high street was far less threatening than that industrial estate in north-west London, so I put the effort in during the interview and actually tried to get the job, which definitely helped. Second, I turned up for the interview wearing a pair of trousers that weren't trying to fly away with every gust of wind and that actually matched the jacket I was wearing, which I think probably helped even more.

My colleagues were nice, although one of the owners of the company would scream down the phone at people to such an extent that it would become uncomfortable to be around. I would have to pretend I needed the toilet just so I could put a bit of distance between me and his spit-flecking screaming insanity. He was always nice to me, but there was something brewing under the surface that just wasn't right and he would very easily slip into full-blown adult tantrums, which is just a bit weird, isn't it?

There was also a lady who worked there who was so bad on computers it was mad that she worked for a software company that did everything on computers. One day she had a bit of a meltdown and claimed she no longer knew how to do anything on her PC any more because the desktop wallpaper had changed. That was it: the picture was different, which threw her entire mind into disarray. It had been a tree but now it was a mountain, and I had to change it back to being a tree just so she could use Microsoft Office again and didn't have to see a therapist about it.

The guy I sat next to was lovely, although I would come to learn that he had a bit of a weird fruit-related issue. One day he told me he had a fear of bananas.

'Surely you don't mean fear?' I said. 'Surely you mean that you don't like them or that they repulse you, but you're not actually scared of them, are you?'

'No,' he said. 'I'm terrified of them. It's an actual phobia.'

I wasn't buying this at all. I mean, who is scared of a banana? It was the maddest, most ridiculous thing I'd heard of. How can you be scared of a banana? What's the banana going to do? Follow you home, wait until you're asleep and then kill your entire family? It's a banana, for God's sake. This was 1998, though, so it's not like I could google it to see if it was a real thing. I had only two options really: take him at his word that he really did have a fear of bananas, or put that claim to the test.

A few days later I was leaving for work from the House of Horrors and a manky old banana was just sat there on the side near the kitchen shower. How fortuitous. I stuck it in my bag and took it into work with me. Later that morning when he was out of the room I snuck it into his bag to prove conclusively that an actual fear of bananas wasn't a real thing, and that at most he just didn't like them very much.

Lunchtime arrived and he put his hand into his bag to

grab his wallet, but instead he pulled out the old manky banana. Here we go – this was going to be brilliant. I waited with bated breath for him to laugh and maybe throw the banana at me. 'Yeah, very funny, arsehole. Have your manky banana back! I've told you I can't stand them.' Or something to that effect anyway.

Instead the poor guy started hyperventilating and seemed to be having a full-blown panic attack, so much so that he hadn't even been able to let go of the banana. He just stood there staring at it in his hand while he freaked out. I couldn't believe it. This guy was good, what an actor, because a fear of bananas wasn't a real thing, was it? Well, it turns out that maybe it can be, because he had to be sent home for the rest of the day to recover.

Writing about this now makes me feel very mean. What a cruel trick to play on somebody who had quite clearly stated that they had a fear of bananas, and I am truly sorry for the distress I caused.

But in my defence, though, come on, I was just a guy working with what he had in the pre-Google era of 1998. I mean, it's not like I could have gone to the library and looked up bananas in an encyclopaedia and it would have explained about the minuscule number of people who have a bizarre fear of them, is it? No, of course not.

OK, seriously, I do like to learn and am always striving to become a better person: googling it now confirms that a fear of bananas does exist and that it is called bananaphobia, so it is a real thing and I was wrong. I honestly just wish I could go back and do things differently.

But come on, bananaphobia? Well, it makes you think it's not even taken seriously within the world of dubious phobias. If it was, it would have an old Latin name like all of the others do, but bananaphobia just sounds like it's been made up by a child to explain the quite frankly bat-shit reaction to a banana of only five people in the world, and possibly that it was made up more recently than 1998.

I do understand, though, that this is no laughing matter, and that the real-life effects of bananaphobia were likely extremely distressing to grow up with, especially to a child. I would imagine that when he was younger he was unable to watch a single episode of *Bananaman* without needing to take a couple of days off school to recover, and even just the idea of 'Bananas in Pyjamas' must have been enough to trigger nightmares for weeks.

All I can say is that I am truly sorry.

If you've been affected by any of the issues in this book, then there are people you can talk to. Just dial 0800 BANANA.

Chapter Twenty

Throughout college and university, and during my time working as a web programmer in Guildford, I had been able to use a computer with magnification software. What this magnification software would do was to magnify an area of whatever was on the screen so that this area would fill the entire screen. I would therefore only be able to see a small magnified area of the screen at any one time but could then move that area around using the mouse.

One of the benefits of magnification software was that as my sight worsened I could simply increase the level of magnification. This would obviously increase the size of text and icons on the screen, but by doing so it would also reduce the magnified area of the screen that I was able to see at any one time to a smaller and smaller square. Inevitably, though, there comes a time when the magnification is so massive, and the area of the screen you are able to see is so small, that to all intents and purposes it pretty much becomes unusable. If you are only really able to see three huge letters on the screen at any one time then all words have the potential to be far too many words. Having 'cat' filling your entire screen could be the start of 'catalogue', the middle of 'education', the end of 'Muscat' or even just a regular old 'cat'. You can't operate with that level of uncertainty every time you move the mouse, you would go insane.

I reached this point around the time I graduated from university. I wanted to get another job as a web programmer but I was no longer able to use a computer in the same way I had, which was going to be a bit of a problem, wasn't it?

Once your sight deteriorates to the point at which magnification becomes useless, the next method of using a computer is with a screen reader. Now I'm aware that I run the risk of becoming a bit techie here, a bit niche in subject matter, but I'm also conscious that not many of you will know what a screen reader is or how anybody blind could ever use a computer at all, so here goes . . .

A screen reader is a piece of software or built-in feature of a modern operating system that speaks everything aloud. It allows somebody who is blind to navigate and use a computer without the need for a mouse, entirely via numerous and often complicated keyboard commands, which can require as many as five different keys being pressed simultaneously, and in ways and at speeds that would blow your fucking mind. It's not without its issues, and it can take a hell of a long time to get to grips with it and reach a decent level of competence and proficiency. I'm not really sure what the difference between competence and proficiency is, even after looking it up, but the sentence feels better and more authoritative with the two of them getting a mention so I'm sticking with them both.

The bottom line was that I had a lot of work to do in order to learn how to use a computer in this new way and make myself employable again as a web programmer. I think it's fair to ask why I didn't see this moment coming. I mean, it's not like blindness was a surprise, is it? My sight had been steadily deteriorating since that delivery room on that almost-Thursday back in the middle of June 1977 and I always knew what the final outcome would be. Maybe it was just part of the denial along the way. Live in the moment, work with what you've got and worry about the future when it happens.

I ended up with a computing degree because that was what I was most interested in. My education was funnelled down and down until just one subject remained, and then that subject got further refined until I'd found the part of it that most interested me. I suppose I took the path of least resistance throughout it all. I could have considered the inevitability of my future situation and studied to do something that relied entirely on my ears and my mouth and not my eyes. I could have worked my arse off to become a French-language interpreter – okay, let's not go that far – but instead I followed my interests and my aptitude for computer programming without any consideration for how I would do that once I was in the dark.

I also think that a part of me had been a little optimistic about some sort of cure when I was younger. The rate of medical development in all sorts of fields had been quite remarkable throughout the nineties and I knew that some very clever boffins were working on the problem, so surely it was just a matter of time before my sight would be fixable. I kind of thought it probably wouldn't be a problem by the time I was a fully grown adult. I mean, these were proper boffins with white coats, safety goggles, clipboards and everything. Maybe I had my head in the clouds, but I was just a kid so I think the clouds are as good a place to have your head as any. If you have your head in the clouds but can keep your feet on the ground you'll be fine.

Even when I'd managed to build up my competence and proficiency, yes, I'm still sticking with both of them, of using the computer with a screen reader, it very quickly became apparent to me that programming just wasn't going to be something I would be able to do well when I couldn't see the code in front of me. Trying to decipher lines of code via computer speech was just far more time-consuming than simply looking at it, and being a tediously slow programmer wasn't something I was prepared to be because of some biological circumstances that were out of my control.

There are many brilliant computer programmers out there who are completely blind, but I would imagine that the best ones read braille so can scan the code in front of them using a computer braille display. I don't read braille and I never have, and trying to become good at that as well as everything else would have been one hurdle too many. It can take years to become even slightly decent at reading braille, and it's probably something that needs to be learned from childhood for it to feel truly natural.

Braille had been there as an option for me throughout my entire time in specialist education, and my mum even teaches it, for God's sake. If I'd wanted to learn it, it could have happened. To a kid who could still see, though, braille was just one of those things that were synonymous with blindness so one of those things that I point-blank refused to entertain.

Why would I want to learn braille when I could see? I didn't need it. Only blind people needed braille and I wasn't blind. The ability to prepare yourself for the future means being able to accept the future, but my idea of accepting the future was, rather ironically, to bury my head in the sand so that I couldn't see it coming.

Admittedly, there have since been many times during my career in comedy when I have wished I had a means of silently reading notes while recording a radio show or giving a speech and braille would definitely have facilitated that. It also would have enabled me to follow my dream of being a programmer to a standard that I would have been much happier with, but the flip side is that if I'd done just that I would likely never have tried comedy at all. So bollocks to braille: I'm glad I didn't bother!

I was still a few years off picking up a microphone for the first time, though, and the idea of becoming a stand-up comedian would have been just as ridiculous to me back then as the idea of becoming a brain surgeon or a rocket scientist. Yes, I am very aware that I have just equated being a stand-up comedian with the two jobs that are often used as examples of the cleverest and most difficult jobs it is possible for a person to do, but this is my book so shut your mouth.

Okay, I had one of those itches in my brain and I needed to scratch it, and you'll never guess what? It turns out that there are actually about six or seven times more rocket scientists and about a third more neurosurgeons working in the UK than there are professional stand-up comedians who are able to make a full living from stand-up comedy. The only conclusion that can be drawn from this data is that it's therefore a lot harder to make it as a professional stand-up comedian than it is to become either a rocket scientist or a brain surgeon, so put that in your pipe and smoke it. Or, as the kids probably say these days, put that in your vape and vape it.

Right, back with the story. I've learned how to use a computer again but realise that I'd make a bit of a rubbish programmer. Ahem . . .

A decision had been made. There was no point in working my arse off to pursue a career as a web programmer when my sight meant I was destined to be worse at it than whoever was sat next to me. I needed to get a job that would allow me to operate on much more of a level playing field. If this was a comedy film, this is where we would cue the montage of me applying for jobs, sitting and smiling and nodding in interviews, and then every so often just smashing my head into a brick wall while screaming incoherent sentences about societal injustices and a basic lack of accessibility!

I applied for countless jobs at all kinds of companies up to some of the very biggest. Even just going back twenty-five years the obligations and desire for equality and access within companies was so vastly different from what it is today. There are still numerous hurdles for people with disabilities to overcome in terms of attitude and access within the workplace but we've certainly come a long way over the past quarter of a century, as I'm sure we did in the twenty-five years that preceded that.

It sometimes felt like potential employers would see my disability as an unnecessary hassle, a problem that was just better avoided in favour of taking an easier option. The truth is that there can be short-term hassles involved in employing somebody with a disability while you get them set up so that they can do the job properly, but people with disabilities are often some of the most creative and determined people you are ever likely to meet. We have to be in daily life and that makes us incredibly valuable people to have on the team. The long-term benefits can easily far outweigh any of those short-term hassles.

Imagine having an employee who is comfortable putting in twice the effort just to meet the same goals, who is used to handling daily frustrations with resilience and grace, who adapts quickly to challenges and solves problems in ways others wouldn't even think of. They sound like a dream employee, don't they? Well, that's what you get from hiring somebody with a disability. You sometimes just need to put a little bit more in at the beginning in order to get all of that out along the way. You know, make sure we can get into the building and access your computer systems. It's not much to ask, is it?

Even when I encountered what felt like genuine enthusiasm from prospective employers, it seemed that access would become the barrier. Technology provides both the biggest gateway and the biggest barrier to opportunity, information and services to somebody who is blind.

In order for a computer to be usable to somebody blind with a screen reader, the operating system, applications and websites need to be built with accessibility in mind. If they aren't, the chances are that we won't be able to use it properly, if at all.

I would do well in interviews, only to find out that access to their internal computer systems with a screen reader would be a problem. And I was getting turned down for jobs that I knew I could do with my eyes shut, if only I could see what I was doing.

I started applying for all kinds of things, whether the jobs were to do with computers or not. Basically my new strategy was to throw shit at the wall and see if any of it would stick.

During this new faeces-flinging exercise I applied to be a spy for MI5. Now, let me be clear, I had harboured no ambitions to be a spy, nor did I think I would make a good spy, or even a mediocre one. It was just meant to be a bit of a joke, a daft idea, just something silly to entertain myself and see how far I could get.

You might have thought that in order to become a spy for MI5, you would probably have to solve a particularly difficult puzzle that's been planted in the back of some obscure magazine, then post your answer to a PO box number to win some book tokens, upon which they would track you down and offer you the job or make you an offer you can't refuse.

'Your country needs you,' or 'We'll make your family disappear,' or maybe a combination of the two.

It turns out, though, that MI5 have a graduate scheme, like lots of companies do, and you just have to fill in a form containing all of your personal information, which hardly seems like the best way to prove you'd make a good spy.

'Name?'

'Chris McCausland.'

'Sorry, rule number one of being a spy, don't tell anybody your name, idiot!'

'Shit! I mean Smith, the Grey Man, the Beaver, something like that, sorry!'

The application form wasn't any more exciting than a regular application form, except it did ask if I'd ever attempted to overthrow the monarchy, something that John Lewis and Lever Brothers hadn't given a toss about.

I wonder if anybody has ever answered yes to that question. I suppose if they had they were probably still contacted by MI5, but just by a very different department from recruitment. I'm sure their families miss them. Meanwhile John Lewis and Lever Brothers could be swimming with potential monarchy overthrowers who have just become fairly comfortable with their pension plans and private family healthcare and don't want to rock the boat.

There were six places up for grabs at MI5 but a whopping three thousand applicants, so really I didn't stand a chance, or so I thought.

Despite applying as a bit of a joke, I soon found myself down to the final thirty applicants. How nuts is that? I was in the top one per cent of best new potential spies that this country had to offer. Me, a man who couldn't even play 'I Spy'.

Well, I exaggerate slightly, because these days I do play I Spy with my daughter, but the problem we have is that I have to pick something I know is definitely there.

We'll be in the car . . .

'I spy with my little eye, something beginning with R.'

'Is it road, Daddy?'

'Yes, it's road, sweetheart. Again.'

'It's always road, Daddy.'

Or we'll play our own version that we have slightly adapted from the original.

We'll be in the park . . .

'I hear with my little ear, something beginning with B.'

The problem here, however, is it has to be something that is making a noise at that precise moment, and in fact throughout the duration of the game, or it becomes impossible to solve.

'Is it birds, Daddy?'

'Yes, it's birds, sweetheart. Again.'

'It's always birds, Daddy.'

It causes a lot of arguments if it's something like 'beeping'.

'But there is no beeping, Daddy!'

'Yes, but there was when I asked. There was a car doing some beeping.'

'That was ten minutes ago, Daddy!'

'Well, you should have remembered. It's not my fault you don't remember everything that was happening at the precise moment I asked the question!'

The MI5 recruitment process started off in fairly standard fashion with some psychometric tests, which I either passed with flying colours or that flagged me as a sociopathic maniac depending on what they were looking for, of course. It could have been the latter.

I then had to sign the Official Secrets Act to say that I

wouldn't tell anybody that I had applied to be a spy for MI5, but as far as I can recall, it didn't say anything about not writing about it in a book some twenty-odd years later. If I should be taken from the streets soon after this book hits the shelves, you know who's responsible. I can't imagine they've ever had a target quite so easy.

I received a letter inviting me to my first of several interviews at MI5's headquarters in London. They don't exactly go out of their way to advertise the fact that it's MI5's headquarters, which makes it kind of difficult to find for an interview. There was no sign outside, and they wouldn't even confirm that I'd found the right place even once I was inside. The only reason I thought I was probably in the right place was because they also wouldn't confirm that it wasn't MI5.

'Is this MI5?'

'We can't confirm or deny that, sir. Do you have an appointment?'

'Great. So it's MI5, then?'

'Sir, if we tell you we'll have to kill you.'

'Great. So it's definitely MI5, then?'

Once inside the building, I was immediately treated as a potential threat to British security until the moment they could get me back out of the building. I had to hand in my bag, my coat, and of course my mobile phone. It didn't have a camera for photographing secret documents, but it had an aerial so large and pointy that it could have been used as a fairly effective weapon if I'd wanted to take control of the building.

'Reports indicate that a man is holding fifteen people hostage inside with the aerial of an Ericsson T28.'

'Jesus, this is bad.'

Interesting fact: there were no answerphones in the building, because they really, really, really didn't want anybody leaving any messages. I suppose they'd figured out over the years that the kind of message somebody might phone up and leave on an MI5 answerphone wasn't really the kind of message you would just want sitting there until you get back from annual leave, while in the meantime an unknown deadline passes and somebody blows something up.

'Shit, sorry. The threat was left on Brian's phone and Brian was away for a wedding last week. We'll build another Big Ben. It was a bit knackered anyway.'

During that first interview a fire alarm went off. My interviewer and I had to leave the building and finish the interview on a park bench, or maybe this was just to see how I fared having secret covert conversations on park benches. It was February and as I'd had to hand my coat in at security, I had to complete the interview absolutely freezing while trying to stop my teeth chattering in that exaggerated comedy fashion.

I must have done all right, though, as they invited me back and I got to complete the next interview entirely indoors. I was told that part of the job, should I get it, would involve running agents. This confused me as I'd always thought that a spy was an agent, but apparently not. An agent, it seemed, was somebody external to MI5 who might have valuable information that they wished to trade or reveal, and running agents meant meeting up with these people in secure staked-out locations to obtain this information.

'I hope you don't mind me saying,' said my interviewer, 'but you being without sight does strike me as being a greater risk in situations such as this than somebody else who is, erm . . . with sight?'

His words but, let's be honest, he had a point.

'So what are your thoughts on that?' he added.

When the thing you are being interviewed for is not your dream, it kind of takes the pressure off a little bit and frees you up to be more yourself and not just the person you think they want you to be. It wasn't my dream to be a spy. In fact, I thought the idea was preposterous so I wasn't really nervous at all.

'Yeah, I see your point,' I said. 'But who would ever suspect the blind guy of being a spy? In fact, what is more undercover than a blind bloke meeting somebody for a pint and a chat?'

My interviewer paused for a moment while he considered this.

'Interesting,' he said, before taking his pen, making a noise of approval, and scribbling something in his notepad.

I never found out what he wrote, but to this day I've always imagined that he simply wrote, 'More blind spies!!!'

The interviews had all gone well, so now the next phase was to take part in a full assessment day where I had to pretend I was an actual spy. This consisted of me having to deal with an inbox of fabricated security documents from various sources, including some of our friendly international allies. I had to decide what was the immediate threat and what could wait, have meetings with various supervisors and try to procure the valuable services of the surveillance team to monitor a target.

Now here's the thing: when somebody with a disability sits an exam or undertakes an assessment like this, if their disability is a hindrance to reading, writing or processing information, 50 per cent extra time is permissible. I was entitled to extra time for exams throughout my GCSEs, A levels and degree. I was also entitled to it for parts of this assessment, which included dealing with that inbox of fabricated security documents.

I did well enough, but I received a letter in the post a few weeks later explaining to me that my disability was a problem, and that they felt my eyesight, or lack of, was going to be too much of an issue for them to put me through to the next phase of the recruitment process. It actually said that the problem was my inability to sift through vast amounts of information and identify a threat in an extremely limited amount of time.

I showed this rejection letter to somebody who had been supporting me in my relentless hunt for work and she was shocked and appalled.

'They can't refuse you employment because of your disability,' she said. 'This is blatant and shameless discrimination. You should sue them for this, sue them!'

I appreciated the moral support but, honestly, I wasn't sure I wanted to live in a country that would give me that job. I was glad that somebody had had the balls to stand up and say no. Can you imagine if a bomb was detonated at a major London landmark, and some poor bloke had to come out on the news and explain exactly what went wrong?

'Yeah, sorry about that. It's just that the guy we had

working on this is blind, and it takes him longer than every-body else to sort through his inbox. Looking on the bright side, though, I am pleased to confirm that we are fully com-plying with EU legislation on equal opportunities and dis-crimination, which is more than can be said for those rotten terrorists who really should have allowed 50 per cent extra time before detonating their bomb. Shame on them.'

Discrimination is never a good thing. Well, usually. Maybe just occasionally, though, a little bit of discrimination might actually be perfectly acceptable for the safety of the nation. Just saying.

Chapter Twenty-One

Just as I'd stopped being able to see anything on the computer screen and had turned to using a screen reader instead, I was also no longer able to see much of anything on the TV so had to change my relationship with television as well.

I can't be entirely sure, but I think the last film I remember actually watching on the screen was possibly *The Matrix* on DVD at some point in early 2000. I had to sit so close to the screen that I couldn't really take in the full picture at any one time and would occasionally be able to feel the static electricity emanating from its surface onto my face, like some kind of fizzy forcefield.

My central vision had always been deteriorating ahead of my peripheral vision so as my sight was slightly better at the edges I would sit side on to the screen and move my head around to follow the action, like a cat with a lazy eye following a ball of twine. Obviously there came a time when those scales tipped again and I thought, what's the point any more? The eye strain caused discomfort while headaches and the effort started to outweigh the enjoyment. Besides, all of that static electricity couldn't have been doing me any good and if I'd got any closer I would have left smudge marks.

Movies and TV had always been a massive part of my life, but now I had to let go of a considerable amount of that. I would still watch stuff I'd seen a hundred times before because I knew what was happening visually, and I would still watch new things that were easy to follow from dialogue alone, like a good old courtroom drama or a film about two blokes trapped in a lift. Anything new with too much action or special effects, though, just became a waste of time. A film that was high on gun battles and explosions but low on dialogue would have been fairly pointless.

'Ratta-tat-bang-bang-boom!'

I would have had much the same experience if I'd just stuck all the knives and forks in the microwave and switched it on.

'Ratta-tat-bang-bang-boom!'

See? It's the same thing.

Audio description had been in its infancy around the turn of the millennium, my first exposure to it coming via the newly emerging home DVD market. It was actually available as an extra language track that you could select on many of the biggest DVD releases of the time.

It was a nice thought, using this new technology to provide an avenue of accessibility to us movie fans who were blind: we could watch a film on our own and not be left completely in the dark during entirely visual moments. How considerate. The only problem with that feature, though, and it was quite a big one, was that you had to be able to see the menus to turn it on. You had to be able to navigate visually through the DVD's audio settings, into language options and down to select the audio description track. Of course, you could take a random punt, but there was just as much chance of ending up with the film in French or hitting play on a behind-the-scenes vignette as there was of getting any audio description out of it.

Even now this oversight makes me laugh – including an accessibility feature but making it inaccessible so you can't get to it. It's a bit like including a lift for wheelchair users but putting all the buttons above head height so nobody in a wheelchair can use it when they're alone.

No more actual watching the TV also meant no more actual watching the football. I had already stopped playing the game, but now my enjoyment of it had been reduced further to absorbing it purely through audio.

Football on the radio is wonderful. It's free, it's lively, and it brings the game to life in ways that are thoroughly captivating. My life would have a huge void if football on the radio was to cease to be a thing.

I miss being able to watch it on the TV, though, because as wonderful as football on the radio is for my own engagement with the game, football on the TV is social, and should be shared with others whenever possible.

The problem is that the commentary on the TV is awful. It is simply there to complement the pictures and barely tells you anything that's happening. If I want to enjoy a game with family or friends, I have to make peace with the fact that I'm putting the social benefits over enjoying the game. It's unfortunately one or the other: enjoy the game on the radio but be on my own, or watch with others but have no clue about what's going on beyond the key events.

One day I thought it would be a good idea to take a mini radio with me to the pub. The plan was to listen to the radio commentary with one earphone in while enjoying the atmosphere with friends.

Liverpool were playing Spurs, and it didn't take me long to figure out that the radio wasn't in sync with the telly and I was probably about eight seconds ahead of the rest of the pub. As the game went on and I became more and more engrossed in my own little world, I forgot about the time delay and the advantage I had on everybody else. And then Liverpool scored!

Obviously my natural reaction was to celebrate, and that was what I did. I went to jump out of my seat and punch the air, but almost immediately I realised that nobody else in the pub knew that this had happened yet.

What happened next was a series of extremely quick events, a chain reaction that began with me simply trying to nullify my momentum but ended in farcical disaster.

I slammed myself into reverse, which caused me to land heavily back in my seat, limbs a-flailing. My legs shot up, connecting with the underside of a table. This sent a number of pint glasses and bar snacks leaping into the air, showering lager and Guinness over the backs of several blokes who were stood in front of me, watching the big screen. These guys yelped in unison as the cold liquid startled them, the glasses smashing down onto the floor as my seat continued backwards, taking me with it.

I ended up on the floor amid smashed glass, lager, Guinness, crisps and nuts. I'd caused a hell of a racket, and everybody turned around to see what all the noise was about. They saw some guys with beer up their backs not looking too happy about it, they saw glasses lying smashed on the floor, and they saw me lying flat on my back with my legs in the air, covered in snacks, still kind of sat on that chair, but not in its usual upright position.

It was then, while they were all staring at me, that Liverpool scored on the screen behind them and everybody missed the goal.

From that day on I wasn't allowed to take my radio to the pub with me for the football. It had been a one-time deal, which is fair enough, I suppose.

Before football moved to Sky and TV later went digital, it was possible to put the radio commentary on and it be perfectly synced with the football on the TV. I could turn down the TV volume and have the best of both worlds, able to watch what was happening but with far superior and more descriptive commentary. This was the preferred method of watching football for many fully sighted people because it was widely accepted that the radio commentary was a much better experience for everybody.

Here's a thought. Hang on, let me just get on my soapbox, ahem . . .

Wouldn't it be nice if broadcasters like Sky offered two live commentary feeds with their games and allowed viewers the choice between the standard minimalist TV waffle and a much more engaging and detailed radio-style offering? I think they'd be surprised by how many of their sighted viewers would opt for the second option. It's an absolute no-brainer for me.

I and many others would be able to regain some of the social aspects of football that we have lost because of poor vision, and could watch games again with family and friends in a way that everybody can enjoy.

I'd love to watch the football on the TV with my dad and be able to enjoy it. I'd jump at the chance to share some of my love of watching the mighty Reds with my daughter. Radio alone won't engage her when she doesn't understand the game, and the standard TV commentary leaves me out of the loop and so unable to help her understand it.

Football has become quite socially isolating for me and many others when it should be the opposite. Are you listening, Sky, and all you other sports broadcasters?

Right, let me get off this soapbox and get back to the pub.

I loved the pub, a little too much at times. It was a place of community, somewhere to belong, a vibrant hub for locals and trades, a place where you could find a man to do a job or just sit there and put the world to rights with whoever wanted to do the same. My hunt for work had continued, but to no avail, and as it dragged on, the pub had become a place where I would go to hang out each day, afternoons stretching into evenings in the absence of any reason to be up early in the morning. All of my friends and peers were beginning their lives, starting new jobs and making new friendship groups, while I had remained stuck at home, jobless and twiddling my thumbs, with nothing more than daytime TV to provide company.

I love *Countdown* on Channel 4: the endless game-play from simply selecting a handful of letters and numbers has made it a staple of British television for over forty years. I have been lucky in recent years to be invited into Dictionary Corner on several occasions to provide a bit of levity and humour for a week's worth of shows. Like *Blankety Blank*, *Countdown* is one of those shows that really does make me feel like I've been magically beamed into the television and I love it.

When I was stuck at home on my own, though, unable to find work, there was only so much *Countdown* I could take. The daily repetition of the same shows over and over became a recurring reminder of the rut in which I was stuck, and if *Countdown* made me feel like that, imagine how *Fifteen to One* made me feel. This was a quiz show that followed *Countdown* every day on Channel 4 and that was truly impenetrable to anybody who hadn't swallowed every single volume of the *Encyclopaedia Britannica,* with a medical dictionary for dessert. If watching *Countdown* every day made me feel I was stuck in a rut, *Fifteen to One* made me feel truly stupid while I was stuck in it. Honestly, I'd be lucky to get one right answer an episode, and even then that usually came from my strategy of shouting 'Edward the Seventh' at the telly to any question that started 'Which king . . . ?'

I would head to the pub in the afternoon before those shows came on the TV, and often end up staying until closing time, caught up in whatever happenings had managed to absorb me. In the absence of work, the pub became my social group and a place to belong. There were those who were between jobs or out of work, and those in skilled trades who were able to start work early and be in the pub by three.

Although this period of my life was evidently difficult for me, and too much pub is never a good thing, it was such a great pub and many of those I got to know became friends over the coming years.

During that time I was probably masking a degree of depression with alcohol, anaesthetising myself to the reality of my situation, losing the remnants of whatever sight I had left while caught in the seemingly futile process of trying to find work. My usual tactic of taking a deep breath, pulling up my big-boy pants and getting on with it had been replaced to some extent with pulling up any old pair of pants and heading to the pub.

Walking in the street during the day was becoming a problem now, as my central vision just wasn't up to the job. I could still see a little better through the peripheral edges of my vision and acting as if I could see normally was still my coping strategy, so that was what I tried to do.

Walking along a pavement, I would often turn my head and pretend I was observing something interesting across the road, but just so I could use that peripheral sliver to get a better idea of what was ahead of me.

Bushes and tree branches that hung over people's garden walls and onto the pavement side became a real nuisance and still are to this day. If you're guilty of having bushes and trees in your garden that spill over like this, please keep them sufficiently trimmed: they're a pain in the arse to those of us who are optically challenged. That's not a real expression by the way: I made it up. Please don't feel you should use it.

If I heard anybody walking towards me on the pavement

the thought of having to negotiate passing them when I couldn't see them approaching made me feel sick. Carrying a white stick would have let them know I couldn't see them and that they should move around me, but I still wasn't ready for that public acknowledgement. I have the same problem with those friendly kisses on the cheek: I never know which way to go. My strategy there was to stop and pretend I'd received a phone call. I would stand to one side and have a completely fake conversation with nobody until they had walked past and I could continue on my way. I'm sure my acting wasn't that great and I likely instilled a bit of panic into some poor sod from time to time, who just saw this dodgy geezer blatantly pretending to have a phone call while he waited for them to draw ever nearer. I bet they were just as relieved to have made it past me without incident as I was to be past them.

My vision at night was pretty much nil by now. When I returned home from the pub I'd try to follow the streetlights but was unable to see much beyond those blurry orange orbs hanging in the sky. Combine that with the fact that I was now operating on an afternoon and evening's worth of alcohol and it's a miracle I'm still alive. One problem I encountered fairly regularly was the inability to tell exactly which one was my house, along the road of seemingly identical driveways. When in the rough vicinity I would have to explore a few until I found the right one. On one occasion I was trying to figure out if a front door was mine or not when the voice of a little old lady came tentatively from the other side.

'Hello?' she enquired. 'Is somebody out there?'

This wasn't ideal. I might have been stumbling my way through life as best I could, but now I was frightening the life out of a little old lady who probably thought somebody was trying to break into her house. It might have been better to sneak off into the night and let her think the noises she'd heard had come from the wind or a cat or a fox but, no, I was answering her before my inebriated mind had allowed me to think it through.

'Sorry.' I said, in a panic. 'Wrong house,' before running back up the driveway to the pavement and dashing further up the road in search of my own front door. That poor old lady probably didn't sleep much that night.

Having a disability often requires bundles of creativity to find novel solutions to the problems and obstacles of daily life. I realised here that I needed a way to identify my house so that I could avoid anything like that happening again, I needed to get my house to make a noise. I figured out that I could use my mobile phone to phone the landline we had in the hallway: I would hear it from the street and could aim for the house that was ringing. Problem solved, brilliant, I'm a genius! Unless somebody at home was on the phone, of course. Then I'd have to loiter in the street until they were off the bloody thing so I could figure out where I lived. Admittedly it wasn't a perfect solution, but it definitely beat frightening the life out of little old ladies.

The longer my unemployment went on, the more the pub became a habit. I would meet new people all the time, but I found that the first three things anybody would want to know about me were usually the same.

'What's your name?'

'Chris.'

'Where are you from?'

'Liverpool.'

'What do you do?'

'Nothing.'

I didn't like not having an answer to all three of these questions. I felt shame, as if not being able to answer all three made me somehow incomplete.

My lifestyle started to clash with the lives of my house-mates, who were trying to live normal professional lives but would have to deal with me arriving home much too regularly in a bit of a state.

I knew I didn't want to continue on this path, where the only decision I had to make each day was whether to stay in and watch telly or go to the pub. I needed a routine and a sense of purpose, a place to go to each day and the feeling of having accomplished something. I had been unable to find employment in anything related to my degree or at a graduate level, but I needed to get a foot on the ladder. Start with something, anything, and build from there.

Chapter Twenty-Two

There are far fewer employment options open to you when you can't see. It's not like I could have got a job in a pub. I would have broken more glasses than my wages could cover.

Stocking shelves in a supermarket? A health and safety nightmare.

Behind the till in a newsagent's? A shoplifter's dream!

Delivery driver? The death toll would be staggering.

I decided the best thing I could do was to work for free, find a charity and offer my services for absolutely nothing. They'd get something out of it, I hoped, and I'd get to lift myself out of this rut, rebuild some confidence and create the routine I knew I desperately needed.

In a huge twist of irony, the purpose of the charity I ended up working for was to help those with sight issues find work. I know: I had sight issues and I couldn't find work, except working for free to help others with sight issues find work. You couldn't make it up.

The charity wasn't exactly local, about an hour each way, but I worked there for about six months, four days a week, not for money but for some of the things I had been missing in my life. I reckon my liver was probably pretty grateful for the change in lifestyle as well.

I was working there on the morning of September the eleventh, 2001, when those planes hit the World Trade Center. I remember two of the office phones ringing just moments apart from each other.

'Oh, my God!' said one of the answerers.

'Holy shit!' said the other.

I thought they'd both been called with equally shocking but very different news at exactly the same time. A bizarre coincidence as they made similar noises of shock and astonishment at either side of me.

The charity was operating out of an office within a London stock-exchange building in Moorgate, so it wasn't long before we were evacuated for reasons that were probably a little bit of an overreaction to something that was happening three and a half thousand miles away.

Having that story to tell when asked where I was when it all happened, though, well it certainly felt better than having to explain that I'd slept through the whole thing because I'd got super-pissed on the Monday night because I had no job to be up for in the morning. It was a small step, but small steps can often make the biggest differences. Having some routine and purpose back in my life was a start, and you can't get anywhere if you don't at least start.

Six months of working for that charity did me the world of good, and I felt like I now had one foot firmly on the bottom rung of the ladder and had rebuilt some of the confidence I needed to get my feet climbing again.

I didn't want to put myself through the process of looking for the same type of graduate work that had proven so elusive and damaged my confidence so much: a career could wait. I was happy to take the next small step rather than trying to leap straight to a destination.

I focused my attention on and around my local area and came across a company that was looking for recruits to their call-centre sales team. This company produced employment-law manuals and health-and-safety administrative software. The subject matter might have been as dull as dishwater but at least the job was selling to companies, not phoning some poor sod at home while they were having their tea.

A recruitment day was held in which around fifteen of us were assessed at the same time for maybe five positions. A lot of the interviewing was done in a group setting – I suppose to see how we all managed in that kind of environment and how confident we were to speak up and be heard.

'What's your dream job?' asked the lady in charge, and everybody took turns to give an answer. So many of these answers were duller than the employment-law manuals we were hoping to sell.

'My dream job is to be a team leader in a call centre,' said one fairly smarmy guy.

I mean, what a load of rubbish. Maybe that's the next aspiration of somebody who just works in a call centre, but it's hardly a dream job, is it? This guy obviously thought that he was playing to the lady in charge and letting her know in no uncertain terms that he was going places.

Granted, I didn't know what my dream job was any more. I was just after a job while I tried to figure that out so I didn't know how to answer the question seriously. Rather than just lying, like Mr Smarmy Pants had, when the focus landed on me I thought I'd take the piss instead.

'Well, I'm from Liverpool,' I said, 'and my eyesight is rubbish, so my dream job would be to play in goal for Man United.'

The whole room broke out into laughter. Honestly, there was so much laughter that I got greedy and went for more.

'Just give me one season, that's all I'd need. One season, I tell ya!'

I know now that this second line is called a topper, or a tag, an extra line added to the end of the main joke to get further laughs out of a premise. Back then, though, I was simply avoiding not having a proper answer to the question by trying to distract everybody from that fact with comedy.

This is probably the first joke I ever wrote, and by 'wrote' I mean thought of. Obviously I'd made jokes in the past, always had a laugh and tried to be funny with mates, but this moment would pop back into my mind some years later while I was a gigging stand-up comedian, and I would use this exact same joke several times onstage, especially when performing in the comedy clubs of Liverpool and Manchester. So, this was the first joke I ever thought of that I would later use in any professional capacity.

The irony is that in avoiding the question about what my dream job would be and making a daft joke, I was spelling it out loud and clear: I wanted to be a comedian. I just hadn't realised it yet and didn't know that it was something that was even possible.

I got the job. Later I was told it was because I was relaxed and funny during the recruitment day and didn't take myself too seriously. Mr Smarmy Pants, on the other hand, was nowhere to be seen.

The decision to enter that world was probably one of the best decisions I've ever made. The materials we were selling might have been dull but the environment was lively and vibrant. Any job that is repetitive and target-focused can have its ups and downs, but overall I loved my time working in that call centre and I honestly can't think of any other decision I've made that has had such a positive impact on me.

When I was unemployed I was able to collect a range of benefits that covered my rent, my council-tax payments, and some moderate living costs due to my disability. And all of this added up. My basic salary was low – in fact, it was less than I was able to collect when out of work – but the difference it made in so many other ways was more valuable.

Working for a charity had allowed me to regain belief that I had something to offer in the workplace, but I think going from being unemployed to having that call-centre sales job did more for my confidence and my sense of self-worth than any other step I've taken since.

All in all I had spent about two years out of paid employment after graduating from university. I had begun my search for a graduate job with optimism and excitement: I wanted to join the rat race and become a successful computer programmer or IT high-flyer. As the search had proven frustrating and often futile while my sight had dwindled to its final dregs, my confidence and self-worth had taken a pummelling and I was becoming more reckless and unhappy in the process.

I realise in hindsight that the stress and anxiety I had been experiencing over that period had been quite significant. It didn't only relate to the practical pursuit of work and attending countless interviews amid an imminent blindness that I hadn't been able to accept or adjust to while it was still happening, but the knowledge that however difficult I was finding things at any given moment, those things were only likely to become even more difficult as my sight continued to disappear.

Intoxication had killed the boredom and allowed me to numb myself to as much of it all as possible, but the mornings would always provide a sober window through which I could truly observe myself and I never liked what I saw.

Those six months of getting myself back on the rails by working for free had helped massively and allowed me to perform a system reset to some extent, but it was going from those last two years, though, to now having this call-centre job, a new friendship group, an income I was earning, and an answer to that third question that made a huge difference.

'What's your name?'

'Chris.'

'Where are you from?'

'Liverpool.'

'What do you do?'

'I do business sales for an employment-law company in Kingston.'

I'm not going to lie, it felt good.

Our big-picture goals and dreams can sometimes feel too elusive or out of reach. The expectations we can place upon ourselves or that we feel we must meet to gain the approval or validation of others can be brutal and punishing, and sometimes circumstance can be a proper bastard. The further our goals and dreams move out of our reach, the more we can feel we are failing in everything we thought would one day define who we were meant to be.

I had narrowed my education down to the point where I'd spent four years studying software engineering at university. My whole identity had become dependent on me becoming a software engineer after graduating, and even though I was hitting brick walls and struggling to achieve this goal amid circumstances that were out of my control, my happiness had become dependent on it.

The most basic and important thing we can do for ourselves is to at least allow ourselves the chance to be happy. If our happiness and sense of self-worth are inextricably tied up with goals and dreams that are too elusive or out of reach, we will never allow ourselves that basic chance.

What I found was that my happiness and self-worth weren't tied up with those big-picture goals and dreams at all, but were just waiting to be discovered with the very smallest of steps, and sometimes just taking a single small step in a different direction can be all we need to stumble across them.

Working in a call centre might not be anybody's idea of a dream job. It can be a fairly transient place to be, bodies passing through while next steps are figured out or as new recruits discover that a pressurised target-focused job isn't for them. Working in a call centre certainly wasn't my dream job, but nothing else I've done has been more instantly impactful and beneficial to me than that job was. It was such a small step, and it was a side-step in a new direction, but it would allow so much to become possible.

The sales environment was incredibly social and alcohol would feature a lot, but now it felt like a reward, a shared celebration of hard work done and targets hit rather than an anaesthetic for life. The job was going well and the commission I'd started to earn meant that I was soon taking home more than I had been when I was collecting those benefits, and this would continue to increase as I hit a rhythm.

During my first year in the job our landlord had decided he wanted to sell the house I'd been living in for the past few years, and my housemates and I had made the decision to go our separate ways as our requirements were all too different. I moved into a small studio flat in the local area, but it wasn't long before my new landlord decided he wanted to sell too. I am often of the opinion that the easiest solution to a problem is often the best, and the commission I'd been earning had allowed me to build a small nest egg. It wasn't tons, but it was enough for half of a minimum deposit on a studio flat. With a parental loan for the other half at a generous 0 per cent APR over two years, I bought that one off my landlord and saved us both a lot of hassle and unnecessary expense.

I loved that little studio flat. It was the sixth place I'd called home since making the move to university, and it might have been small but buying it gave me a real sense of security and peace of mind, that I would only ever have to move again if I wanted to, and not at anybody else's whim.

It might seem strange to learn that this was a really good period of my life, even though it was the period over which my sight would leave me completely, but it was. I appreciate that people can lose their sight in much more abrupt and immediate ways, and that the sense of loss they experience must be overwhelming, but my deterioration had been so slow and drawn out over the years, and I had become so numb to the idea of it, that it felt like something that was happening in the background while life continued on top.

My sister had developed a love of rock and metal music and I used to love buying her CDs for Christmas and birthdays. I would take great pleasure in being able to drip-feed my own musical tastes into my younger sibling.

By the age of seventeen Louise had become quite the Marilyn Manson fan, and it just so happened that the cultural provocateur and self-proclaimed Antichrist Superstar was to play the Reading Festival that year. One of the very last things I did with my vision was to take my little sister to her first festival. To be honest, she provided most of the vision, but I brought the experience and camping knowhow, as I had become quite the expert since that first attempt when I'd turned up with her pathetic child's tent and shared use of a single sleeping bag between three blokes.

This is one of my favourite memories from around this time, of approaching the cusp of blindness, but of standing for an hour with her down near the very front so she could see Marilyn close up. The security at the front were throwing plastic pint glasses of water into the crowd to provide some form of cooling effect in the hot sun, and I must have become somewhat of a target for them, as I couldn't see them coming, and took a statistically high number of full plastic pint glasses in the face without so much as flinching. At least I wasn't going to get hot standing there – bashed and bruised maybe, but not hot.

I may have perhaps taken one too many impacts to the head as, in a moment of spontaneous madness, I charged into a mosh pit with Louise on my shoulders for an entire song of smashing into oncoming bodies I couldn't see coming, then being congratulated by those around me for remaining upright with her on my shoulders throughout. If only they knew the whole story.

I was able to lift her on top of the crowd so that she could surf to the front and have that same moment of awe that I'd had all those years earlier. We'd find each other later – somehow.

When I'd first started working in that call centre I'd been doing the fifteen-minute walk to and from the office each day, but it wasn't long before that had to stop. As I've said, it often took incident, injury or close shave for me to understand that I shouldn't be doing a particular thing any more, and this time it was almost getting hit by a bus while crossing the road, then nearly knocking over a little old lady on the pavement while hurrying not to get hit by that bus. I decided to take myself off the streets, opting instead to get taxis to and from work rather than being a danger to myself and others.

Knocking people over in mosh pits was fine, but not little old ladies who were waiting to cross the road.

Those final dregs of sight were disappearing now. In one way this was to be the beginning of an end, but in so many ways, it would also prove to be the start of a new beginning.

Chapter Twenty-Three

I interrupt this broadcast to bring you an important message . . .

Sight loss might have been difficult at times and plenty frustrating along the way, but it could also be pretty damn funny as well. While I was running on those final dregs of sight, I got myself into so many farcical situations that I thought I would just stick a few of them together into one bumper bonus chapter, for no greater reason than to give you a laugh before we crack on with the story.

So, with that in mind, let me start by telling you about the time I went to the undertaker's for a haircut. It was a brilliantly sunny day and I was in desperate need of a trim, but with my sight being not fit for purpose and with the bright sun shining in my eyes, I couldn't see a thing. I walked right past the door for the barber's and into the premises next door. Next door was the undertaker's, obviously, and as I entered the place it seemed very quiet indeed, which, of course, it would be, because it was an undertaker's.

At the time, I thought I was in the barber's and was trying to figure out whether the place was just empty or whether people were waiting quietly in the way that people can wait quietly in a barber's, when a man appeared from the back of the shop.

'Can I help you?' enquired the man, which unfortunately for me was not only the kind of thing that an undertaker would say in this situation, but also the kind of thing that a barber might say if it was a barber's, which it wasn't.

Even more unfortunately for me, I replied to him with a question that was a perfectly acceptable and normal thing to ask of any barber but just so happened to be one of the most inappropriate and obscure things you could ask of any undertaker.

I asked him, 'Have you got many waiting at the moment?'

That's it. That's what I asked this undertaker. That is what I asked this man who prepared the dead for burial or cremation. I asked him if he had many waiting at the moment. The poor guy didn't even answer with words, he just made a confused noise, which immediately told me this wasn't the barber's. In a moment of horror that punched me right in the gut, I suddenly remembered what was next door to the barber's, and where I was almost certainly stood in that moment.

I felt like I was about to drop dead from embarrassment, which wouldn't have been that bad, I suppose, because at least then he would have been qualified to give me a haircut.

Then there was the unforgettable afternoon when I was dragged into somebody else's emergency and couldn't have been more the wrong person in the wrong place at the wrong time for one unlucky lady.

I was walking home from our local supermarket, just minding my own business and swinging my one carrier-bag containing my one and only purchase; a foil tray full to the brim with whatever their Curry of the Day was. I never knew what their Curry of the Day was: there was only ever one available from the hot counter, and although its name and ingredients were displayed for all to see, I made my decision based on what shade of brown it was. If it was a dark, rich brown I'd buy it, and if it looked fairly light and beige I'd give it a miss – that probably meant it would be full of cream or coconut or, even worse, both.

As I was walking home along a tree-lined residential street with my steaming hot tray of deep-brown mystery curry, a young woman ran out of one of the houses screaming and headed straight for me. She was foreign, that much was immediately obvious, eastern European if I'd had to guess, which I didn't, but I still like to. I doubt she'd been here long as she didn't seem to know many words at all. She let out a guttural scream as she ran straight for me.

'Come! Come!!' she said, through tears, as she grabbed my arm and dragged me with her back into the house from which she had just emerged.

This was almost close to being a young man's fantasy. A woman with a striking foreign accent spots you passing her house and rushes out into the street to drag you inside with her, to fulfil some desperate need that she is unable to satisfy on her own. Unfortunately, the screaming and the tears made it clear that this was definitely not that, and something had happened inside that was probably quite bad.

Into the house she dragged me and straight through into the back room, where I almost went crashing straight over a workman's ladder that was lying on its side, and then almost straight into what I think is known in the building industry as a massive hole in the floor.

'You help! Help!' she said, still sobbing uncontrollably.

I peered into the hole, but I couldn't see anything at the bottom, or in fact the bottom at all, just a blurry darkness. It didn't take a rocket scientist, or indeed a stand-up comedian, to figure out that there had probably been a person on the ladder and they had either gone through an already existing hole in the floor, or straight through the floor creating the hole.

It was lucky for both of us that I was just about able to make out the hole. Can you imagine if, in her panic, she'd unknowingly dragged a blind man off the street, all the way through into the back room, then thrown him into the hole as well?

Who knows? Maybe she had. Maybe at the bottom of that hole was the man who had been on the ladder, along with a blind man she'd already dragged in off the street and flung into the hole on top of him and this really wasn't her lucky day.

'I'll phone an ambulance,' I said to her, showing her my mobile.

'What's your emergency?' asked the voice at the other end of the call.

'I'm in a house,' I started. 'It appears that somebody, maybe a builder or something, has fallen from a ladder straight through a hole in the floor.'

'Okay,' said the voice. 'Is he moving?'

'I don't know,' I said. 'I'm sorry but I can't see very well,'

(I still wasn't saying 'blind'.) 'so I can't see the bottom of the hole to tell you what's happening down there.'

'Okay, not a problem,' continued the voice. 'I can work with that.' God, they were good. 'Are you with anybody in the house who can see if he's moving?' they asked.

'Yes, I am.' I replied, 'But you're not going to believe this. She doesn't speak any English, so she can't tell us.'

'Right,' said the voice, in the drawn-out manner the bloke had used when I'd claimed I'd never used Windows 95.

It sounds like a comedy sketch, doesn't it? You've got two people present at an emergency, one who can't see what's happened and one who can see what's happened but can't say what's happened.

'Basically, we've got a situation here in which somebody has fallen through a massive hole in the floor and needs urgent help,' I explained. 'I can't see him to tell you anything about what condition he's in, or even to confirm if he is a he or he is a she, and the only other person here with me can see him, or her, and everything you want to know, but is unable to tell either of us what that everything is. You need to send an ambulance right now, and probably a fire engine to get him or her, but probably him, out of the hole!'

'Okay,' said the voice, obviously deciding this was as good a plan as any. 'What's the address?'

'I don't know,' I said. 'I've literally just been dragged in off the street, and it's not like I can ask her, is it?'

'Well, I can't send an ambulance without an address,' said the voice.

'I can tell you where it is from the local Waitrose,' I suggested.

'I can't put directions from a Waitrose into the computer,' said the voice, 'That's not how the computer works. I need an address.'

'Can't your computer triangulate my mobile-phone signal or something?' I asked. 'That's what they do in the movies.'

'No, I need an address,' said the voice again, 'or at least a street name.'

I knocked on the neighbour's doors but nobody was home. I realised that the house was on a corner, though, so I went to see if there was a street sign on the wall – and bingo! The big problem? I couldn't read it.

If Liam Neeson had a very particular set of skills and he would use them to find you, I was certainly lacking some very fundamental ones and was finding it difficult to find myself.

I ran inside, grabbed the woman's arm and took her back to the road sign with me, where I then had to try to ask her to spell out the name of the road to me through a series of exaggerated mimes. I pointed at the sign, and then I pointed at my eyes, before shaking my head. 'No see,' I said. Then I pointed at her, followed by the individual letters, then back at me before doing the universal hand sign for a speaking mouth.

Thankfully, she understood, and after a few goes I was finally able to give the voice at the other end of the phone something to type into the stupid computer that was unable to handle directions from a supermarket.

It turns out that there *was* a man down the hole. He was winched out on a stretcher and was conscious as he went into the ambulance. I've no idea what happened to him, or indeed to her, but I do wonder whether she's ever told this story to anybody since. About the time a builder fell down a hole and she dragged a blind man off the street to help, who didn't have a clue where he was or what was going on.

'What are the chances?' she will say to people, through tears of laughter, adding, 'I wanted to make love to him all day once that ambulance had gone, but he disappeared so very quickly before his curry got cold.'

Bugger.

I didn't need to be dragged off the street to become caught up in farcical situations, though. I was more than capable of creating my own, thank you very much. This was certainly the case when I went to watch the entirely wrong band play a live show because I'd kept their CD in the wrong case for two years.

It wasn't just that I went to watch the wrong band. I went to watch a band I knew I didn't like, but I had spent two years believing that the two bands were each other, if that makes any sense to you.

I had bought a couple of CDs on the same day from a local record store, Beggar's Banquet, now known as Banquet Records. If you watched *Strictly,* you might remember one of the video inserts of my dance partner Dianne Buswell and I playing some classic rock vinyls in a record store as part of Icons Week when we danced our tango to Kiss. Well, that VT was filmed in this very store.

This bit didn't make the edit, but this is where Dianne revealed to me that she not only didn't have a clue that Ozzy Osbourne was the lead singer of Black Sabbath, the Prince of Darkness and the godfather of heavy metal, but she'd thought he was only a reality-TV star, the husband of Sharon Osbourne, and nothing else, that's it. Honestly, where to start with that girl?

Anyway, back to the story . . . I'd gone in there looking for recommendations for a couple of new heavy bands to get into and the guy behind the counter suggested two I'd never heard of. After listening to a small sample of each I purchased the two CDs and left with a big smile on my face. When I got home, though, and listened to the albums in full, I discovered I loved one of the bands but wasn't keen on the other. This was back in the days before streaming, when music was far less disposable: if you bought an album you weren't that keen on, you gave it a chance – you gave it a good few plays as it could have been a grower.

The problem I had created for myself was that I had returned those two CDs to each other's cases from that very first day, so the CD of the band I liked was kept in the case of the band I didn't like, and vice versa. That meant I spent two years believing that the band I liked was the band I didn't like, and that the band I didn't like was actually the band I liked. I hope you're keeping up with this as it's about to get a bit more complicated.

The band I didn't like was on tour and happened to be playing a live music venue in my very own Kingston-upon-Thames, which, under any normal circumstances, I would have ignored, but I'd thought this was the band I liked because I'd spent the last two years keeping the CD of the band I liked in the case of the band I didn't like and who were now playing live near where I lived.

Obviously I bought tickets. I bought tickets because I thought I liked them, and I persuaded the one and only Dave Knight Rider, of basement-floating-poos fame, to come along and watch this great band with me that he'd never heard of but that I'd told him were great even though I didn't like them but thought I did.

The venue was quite small, with just a couple of hundred punters in attendance and the band played two sets with an interval. I don't think it's going to be any surprise to learn that I didn't like it. I didn't like it because I didn't like the band. I knew I didn't like the band but their CD had been safely stored away for two years inside the case of the band that I really did like but who weren't on tour and definitely weren't playing there.

The band I didn't like weren't as good and they weren't as heavy, but I hadn't yet figured out any of this. I only owned that one album by the band I liked, whom I thought I'd come to see. My first assumption wasn't that I'd had these two bands confused for two years, but that the band I liked must have changed their musical stylings from the album I liked, and just weren't as good and weren't as heavy any more. It didn't occur to me that this wasn't that band, even though I hadn't recognised a single song.

That wouldn't occur to me until sometime during their second set, when finally they played a song I knew . . . but, hang on, where did I know this song from, because it wasn't off their album?

Honestly, my thought processes here were so slow and laboured that it took quite a while for the penny to drop.

This was how my brain figured it out . . .

'Oh, finally, I know this one.'

The song played for a while.

'Hang on, this isn't on their album, though.'

The song continued to play.

'But I only own the one album by these guys, so this can't be their song.'

I continued to listen.

'I definitely own this song on CD, though, I'm sure of it. They must be playing a cover version, a cover version of a song I own from another band.'

I concentrated harder and tried to figure out where I knew it from . . . I got it, kind of.

'Ah!' I realised. 'This is on that album from the band I didn't like. That's where I know it from!'

Even then, though, the penny hadn't fully dropped. For a few seconds after this, I genuinely had the following thought speak itself out loud in my head . . .

Wow, I bought that album from the band I didn't like on the same day as I bought the album from this band. What are the chances of this band playing a cover version from the band I didn't like, whose album I bought on exactly the same day? What a coincidence!

Honestly, I thought, what a coincidence!

Before five, four, three, two, one, and the penny dropped . . .

'Shit!' I finally realised. 'This is the band I didn't like. No wonder I don't like them!'

That wouldn't have been quite so bad if, during that break between sets, the band hadn't made their way out front to the bar, right next to me, and I hadn't maybe mentioned to one of them that they possibly weren't as heavy as they used to be.

I'd had a few beers by this point and was feeling bolshy.

'What happened to your music?' I said to one of the band members, who was stood beside me.

'What do you mean?' he replied, pretty confused by my question.

'Well, you used to be a lot heavier and you're not any more. What happened?'

'I don't know what the fuck you're on about,' he said as he turned away from the complete lunatic who was trying to complain to him that his band just wasn't as heavy as an entirely different band.

'Dave,' I said, 'we've got to get out of here.'

For you music nerds out there, the bands in question were called Errortype 11 and Eyelid. I'd spent two years thinking I liked the former, when in fact I liked the latter, so it was the former of these two that I went to watch believing them to be the latter. What an idiot. What an almost blind idiot.

You've got to laugh. Honestly, you've got to laugh. I mean, what else are you going to do?

End of important message.

Chapter Twenty-Four

When blindness finally came it was a relief. I might not have realised this at the time, but I would look back at it as a turning point, as the moment when I would start being able to get better at something rather than being caught up in deterioration and denial.

For my whole life I had only ever been getting worse at being able to see, at being partially sighted, coping as best I could as my sight continued to worsen, always playing catch-up and trying to adjust to something that was in a constant state of change as the goalposts were for ever moving.

For the first time I had reached a plateau, a state that would be unchanging and that I could now start to adjust to. I could start getting better at being blind, because blind wasn't going anywhere, blind wouldn't be changing in any noticeable way, and those goalposts would be staying firmly put.

Blindness wasn't a glorious warm bath of acceptance that I plunged into. I'm just able to see all of this for what it was now that I've lived through it and can look back with some years under my belt. In truth, I'd already started to get better at elements of being blind but just hadn't put two and two together to give me four. I had already started using speech on the computer rather than relying on sight. I had already given up many parts of myself and things that I could no longer do and replaced them with other forms of socialising and entertainment. I had already learned to give over significant parts of my independence for dependence on others.

Despite these shifts, though, I had still never thought of myself as blind, not while I could still see something that was of some use, not while I could still see enough to try to cope. Blindness brought with it a new identity, an identity that was fixed and that I could no longer deny. I was blind.

Blindness is not just seeing black. In fact it never is. Blindness is either the total absence of any visual experience, or being able to see something that is nothing of any use.

Many people assume that total blindness must be black, but to be able to see black your brain needs to be interpreting light to see the absence of it. Those who are born completely blind will not see black, or even nothing, because they can't see to see that there is a blackness or a nothingness to see. The reality is that they can't see anything. There is a difference.

It's difficult for somebody sighted to understand the idea of not being able to see anything, because an equivalent experience to them is usually due to it being dark, and so therefore black. A total blackness has therefore become the representative placeholder for the idea of not being able to see anything and so, by extension, total blindness.

We more readily accept that total deafness is an absence of hearing without having to insert a silence for the deaf person to listen to, but with total blindness those who are sighted find it difficult to detach their own experience of sight to be able to appreciate an absence of it.

Place your hand behind your back. What can it see behind you? Precisely. It can't see anything, because it can't see. It's a ridiculous example to be honest, but it's the best I've got.

I will never fall into this category of blindness as I will always still be able to see something, but my something is nothing more than a swirling, murky, fuzzy soup of shadow and light. My eyesight is still deteriorating to this day, possibly still degrading by half every five years or so, but it has long since passed the point where any of that is noticeable to me. That swirling, murky, fuzzy soup might have intensified over the years, since it consumed my useful vision, more swirling, more murky, more fuzzy, more soupy, but one swirling, murky, fuzzy soup is much like any other.

I think that joke about trying to look through a bathroom window might actually be a half-decent analogy, to be honest. If you have ten different levels of frosted glass and you can't make anything out through level three onwards, the severity of the frosting becomes irrelevant to the experience of trying to see through it. I could be on level seven by now and still increasing the frosting, but I hit level three over two decades ago and it's all been pretty damn frosted since.

I know it sounds a bit mad to say that life got easier once I became blind, but it really did. I know that from the perspective of losing my sight I never could have foreseen that being the case: wishing I could reach blindness sooner for the relief and the opportunity for growth that it would bring.

I finally started carrying a white stick around with me and

even had some training on how to use it, but I was never very comfortable with it and would only resort to using it when I had no other options. I didn't have the confidence to be using one to get to and from work every day so I stuck with taxis, figuring that I'd be no use to anybody if I arrived every morning feeling completely frazzled before I'd even started.

The point of a white stick is to identify and locate obstacles before you walk into them or trip over them, but in practice that means you must hit the obstacle with the stick before you can navigate around it. Basically, you have to walk into something a little bit so that you can avoid walking into it a lot. I never liked this method of mobility as it all felt very clumsy to me, like I didn't really know what I was doing, which I didn't, but that wasn't the point.

To anybody born blind or blind from a young age, navigating with a white stick is usually second nature. They are a different animal entirely from somebody like me, who has tried to pick it up later in life and often with reluctance. I was very self-conscious and didn't have anywhere near the level of confidence or skill required to navigate outdoors under the gaze of others. On those occasions when I had no choice, I would walk slowly but sometimes struggle to maintain a straight line and from time to time would end up in somebody's front garden. I honestly think I might have one leg shorter than the other as I was like a trolley with a wonky wheel, which makes *Strictly* seem even more of an achievement, doesn't it?

I was looking over some old blog posts I had written almost twenty years ago and I came across this paragraph, which I think really gets across the difficulties I would encounter trying to be independent back then.

I needed to get a haircut and so decided to take a walk down there using my white stick. I did a rough step count on the way and would estimate that the walk is about seven hundred steps from my front door along three suburban streets. Within this short quiet walk I clattered into three cars that were parked with their ends sticking out of driveways blocking the pavement. I don't mind giving these a whack. Four sets of bins were left blocking the pavements, okay, yes, today is bin-collection day but that's still one out of seven days that this is an issue. On twelve separate occasions I was hit in the torso or face by bushes and branches that reached way beyond the boundaries of a private garden wall, and as I got close to the barber's and in among the shops I also hit two advertising boards. In total that is twenty-one separate obstacles in just that short walk, and that's avoiding the high street and any cafés.

This really shows its age, doesn't it? Weekly bin collections? My goodness. These days, those bins would only be a problem once every four weeks or so, if at all.

There is the common misconception that if you lose your sight your hearing will compensate, and this isn't entirely true. My hearing is no different from what it ever was. In fact, if anything, it's probably worse, due to a lifetime of heavy-metal music. The only thing that changes is the attention I place on what I hear. If I've got nothing to look at, it stands to reason that my focus is mostly going to be on what I'm listening to.

Rain becomes a problem as its relentless pattering and pummelling is like a blanket of static interference distorting and masking the sounds of traffic and pedestrians. Car tyres on wet roads throw up sounds that seem to emanate from different directions all at once, and shops that normally keep their doors open will shut them during a downpour, removing smells and sounds that may have provided signposts along the way.

You can usually smell the pastries and bread as you pass a baker, or the stuffy leatheriness of a shoe shop, or you can hear the chatter and clinking of knives and forks outside a café. The rain can remove all of these clues and leave you just counting your steps.

Similarly, a gentle breeze can add some beauty and bring the trees to life, but anything too gusty will obliterate the entire sonic landscape.

These days, I'm lucky because my need to venture out alone on foot is pretty much zero. I work a lot, and any home time is spent with my family. In the past I would have had to head out to get supplies from the shops, but now I can pretty much have anything urgent brought to me within the hour via any one of a number of food-delivery apps, and for anything that can wait until tomorrow, there's Amazon.

If I need to go anywhere I can have a cab at my door in a matter of minutes, the immediacy of ride-hailing apps offering me the luxury of spontaneity that just wouldn't have been possible twenty years ago.

Technology has been a huge enabler for me, the single biggest game-changer being the iPhone. This was the first phone I was able to buy from a shop and use straight out of the box without requiring any adaptations. When I got my first mobile phone almost thirty years ago, I was able to dial phone numbers on the keypad, but I couldn't see well enough to send texts or access the contact list. This meant I could only phone people whose numbers I could remember, which meant I could only phone about eight people. After about five years of this highly restricted use of a mobile phone, there was a piece of software I could buy for £150 that could be installed onto some specific models of Nokia phones. It allowed the menus and contact list to be spoken out loud in a Stephen Hawking-type voice. It made such a difference, as for the first time I could phone more than eight people and send text messages like everybody else.

Apple was the first company to consider accessibility on-device, and in 2009 I bought my first iPhone and never looked back. To take a device that appeared entirely exclusionary to the blind, a glass-fronted phone with no tactile keypad or buttons, and to make that the most accessible tool I have ever encountered in the decade and a half that has followed, well, it would prove to be a real turning point in the way the world would come to view accessibility.

Pretty much all of the tech I use is Apple, and it is all usable to me straight out of the box. The phone, the watch, the laptop, everything talks. Even when I'm at home on my own I never get a bit of peace and quiet. People will often ask how I type on a laptop. Well, I touch-type just like other people do: not looking while typing is a normal thing, not a blind thing. Most things aren't that different, really, and I'm typing every word of this book in the good old-fashioned way with fingers on home keys while my Mac kindly reads everything out to me.

The access and autonomy that technology gives me to live my life with independence and spontaneity can't be over-stated. Whereas in the past a device costing thousands of pounds would have been required for me to scan my mail in and have it read out loud, now I just do that with my phone. I access my banking, the internet, do my shopping, order food, taxis and pretty much everything else through my phone, just like everybody else does. That is why it has been such a game-changer, because before the iPhone, 'just like everybody else does' wasn't really possible.

I've tried to cover a lot here to give you an idea of what blindness is, what it meant when it finally arrived, and what was to come over the years as I adjusted to life without sight. I never did get to grips with a white stick and haven't used one for years. I still carry one about with me sometimes as an indication to others, but I've found other ways of achieving enough independence that don't involve having to clatter into quite so many bins and inconsiderately parked cars. It's not complete independence, in fact far from it, but it's enough, and often enough is all you need.

Over those years that lay ahead of me at the age of twenty-five, my adjustment to blindness would manifest in so many practical ways, but the most valuable and impactful adjustment would come from my acceptance of this new identity.

My intention is not to make out that blindness is easy, because it's not. If anybody reading or hearing these words has experienced or is going through sight loss, just know that it's a bastard. It's fine to feel lost, helpless and frustrated at times, and there will be good and bad days along the way. The one thing I can guarantee, though, is that you do just get used to it. It's as simple as that, really. You get used to living without sight, you get used to relying on others and finding new ways to accomplish things that today may seem beyond your grasp, and you get used to managing those moments of frustration that are both frequent and inevitable along the way. Even for me all these years in: I still get overwhelmed by situations and some of the enormous efforts I have to go to in order to achieve seemingly simple tasks, and I still swear at items of furniture and kitchen-cabinet doors with the same alarming regularity that I always have.

The other thing that happened was that I started to grow more comfortable in my own skin, with shame and embarrassment becoming the faintest of echoes from a life left behind. Many factors contributed towards this positive shift, from the natural march of time and the maturity that ageing brings, to getting married and becoming a dad.

More on this in a little bit, though, because I was about to find my purpose. I was about to find stand-up comedy.

Chapter Twenty-Five

One day in March 2003 I woke up with a strange sensitivity on my left-hand side, around where you might imagine one of your kidneys to be, or something similar that is equally important. It was like a perfect arc of sensitive spots, a rainbow of pimples that started from around my belly-button and arced around the side of my torso before curving back down towards my lower spine and coming to rest in exactly the same place where it had started, but on my back.

That's it, I thought. I've got some kind of kidney disease. I'm doomed!

It wasn't just some random rash. It was far too precise, clearly following the path of something internal. Something inside me was broken and this was the outward symptom of that internal failure. Probably a kidney or my pancreas. Isn't that in the same general area? What side was the liver on? Shit. Why did I only get a D in GCSE biology? For the first time I was beginning to lament my casual attitude to the study of the human body all those years earlier.

As it turned out, I had shingles, which was good, I hoped, although I didn't know what that was either. The doctor could have told me anything.

'Ah, shingles, a very rare spleen-eating disease that starts at the spleen but will have consumed all of your internal organs within about three weeks. Sorry, there's nothing we can do. On a brighter note, though, you can eat and drink and smoke whatever you like. It doesn't really matter any more.'

Shingles is actually related to chickenpox in some way, I'm not entirely sure how, bastard cousins maybe, and is brought on by stress.

'Has anything happened recently that has caused you unusual levels of stress?' asked the doc.

'Well, I went blind,' I said

'Yeah, that'll do it, I suppose. I'm going to sign you off work,' he said.

That wasn't ideal. Sure, being signed off work might sound like a dream if you're still getting paid a full whack, but I was on commission. My basic salary would continue but my income and targets were bound to take a hit.

'How long are you signing me off for?' I asked.

'Three weeks, maybe four,' he replied. 'You need to rest in order to get better. You need to lower those stress levels and, erm, you know . . .'

It sounded like he might have been about to say 'stop being blind' but had decided against it at the last moment.

'. . . erm, you know, stay at home and don't be going anywhere.'

Good save, Doc.

I loved my little studio flat but the thought of being cooped up there for three or even four weeks was quite a daunting prospect. Little did I know, though, that this relatively brief period of enforced rest would be the catalyst that would cause me to consider stand-up comedy in a very different light. I started my rest period by binge-watching loads of it, working my way through the ample collection of DVDs and videos that I had amassed over the years. Even now, as a stand-up comedian with more than two decades under my belt, I'm still a huge fan of the art form. Yeah, that's right, art form!

Over those last twenty-odd years, a lot of my friends and contemporaries have gone on to achieve great success, and I love sitting down as a comedy fan and getting to watch what they have produced. I've always felt so much excitement and pride watching Michael McIntyre, Micky Flanagan, Kevin Bridges and John Bishop filling arenas, and more recently comics like Tom Allen, Rob Beckett and Joe Lycett smashing the shit out of it. Even though I have absolutely nothing to do with any of their success, I always feel a rush of vicarious joy that somebody I used to play the clubs with has become a household name for a new generation of comedy fans to enjoy, and that I was stood somewhere nearby when it happened.

I still enjoy discovering new comedians, although my tolerance for successful mediocrity isn't what it used to be. The number of American stand-up specials I've had to turn off after fifteen minutes or so because their very existence irritated me are too many to count.

After a couple of weeks of working through my collection I'd run out of stuff to watch and turned my attention to this relatively new thing called Google. Google was a few years old by this point and rapidly growing in popularity so, armed with my very first broadband connection, I started having a little mooch around on the internet for anything stand-up related that was new to me. We were still a way off YouTube being a thing, and finding videos was a lot trickier back then, but a few sites hosted some short clips of mainly American comics I'd never heard of before.

One of the things that caught my eye, or my ear – I was using a screen reader by this point, remember – was a sponsored search result that claimed you could become a stand-up comedian in just seven days, or something ridiculous like that. Yeah, right. What a load of rubbish. Like you can become a stand-up comedian in seven days.

I wasn't just being dismissive about the time frame, though, but about the audacity of the suggestion. Become a stand-up comedian? You can't just become a stand-up comedian. I had just spent the last two weeks binge-watching stand-up comedians. I had seen Eddie Izzard live, for God's sake. These guys had confidence by the bucket load. They had showmanship in their DNA – they had an X-factor that your normal regular guy, who worked in a call centre but was at home looking up stand-up clips on Google because he had shingles, just didn't have. You couldn't just learn these things in seven days!

Of course you couldn't, but what hadn't occurred to me in that moment was that I had been binge-watching stand-up comedians who were at the very top of their game. The top few per cent of professional comedians that had managed to infiltrate our homes. The only comedy club I'd ever been to was the Comedy Store, the premier stand-up comedy club in the entire country for the very best and most experienced comedians on the UK comedy circuit. I didn't even know there was a comedy circuit!

Eddie Izzard was the UK's first comedian to take stand-up into arenas and set the new elite precedent that others would follow. Of course you couldn't do that in seven days, but I didn't know just how much comedy existed beneath Eddie.

I clicked on the link and there was a downloadable course. I can't remember exactly how much it was, but I think maybe around eighty to a hundred quid. I wouldn't have paid that kind of money but there was also a free downloadable sample of the course, so I clicked to download that free sample.

The internet has become awash with crackpot claims that promise ridiculous results, if you'd only part with some of your hard-earned cash for the full course after reading the handy sample or watching the introductory video. Immediately, though, that free course sample captivated me. I read about what it's like to start off in comedy and do your first gigs, which was something I'd never really considered before.

Yeah, you can't become Eddie Izzard or Lee Evans in seven days, that's preposterous, but even they must have started somewhere, mustn't they? Surely there was a time when even they weren't that great or had maybe even been a bit shit. On that day, as I sat in my tiny little studio flat with shingles and nothing else to do, I gave myself the time to think about this. My immediate dismissive reaction to the suggestion broke down as I started to think about it as a much larger picture.

Surely everybody must start somewhere. I'm just seeing the professionals. Even at the Comedy Store in London, they might not have been household names but they were professionals who were just as good as many of those household names, blisteringly funny and at the very top of their game, but the free sample of that course, with its ridiculous claim of seven days, had opened my eyes to the idea of amateur comedy, open-mic gigs and a ladder to be climbed.

I realised that, just like any industry, comedy had a ladder to experience and success, and what I and the vast majority of people tended to see was just the very top of that ladder poking through the clouds. Most of us only saw those comedians who had manage to gain access to our living rooms either via TV shows or their stand-up comedy videos and DVDs.

All of this might be far more obvious, these days, with comedians at all levels having a social-media presence, and the enormous amount of stand-up posted online that has exposed the ladder in full.

I finished that sample, went back to the website, clicked the link, stuck in my card details and paid for the full course. I had never read about stand-up before or ever considered the mechanics behind it. I'd always just enjoyed it exactly as intended, entirely as a form of entertainment. I'd never thought about what made jokes work or how they were constructed. But the course talked me through a lot of that. It captured my imagination and ignited my enthusiasm immediately.

I spent the next two weeks of my recuperation working through the course and re-watching a lot of those videos and

DVDs I'd only just enjoyed, but now I watched them as a new student of comedy, not purely as a fan.

I wrote some bits and pieces of my own, but had absolutely no idea whether any of it was any good or even remotely funny. I'd thought I had the kernels of some amusing ideas when I wrote them down, but it wasn't long before I'd got inside my own head and was doubting every last word of it. I didn't realise that the longer you spend working on something you think is funny, the less funny it will inevitably become to you by the time you've finished working on it. Once all of the initial excitement, spontaneity and freshness of an idea has dissipated over time, with every tweak and rewrite, you can very easily find yourself wondering what the hell was funny about any of it in the first place.

With experience, though, you learn to understand that this is just what happens, and to trust yourself more and more. You become better at being able to see the comedy in ideas and words and to understand how they might be received by an audience hearing them for the first time. Back then, though, I didn't know any of this. I had this stuff that I had written and all I knew was that I'd found it amusing when I'd written it but now I didn't feel quite so sure.

My four weeks were up and I returned to work shingles free. I continued making phone calls and hitting my targets, but now with an itch in the back of my mind, an itch that wouldn't leave me alone. What I needed was some external validation that what I had written might be funny but I certainly wasn't going to show any of it to friends or family, I needed to try it out for myself and see if anybody laughed.

It's amazing how the idea of trying stand-up in front of a room full of strangers felt less daunting than sharing what I'd written with the people who were closest to me, but that is even the case today. Even now after more than twenty years of performing, I still won't share jokes or ideas with friends or family before trying them out on stage. If I have an audience of just one and they don't laugh at a new joke or idea, it's died a death and that will dent any confidence I have in it before I get to try it out for real. In a room of a hundred people, all I need is for some of them to laugh to know that the bit might have legs if I maybe tweak it a little.

I can't exactly remember how, although I would imagine probably Google again, but I found a one-day crash course in stand-up that was taking place one Saturday morning in a village hall and signed myself up. This course was run by a lovely couple called Marek and Alice, who were incredibly supportive. The experience ended up being really good for me. We spent a great deal of the day working through the comedy material that we had each brought with us, then all got a chance to stand up in front of the class and deliver our material. A local neighbour to the village hall came in to complain about the noise and ask us to keep the racket down – but I was used to criticism like that, wasn't I?

'Defect! Defect!'

I thoroughly enjoyed the opportunity to share the ideas I'd thought might possibly be funny all those weeks ago in my studio flat and to get to say them out loud in front of others, and I left Marek and Alice with that comedy itch even itchier.

Technically, I suppose, that was my first gig. Standing up

in front of the rest of the class and delivering my first attempt at stand-up comedy. However, it wasn't really, was it? Everybody laughed at everything, partly because we were all being ultra-supportive of each other, but also probably because we thought that if we laughed at everybody else's jokes they would laugh at ours. It still wasn't a genuine indication of whether anything I had written would work in front of a room full of strangers who had paid money to be there and didn't want anything back from me in return.

The idea of this was terrifying, though. Plus, how would I be able to make the logistics work? It wasn't like I could just take myself off into London and do a gig on my own. I would never find the place, and if I did, I wouldn't be able to navigate myself around inside. I would probably have to get a friend to accompany me, which would add further stress and would mean that I wouldn't be able to fail miserably in secret without anybody knowing about it.

Then something happened, a coincidence. A coincidence like no other coincidence. It was a coincidence that was such a phenomenal coincidence that it almost made me believe in angels or fairies, or both, before deciding that it was probably just a coincidence after all.

Back in the call centre I was having a chat with a guy who had recently started, and who was sat opposite me on our workstation. His name was David and he was about my age and from Birmingham.

'What's your dream, Chris?' he asked.

'I don't know, Dave. I'm still trying to figure that out,' I told him.

At this point, comedy wasn't really a dream. It was more of a dare that I'd decided I'd quite like to make myself do, even just once.

'What's your dream, Dave?' I asked back.

'I feel a bit silly saying this' he said, 'but I'd love to try stand-up comedy.'

What a coincidence!

Chapter Twenty-Six

David and I made an agreement that together we would scratch this itch and give stand-up comedy a go in front of a room full of people. My fear, of course, was that I would be terrible, and not just terrible, but the most terrible person ever to have tried stand-up comedy. The truth is, though, that even if you are shit, nobody really cares. The world just moves on and nothing bad happens. It's not like people will be pointing at you in the street for years to come.

'There he is. That's the guy who died on his arse in that little room above the Duck and Whistle back in 2003.'

With hindsight it's easy to see how insignificant an event me appearing at an open-mic comedy night was to everybody else in the world who wasn't me, but at the time it felt so monumental that the pressure I placed on myself almost ate me alive.

Thankfully, David shared that same fear, which was quite reassuring for both of us, as we couldn't both be the worst person ever to have tried stand-up, could we? Just so long as we both did the same gig, we would instantly halve our odds of that being the case.

What neither of us knew was what the standard of

comedy was like at any of these open-mic gigs. We didn't have a clue how good we'd need to be to hold our own, or how bad we'd have to be to be the worst, so we decided to get out there for ourselves and find out.

We went to an open-mic night in a room above a pub in Wimbledon, which turned out to be exactly what we needed to allay any fears we had about what might happen if we were to experience a catastrophic and very public failure onstage. First, there were only about fifteen people in the audience, which was hardly very public, and that modest total included us, so really about thirteen proper audience members because we were just there to check out the standard.

There were some good acts on the bill, but far more importantly for us, there were also some absolutely terrible ones. There was one poor guy who didn't get a single laugh. Absolutely nothing. He just slowly crumbled in front of us before walking off to the sound of his own footsteps. It was bad. It was terrible. It was incredibly uncomfortable to sit there and watch the slow disintegration of a man's confidence and resolve happening right in front of us, but it was also hugely reassuring.

It was reassuring because I couldn't even remember what his name was by the time I was on the train heading home, and for me that was the real eye-opener. Here was a guy who had just lived the exact same nightmare that I was terrified I might have, and I wouldn't have been able to tell you who he was even if you were paying me for the information. Suddenly, this all felt a lot safer.

So, with the reassurance that failure would likely be met

with almost instant disregard by whatever small number of people were present, David and I made good our plans to get up there and give it a go for ourselves.

Armed with a copy of *Time Out,* a magazine dedicated to the live-entertainment scene in London, we combed through the comedy section and phoned anywhere that had a number listed. David did the combing and I did the phoning.

'Sorry, mate, you need at least thirty gigs under your belt before you can play here,' said one guy to me. 'It's for new comedians, but not that new.'

'This is a club for professional comics, not open spots,' said another. 'Phone me back when you're doing paid twenties.'

Paid twenties? What the hell did that mean?

'Okay,' I said back, 'but can I just ask, what are paid twenties? Hello? Hello?'

There was a lot of lingo involved that I just didn't know.

'Oh, fuck off,' shouted another guy I had evidently just woken at two in the afternoon. 'I was in Lincoln last night.'

'Okay, sorry to hear that.'

'I have to answer the phone just in case it's the Comedy Store wanting to book me for tonight. Next time you want to find out about spots at my club, phone at a reasonable time.'

'Right, will do. What time would be reasonable? Hello? Hello?'

This wasn't going great.

'I don't know you, do I?' said a lady.

'Err, no, I'm a new comedian and –'

'Well, you can't just phone me out of the blue asking for a gig. You're not Micky Flanagan,' she said.

Who the hell was Micky Flanagan? This wasn't going well at all.

'Yeah, of course,' said a guy.

'Sorry?' I said, a little bit taken aback by his positive response.

'Yeah, of course. I can put you in for a five-minute spot in six weeks' time.'

'Six weeks? I asked. 'That long away?'

I was ready to do it there and then and was worried that any delay to this would have me doubting myself to the point at which I would change my mind.

'Yeah, sorry about that. Six weeks is all I've got. Take it or leave it, I suppose.'

'Okay, I'll take it,' I said. 'Oh, and there's just one thing.'

'Yeah?' said the voice.

'Could you stick two of us down?'

'Are you a double act?' he asked.

'No. There are just two of us, two separate people, wanting spots. We've just decided to share the phoning around.'

'Ah, yeah, okay, good idea, not a problem. You're both in for five minutes in six weeks' time.'

I gave our names and hung up. We were in. In six weeks' time we would be absolutely shitting ourselves.

Those six weeks went both slow and fast at the same time. The time seemed to drag, but then I couldn't believe the date had come around already. Time is a strange and often bewildering phenomenon that always seems to show itself differently depending on when and in what state of mind you look back at it.

That first gig was at a new-act night, held at an absolutely massive pub called the Bedford Arms in Balham, south London. The Bedford was and still is home to the incredibly long-running Banana Cabaret comedy club, which runs on a Friday and a Saturday night and is for professional comedians who are established on the circuit. I have gone on to perform there over many weekends, but on that first tentative step into the world of comedy I was performing at a completely different and much smaller new-act comedy show that was held at the same venue every Tuesday night.

The Bedford might be the biggest pub I've ever been in, or certainly the pub that has had the most going on at the same time. It has a large performance room with a balcony running around the top, which is where the Banana Cabaret takes place. It has a ballroom and a much smaller performance room up the top. I've been in there on a Tuesday when they've had a live music event in the main performance room, ballroom dancing in the ballroom obviously, an Irish band playing in the main bar area, and the new-act comedy show taking place in that small upstairs room.

And all of that happening on a Tuesday?

On that particular Tuesday the new-act comedy night was taking place in the main performance room, although most of the space wasn't needed. I'd ended up having to take both the Monday and the Tuesday off work as I was much too nervous to be any use to anybody and I needed the time mentally to prepare myself for what was about to happen. For somebody who had already decided that failure wouldn't be the complete catastrophe I'd originally feared it might be, I was so nervous that I could barely eat on the Monday and didn't manage to eat a single thing on the Tuesday, surviving entirely on coffee and cigarettes.

I spent the entire Tuesday just pacing my little studio flat in the smallest of circles, reciting my words over and over to myself under mumbled breath and feeling grateful that I'd had laminate flooring fitted as I would have worn through any carpet. It's quite ironic how that four-week period off work to recover from shingles, caused by stress, had ultimately led to me doing the most nerve-racking and stressful thing I'd ever been compelled to do in my life so far, and that would remain the case until *Strictly*.

We arrived at the venue and I was honestly so sick with nerves that you could have pushed me over with a single finger. Not eating properly for two days and likely being in the midst of a fairly significant caffeine and nicotine overdose probably didn't help. The guy I'd spoken to on the phone and who ran the night was called Ed Balls – no, not that one. This Ed Balls was a laid-back Aussie who loved his comedy and had a heart of gold.

I would find it wasn't uncommon in the world of open-mike shows and lower-end-circuit gigs to encounter gatekeepers to stage time who enjoyed the power they felt the position allowed them to wield over new and inexperienced comics. There were a lot of nice, kind, genuine gig promoters whom I would encounter over the coming years, but there were also a lot of arrogant arseholes with egos far above their station.

Ed fell very much into the first category of nice, kind, genuine souls, which was lucky for me as he was not only my gateway to my very first five minutes of stage time, but he was my introduction to the comedy scene as a whole.

'So how does this work, then?' he asked me.

'How does what work?' I asked him, not sure what he was on about.

'How does it work with you being blind?' he said. 'When you're doing other gigs, how do you get up to the microphone?'

'Oh,' I said, as I tried to think of the best way to break the news. 'I don't know, I've never done this before.'

There was a silence for a moment or two while Ed processed this new information.

'Right,' he said, in that long drawn-out way I was becoming accustomed to.

'Do you think you could come and get me?' I asked, without really understanding how the logistics of that might interfere with the flow of the show or his ability to build the energy in the room between acts without it being a bit awkward.

'Yeah, okay,' he said, without a moment's hesitation, and sat me at a table near to the stage so that he could retrieve me without too much fuss and disruption to the show.

There were about forty people in the audience, a lot more than had been at that open-mic night in Wimbledon, but it felt quite empty in that massive room. David and I sat off to one side at a table with a couple of other guys on the bill. Everybody was fairly new but nobody aside from us was doing their first ever gig.

Ed had put us both somewhere in the middle of the show, but not straight after one another – I imagine just in case we were both super-shit and tanked the whole night for a solid ten minutes straight. I wasn't able to pay attention or enjoy any of the show as I was so nervous about my own spot coming up, but I remember that everybody kind of did all right. My turn came and I prepared myself for Ed to nip over and grab me.

'Okay, guys,' he said. 'Our next act is doing his first ever gig.'

The audience whooped.

'I'm gonna introduce him now, and then I'm just gonna go and grab him but you'll see why, so keep that applause going all the way to the microphone. Ladies and gentlemen, please welcome to the stage Chris McCausland!'

There was no actual stage in a physical sense. The microphone stand was on the floor in front of the small audience, but as they started applauding Ed nipped across and gave me a hand over to it.

I don't have a set list to remind me of exactly what material I did on that first gig and in what order, but I do know that I definitely opened with a joke that dealt with me being blind. My plan had always been to do this first, and then to move on to other stuff and not mention it again. I was there because I loved stand-up and wanted to see if I could perform stand-up. I wasn't there to see if I could be funny about being blind for five minutes or because I thought I had something I could milk for a few laughs.

I understood that I couldn't just go onto a stage when

there was quite clearly something different about me, then not reference the thing that made me different. I needed to make a joke at the beginning. I needed to put the audience at ease and break the ice. I needed to show them I was comfortable with whatever was going on, and here lies the crux of that, I suppose: I needed to make myself feel comfortable with being blind in this situation and put myself at ease. Then, hopefully, the audience would be able to follow suit.

I had a bit about those new warnings that were now being printed on cigarette packs, but I can't remember exactly what the material was. There were never any set lists on pieces of paper or notebooks of ideas for me to keep hold of: everything I ever wrote had to be on my computer, and about two years into comedy I lost the contents of my hard drive, with the details of all those first gigs and earliest attempts at writing stand-up comedy material. I do remember, though, that it had something to do with stunting your growth and jockeys, something along the lines of cigarettes being the ideal performance-enhancing drug for a jockey who wants to remain as small as possible. The idea was fine but fairly average, and I soon realised that lots of comics had material about those new warnings on cigarette packs. Even though the angle might have been different, the subject matter was pretty well trodden in comedy back then.

I had a bit about bombs in movies, which I'm much clearer on because it was good, and it would survive with me for some time as I developed it and built it into a solid piece of stand-up. The basic premise was that whenever there's a bomb in a film and the good guys are trying to defuse it, they're always faced with the choice of whether to cut the red wire or the blue wire.

'Shall we cut the red wire or the blue wire?' I would say. 'Red or blue? Red or blue?' Then, 'Here's a thought,' I would add. 'Why don't the bad guys just make the wires all the same colour? Then they'd get to the bomb and go, "Shit! They're all brown! I can't deal with this. I can only do red or blue."'

This was the idea for the initial premise, but as I said, I would go on to develop it to include further anomalies like why the bad guys always include a handy digital countdown timer so that the good guys know how long they've got left.

I remember at some point around two years into comedy, an established and really brilliant comedian and lovely guy called Martin Beaumont telling me he thought the bomb stuff was really great. He also told me he thought I needed to smarten up onstage and not look like such a scruff, and he was right, of course.

Around 2019, just prior to Covid, I was performing at a gig up in Grantham in Lincolnshire, and there was a guy in the audience who worked in bomb disposal. I've never had the kind of brain that can just pull an old bit of material out and perform it if the opportunity calls for it, but I told the room how one of my very first bits of material ever was about that very subject, which gave me the leeway I needed to work my way through that old bit of material as best as I could remember it. It still worked really well all those years later. Obviously there is always a boost to the comedy in something spontaneous, when the audience feels something is happening in the moment and just for them, but the premise still brought laughs a good fifteen years after I'd first thought of it.

Rewinding back to that Tuesday night in Balham in 2003, and the one thing that no amount of good ideas or comedy premises could make up for was a complete lack of stage presence or performance experience. I had spent so long reciting my words over and over to myself, and was so hung up on getting those words right on the night, that I had barely any stage presence at all. I just worked through my set without any nuance or expression whatsoever. My performance was so monotone and flat that I would later come to think of it as being like the stand-up comedy equivalent of a song by the Lighthouse Family, all seemingly performed on just the one note and without any real enjoyment exhibited throughout any of it.

I got laughs, though, several laughs. I wouldn't go as far as to say that I smashed my first ever gig and took the roof off the place, but I certainly did okay, and okay was absolutely 100 per cent good enough for me.

I left that stage to a round of applause and a cheer, as Ed returned to the microphone once he'd helped me back to my seat.

'His first gig, guys!'

The crowd whooped again.

'Shall we get him back for more gigs?' he asked the room, and the audience cheered their enthusiastic approval.

Ed's real name was Ed Rikard Bell and he died in early 2013 due to a brain tumour. Ed was an incredibly integral component to me being a stand-up right now. If it wasn't for him giving me that first gig, and for his kindness and support during my first ever steps onto a comedy-club stage, maybe I'd never have tried it a second time. During my early years on the circuit I returned to that new-act night many times to get stage time and try out new material, sometimes in the big room and sometimes in the little room upstairs, but always with Ed.

Thanks for everything, Ed.

Chapter Twenty-Seven

The desire to give comedy a go had been just that, a dare to myself to try it at least once. It was never intended to be the beginning of me building a career in comedy. I just wanted to get up there, have a go and see if I could make an audience laugh. It was to say that I had done it and maybe have a story to tell. After that first attempt, though, I wanted to do it again as soon as possible, to see if I could enjoy it a little more this time with fewer nerves, and see if I could get more laughs along the way.

This is how it grabs you and reels you in. You might have heard other comedians talk about how they very quickly caught the comedy bug, and in the beginning it is just that: the desire to do it again, to chase that high and try to do better the next time around. I went back to work on that Wednesday morning but performing stand-up again was all I could think about while I tried to sell employment-law manuals to human-resources managers. David had also enjoyed the experience and performing again was all that was on his mind as well. We kept our comedy adventure completely secret from our colleagues in the call centre, but would sneak opportunities to reminisce covertly about what we had just done and talk about our desire to do it again.

I don't think I ever told David this, but I was extra relieved that he'd done well: his idea of stand-up material was so off the wall and batshit crazy that when he was running his ideas past me I couldn't tell whether I thought any of them were funny or not. His idea of comedy lacked any conventional jokes or recognisable punchlines, instead veering towards surreal flights of fancy that would spontaneously break out into urban song with a hip-hop vibe. Think Noel Fielding crossed with Lenny Henry and you might get a rough idea of where he was aiming for. Honestly, though, it might have been daft and more than a little unconventional, but it definitely turned out to be funny.

It was precisely two weeks later that we would get to do it for a second time, and again this would be as a double booking with the two of us featuring somewhere in the middle of the bill to cause minimal damage if we were shit. The second gig was for the Laughing Horse chain of comedy clubs, which offered a fairly substantial number of open-mic and semi-pro nights that were typically held in function rooms of pubs in and around London. Ed Balls wasn't the only good guy on the open-mic scene: the Laughing Horse empire was run by a guy called Alex Petty, who loved comedy and operated this quite significant part of the open-mic comedy scene alongside his day job. I think it would be hard to overstate the impact that Alex had on grass-roots comedy in the south-east when I was starting out and throughout my early years. The opportunities and stage time he was able to provide to hundreds of us through a substantial roster of well-run shows meant we could often at least half fill our diaries just from Alex alone.

This second gig was at a pub called the Coach and Horses, which was somewhere behind Oxford Circus tube station. It was a tiny cosy room above the pub and it would become one of my favourite tiny places to return to and play over the next few years. The room held forty or fifty people, which doesn't sound like much, but this was a super cosy little space. There was a tiny bar up there and all of us comedy newbies would gather in front of it to watch the show and wait our turn.

There was a guy called Ed Petrie on the bill, who I would go on to do several gigs with over the next couple of years, a really funny guy who used a flip chart and drawings as part of his comedy, and very quickly moved on to have an illustrious career in kids' TV.

There was also this strange German fella called Henning Wehn, who sounded like he'd just arrived in the country for the first time on that morning. Henning was hilarious even back then, and although his comedy has got even sharper over time, more than twenty years have passed and he still sounds like he's just arrived in the country on any given morning. I think surely he must be putting on the accent a little bit by now, but don't tell him I said that.

Headlining the show was a comedian called Kevin Shepherd, who is both incredibly funny and warm in equal measure. Kevin is a brilliant comic and is still going strong to this day, although he's easily responsible for the single most un-rock-'n'-roll thing that anybody has ever done backstage in my presence. It was about ten years ago at a gig when Kevin pulled a travel blender out of his bag and proceeded to blend himself a healthy smoothie from fruit he'd brought along in a range of Tupperware containers.

'I'm on a calorie-controlled diet,' he explained, as he began the blending process right in front of me.

'Why didn't you just blend it at home and bring the smoothie with you?' I asked him.

'Because it wouldn't have been as fresh,' he replied, with an ultimate seriousness to his tone.

Okay, this might be technically right, but in the eighties and nineties there would have been somebody racking up lines of coke in front of me while supping a straight Jack Daniel's, but now it was a guy preparing a healthy smoothie in front of me like I was sat in a juice bar.

I told Kevin I was including this bit in the book and he tried to claim he was just ahead of the curve all those years ago. Yeah, maybe everybody is a lot more health-conscious than they used to be, Kev, but still nobody else has ever brought their own blender and made a smoothie right in front of me while I was waiting to go on stage.

Kevin was ridiculously funny on that night, and I was relieved that he'd been the headliner as I think it would have sucked what little confidence I had right out of me if I'd had to watch him destroy the room before I was due to go onstage. As it happened I followed a guy dressed as a wizard, so all good. This guy wasn't just dressed as a wizard, he did jokes as if he was a wizard, a wizard that had obviously decided to ditch a life of wizardry and casting spells in favour of giving stand-up comedy a go instead. The irony was that if he'd only cast a spell on the audience he might have had a better chance of making them laugh than he did with his actual material.

I did the same set I'd done on that first gig, except I'd been over it to try to improve on the bits that hadn't got any response from the audience. The difference in nerves from that first attempt was night and day. I was still nervous, but I was actually looking forward to doing it again, which allowed me to add some level of performance to my material that I had been unable to access on that first attempt. I'd also been able to go to work earlier that day and eat solids, which probably contributed to my energy levels and me feeling more like an actual human being. The gig was good and I not only did better than the wizard, but I did better than I'd done on that first gig. That was the main thing. There had been progression.

It was the third gig that was a real step up for the two of us, though. I think it's the same with anything really: when you start something new you can see the vast difference and improvements quite significantly early on. The leaps forward reduce in size as you continue and your efforts make for smaller and smaller margins gained. This, though, felt like a huge leap forward, and it wasn't just down to the audience or the room but to our comfort with a microphone and our ability to perform and enjoy the experience of being up onstage.

London's West Hampstead was the destination and this time the gig was a free-to-enter show in the basement of a bar. As I would learn over the years, free to enter usually means avoid, avoid, avoid. If audience members haven't paid, even just a couple of quid, this can hugely reduce the level of expectation they have for a good night and subsequently their investment in the whole enterprise. This one was an exception, though: the audience was really great and up for it from the start.

Waiting in the little cubby area next to where the stage was set up, I was sat next to a guy by the name of Tom Wrigglesworth. I knew of Tom because I'd just read that he'd won a national comedy competition called 'So You think You're Funny?', a competition I would enter the following year. Wow! Here I was only on gig three and I was already sharing the bill with a national competition winner.

Tom was brilliant, and still is. We would work with each other a lot over the coming years and he would go on to have a great deal of success up at the Edinburgh Fringe and make a name for himself on Radio 4.

David and I were both on cloud nine after our performances on that night, when the headliner turned up. Lee Mack arrived and performed a twenty-minute set that just took the room to a whole different level. I knew of Lee from the rather imaginatively titled *The Sketch Show* on ITV and couldn't believe I was sharing the bill with somebody off the telly and this was only my third gig. Bloody hell, comedy moved fast, didn't it?

Well, maybe not. It would be sixteen years before I next crossed paths with Lee, but more on that later. There's still a bit to get through first.

Don't worry, this isn't going to turn into a gig-by-gig

account of my entire career. To be honest, I remember my first three really well, but then they all just start to become a little murky in my mind.

It wasn't long before David decided to move back to Birmingham. It felt like no sooner had we set foot in the world of comedy together than he was leaving me to explore it for myself.

I never heard from David again. It's almost like he appeared just to facilitate my start in comedy, then vanished into thin air. A more spiritual person might say it was like he was a guardian angel, sent down to get me moving on the right track and in the right direction, but this isn't that kind of book and I'm not that kind of person. He was definitely real, 100 per cent.

Honest.

Maybe.

For me, comedy had started as a dare but had become a hobby, and for my first two years on the open-mic circuit that was what it remained. There were new acts at this level who would refer to themselves as stand-up comedians, but I didn't buy into this. Stand-up comedian was a job, and I already had a job. I worked in a call centre. That was what paid the bills. I was just somebody who did a bit of stand-up comedy, not somebody who was a stand-up comedian. In my opinion there was a huge difference.

The very first time I was paid anything for a gig, it was five pounds and I was paid it by a lovely bloke who was an open-mic act and promoter called Dave Dynamite. I was so excited by this progression in my new hobby that I vowed never to spend that five-pound note so I put it away somewhere so incredibly safe that I forgot where it was and never saw it again.

I applied to several of the national new-act competitions in my first year of comedy and received a third, two seconds and a first-place finish in four of the big ones. These competitions are important for new acts as they can give you a small amount of exposure to industry and promoters, and when you're starting off in comedy, a small amount of exposure can be all you need to get a leg up.

With the company and generosity of friends, and by meeting up with other open-mic acts to head out on car-share trips to gigs outside London, I absolutely hammered those first two years in comedy. I enjoyed the buzz of performing and the sense of community on the circuit, but I was driven by progression. Promoters started booking me for longer sets and soon I was being paid multiple five-pound notes per gig to do anything up to twenty-minute sets – that's what paid twenties were!

This hobby was now starting to pay and I was receiving offers for work that I had to turn down because I still had the day job. I had hit a dilemma: I couldn't give up the day job until I was earning enough money from comedy to live, but I couldn't guarantee being able to earn enough money from comedy to live while I was still tied to the day job.

I had been unemployed for two years before I took the job in the call centre and it had been the best decision I had made, but I knew it wasn't a dream. I had thrown myself into the job and the culture and the social life that came with it, and it had not only done me the world of good but I had bloody loved it all. Now, though, I had a choice: stick with what was safe and continue working in the call centre and performing a bit of stand-up but with limited opportunity for progression, or take a chance and throw myself into comedy.

I applied for a credit card and kept it in a drawer at home, just in case. That was my emergency back-up plan: that was how I was going to afford to eat if this risky move didn't work out how I hoped it might. I handed in my notice at work and they even let me drop down to three days a week over this period so that I could make a start on building that comedy work before losing my income. It was a lovely touch from my employer and I managed to make the transition into comedy without ever needing that emergency credit card.

This was the start of a brand-new life and it had come almost completely out of the blue, and I now had a very different answer to that third and final question.

'What's your name?'

'Chris.'

'Where are you from?'

'Liverpool.'

'What do you do?'

'I'm a stand-up comedian.'

Chapter Twenty-Eight

I feel very lucky to be a stand-up comedian, to have made it off the open-mic circuit to reach a professional level, because as hard as I worked and as much talent as I was able to develop over those first couple of years, I can't help but marvel at the element of chance that more than played its part.

There were some truly terrible amateur gigs out there, and some pretty awful professional ones as well, to be honest, but those first attempts to perform stand-up comedy can be make or break as to whether you think stand-up is for you. I just happened to pick the right gigs to make it through unscathed.

My first fifteen or so gigs were actually really enjoyable, and I didn't have what I would consider to be a bad one until maybe somewhere around the late teens.

Nobody avoids bad gigs and nobody avoids absolutely dying on their arse. I don't care who your favourite comedian is, how good or successful they are, or how many arena tours they have under their belt. All professional stand-ups share one thing in common, and that is that we have all died onstage and had more bad gigs than we can remember.

I am one of the lucky ones who didn't have one of those

experiences until I'd already discovered that stand-up was something I could do. I think with comedy it can be the luck of the draw like that. There are probably tons of people out there who have tried stand-up once or twice, had an awful experience onstage and thought stand-up wasn't for them. I've played some terrible rooms along the way, and if one of those gigs had been my first time onstage, there isn't a chance in hell that I would have done it again.

If you're thinking of giving stand-up a go, get out there and try your hand. If it goes terribly, do it again. If that goes terribly, do it again. If the first twenty go terribly, maybe try a different approach or call it quits. There is, of course, the chance that you might just be terrible.

My first truly awful gig was around number eighteen or nineteen, but after a run of enjoyable experiences of varying success, I was able to rationalise the idea that bad gigs were just something that happened, and that the best thing I could do was to get back on the horse and carry on.

When you first start out in comedy there are so many factors working against you that awful gigs are inevitable, but they will become rarer and rarer with experience and progression. The only thing that defines a death onstage is whether the audience laugh or not. Silence or mob animosity generally equals a death, while any amount of laughter at all is a value to be placed somewhere along the expansive scale that runs from 'shit' through to 'smashed it'.

Obviously the biggest contributing factor early on to having a terrible time onstage is your own lack of experience, but so many other factors can make comedy tougher for newcomers. I've performed at countless comedy nights in rooms that were far from ideal for comedy. I've told jokes across open bars while people were being served drinks, to rooms in which a significant proportion of the audience were hidden around a corner, and more gigs than I can remember where you could count the number of audience members on one hand without using all your fingers.

During my first run at the Edinburgh Fringe I was performing each night in a small fifty-seater room. On the second weekend it was completely full and I received an incredible review from *The Edinburgh Guide* that claimed my show was surely a shoo-in for the Perrier Best Newcomer short-list. Even the idea that somebody would think that about my show felt amazing and had me on cloud nine for days. When a judge from those prestigious Perrier Awards came to watch my show several days later, it was on a Wednesday evening and I had a grand total of just two audience members, one judge, and one other person who was there on their own and clearly didn't have any friends.

I've done gigs where there was so much noise pollution that I felt like I was shouting about Jesus outside a nightclub. I've performed onstage while pounding baselines and rowdy gatherings have been leaking through from the party downstairs, the venue next door, or sometimes even from something else going on in the same room. I've performed in rooms where the only barrier between the comedy and the football on the big screen was the Boston-style bar in the centre with clear space above and around it for the commentary and the noisy football rabble to be a constant presence.

I've performed on the mezzanine balcony of a pub while a couple of hundred or so punters were having a completely different and noisy night down below, which was pretty much unplayable.

What you do as a new or amateur comedian in these situations is you stick it out and take the stage time, and possibly the money, if it pays at all, that is. Then maybe you just don't return to that comedy night or work for that particular promoter in the future. Because what these gigs do is they toughen you up. They make failure feel less important each time you have to face an environment like that, and you start to develop strings to your bow that mean you'll start being able to manufacture moderate victories out of circumstances that would have spelled certain defeat in the past. Those awful rooms are training grounds where you develop strategy and tactic, and where you learn how to become bullet-proof and earn your stripes along the way.

On a very basic level, I suppose, stand-up teaches you to become immune to humiliation, to stare into the faces of a hostile or apathetic audience and not let it faze you. Every mistake you make as a stand-up comedian will be public and in front of a room full of people, and all of those mistakes and bad experiences ultimately carve you into a more confident, versatile and unfazeable performer who will start to be able to pull nuggets of gold from a bog.

It's difficult to say what my worst gig was because bad gigs were bad for so many different reasons. But one does stand out because the circumstances were so bizarrely ridiculous as to relieve me from any real responsibility for its badness.

I'm the poor unfortunate victim in this story and it was so comical as to be almost unbelievable in its preposterousness.

In a nutshell I was compèred onto the stage by an escapologist who locked himself in a box and couldn't get back out.

An RAF officers' Christmas party sounds as ominous as anything, but when you're existing hand to mouth as a jobbing comedian you take the work where you can get it, especially when the job paid a lot more than I would have been lucky to earn in a week.

I'd been performing stand-up for a few years by now and I was to be paid a thousand pounds for the gig. It was all the way up in Lincolnshire and hardly enough to change my life in any significant way, but a thousand pounds for a single night's work was certainly not to be sniffed at.

The booker had decided to build a variety entertainment evening for the lovely officers of Her Majesty's Royal Air Force, and I was the only comedian among some very varied acts that included four young female exotic dancers.

I had never been introduced onto the stage by an escapologist before, and I'm happy to report that I never have since. I would say that part of the job of being a good compère is maintaining the energy and attention of a room while you're onstage, and what I learned on that night is that one sure-fire way to lose both of these things is to lock yourself in a box. In fact, I would go as far as to say that locking yourself in a box is probably one of the worst things you can do, especially when you can't get back out.

I'm no expert, but I do know that the number-one and non-negotiable aspect of being a half-decent escapologist is that you're able to escape from whatever space you've locked yourself into, and that you're able to do this within a reasonable and fairly impressive short period of time.

What doesn't work, especially in a room full of RAF officers who are all hell-bent on getting shit-faced for Christmas, is that you lock yourself in a box for a truly unreasonable amount of time while the room around you descends into festive chaos.

After a few rubbish jokes, he got an audience member to fasten him up with handcuffs and chains and in he went, almost never to be seen again. For a while everybody just stared at the box. We knew he was alive in there because he'd been thoughtful enough to take his microphone in with him, so we could all hear the sounds and grunts of his efforts, which became sporadically interjected with apologies for how long it was taking.

Having never seen an escapologist perform live before, I thought that maybe this was how they all worked, that maybe this was where the 'apologist' part of the job title came from.

'Look, I'm really sorry about this, but you'll have to give me a little time,' came the voice from inside. 'It's a bit tighter than I'm used to.'

In fairness to the room, they did give him a little time. They actually gave him as much time as he needed, by completely forgetting that he was even in the box. Everybody in the room just got up, started to mingle and have a far more sociable evening than they had been banking on.

I was stood at the side of the stage with those four exotic dancers and we were becoming a little concerned that we could be stood there all night, as he still remained in the box.

'If I can just get my arm through here. Oh, bugger,' came the voice, but nobody was listening apart from those dancers and me.

By this point the room was just doing its own thing when . . .

'Da-dah!' came the voice, as he pretty much fell out of the box onto the stage.

He took the microphone and placed it back in the stand, looked out at the Christmas party, which was now in full swing, and said the following words:

'Ladies and gentlemen, please welcome to the stage Chris Macalaclacle.'

Well, I'd come all that way and I wasn't going home without my thousand pounds, so on I went. I stood up there and did my time. I talked and nobody listened. I said my jokes and told my stories without anybody hearing them or caring. Well, nobody apart from the dancers, of course. They were watching from the side of the stage just as they had for the man in the box.

I died on my arse with just four young exotic dancers to watch it happen. Oh, well, at least they thought my name was Chris Macalaclacle, I suppose.

Chapter Twenty-Nine

Despite bad gigs being part of becoming a comedian, the overwhelming majority of the gigs I've done throughout my career have been absolutely lovely, or at least on the better side of fine. Of course they have, or I wouldn't have made it this far. It's just that the bad experiences are way more entertaining to read about than the good ones.

If any two comedians are chatting backstage and one tells the other about a gig they did recently where somebody smashed it and somebody else died on their arse, you can bet your life that the only question that follows is 'Who died on their arse?' because that's where the story is.

The more established I became as a stand-up, the better the gigs I got to play. I grew to be more capable and versatile as many of the rooms I performed in got bigger and more professional.

There are so many brilliant independently run comedy nights all over the place, but the golden ticket as a circuit comic was to get full weekends at the big clubs. Jongleurs was a chain that had twenty or so comedy clubs across the UK. They had a bit of a reputation for prioritising the drinking and dancing over the actual comedy, though, and were a prime hotspot for stag and hen parties, which could make them lively indeed.

I've played a night in Nottingham when a bar-room brawl broke out during my set and I had to leave the stage while it was brought under control.

On one night in Birmingham a drunk punter got onstage and thought he could prove to everybody that I wasn't really blind by trying to punch me in the face, which didn't end too well for him. I was in the middle of performing when the audience universally made a noise that let me know something less than ideal was happening. Just then this idiot grabbed me from the side so I grabbed him back. We tussled for several moments as he tried to wrestle the microphone from me, and I was later told that he had pulled his fist back ready to land the punch that would prove to everybody once and for all that I was nothing more than a rather peculiar character act. In an instant he vanished from my grasp as two huge bouncers charged the front of the stage and splattered him into the back wall, like a bug hitting a windscreen.

'Sorry about that, Chris,' one of them said afterwards. 'If it's any consolation, he fell down the stairs a few times on the way out,' he added, with a chuckle.

Portsmouth Jongleurs had a reputation for being one of the worst. Held in what felt like an aircraft hangar, the nights in that room were rarely good or even remotely enjoyable and often just seemed to serve as something to fill the time before the students would be let in for the club night that followed.

I remember headlining one night in that room and being expected to do thirty minutes. I'd set the timer on my watch to vibrate after twenty-five minutes to let me know I should start wrapping up, but I'd decided to call it quits much earlier and left them all to get on with the debauchery. It wasn't that you played to silence or animosity in there, just that the room did not suit comedy. By the end the audience were usually beyond drunk and whatever else they'd been taking, and their attention was not at the required level for half an hour of structured sentences. You know it's not been the best night when your watch vibrates to let you know you've got five minutes left while you're paying for the car park.

Despite this, most Jongleurs gigs were fairly decent and once you were in with them it was easy to fill about half your weekends with their shows alone. I think I would have struggled to make it as a professional comedian as early as I did if it wasn't for all the work I was able to get playing shows for Jongleurs.

There were fantastic clubs like the Glee Clubs in Birmingham and Cardiff, Rawhide in Liverpool, the Frog and Bucket in Manchester, and Komedia down in Brighton. I started working weekends for those clubs from 2006, and over the four or five years that followed I built myself up to be a headliner at all of them.

The most prestigious of all the clubs was the place I had spent many a night at as a fan before even thinking about touching a microphone: the Comedy Store in London.

Less than three months into comedy I had put my name down for the gong show, a brutal showcase for new acts that was held at the Store on a Monday night once a month. The aim was to last five minutes on stage. Yes, you read that right:

last. There was a gong onstage and if the audience didn't like you or got bored of you, the gong would sound and you'd be on your way. How it worked was three audience members would be given a card, and if all three cards went up, the gong would receive a whack from whichever established Comedy Store comedian was hosting the show. It would get noisy if all those audience members who did not have one of the three cards decided they wanted you gone, because they would become very vocal about it until those cards were raised. See what I mean? Brutal!

Several guys got gonged off before they'd even reached half a minute because the audience didn't like them almost immediately, and one poor bloke got gonged off before he'd uttered a single word because the audience didn't like him exactly immediately.

I was among three from at least twenty fledgling comedians who managed to last the full five minutes without hearing the gong, and at the end the audience were asked to show their appreciation for which of us they wanted to crown the winner.

Well, obviously it was me, wasn't it, or I doubt I'd be writing about it here, but this was my first experience of setting foot on that stage, a stage that would be the focus of every goal in comedy that I had for the coming years.

After my gong experience I performed a five-minute try-out on a Thursday night. This was on a full proper comedy night among those incredible Comedy Store regulars.

The progression was to do some ten-minute spots

on a weekend, before getting a twenty-minute spot on a Thursday, then hopefully those glorious full weekends. The gaps between the points of progression were big, six to eight months each time, such was the hunger for these opportunities from newer comedians.

I can only imagine that progression is even slower, these days, as the number of those entering the world of stand-up seems to be magnitudes greater than it was twenty years ago. Although only a fraction of those who try stand-up will make it to a professional level, the battle to reach that goal must be fierce. For all those who don't make it, just remember that there are always the slightly easier options of brain surgeon or rocket scientist to pursue.

From about five years into comedy I became a regular face at the Store for well over ten years, and that for me was the absolute pinnacle of comedy at that time. To be in that dressing room listening to the show through the stage door, waiting for my name to be called before pulling that door back and emerging through it to stand on that stage, with four hundred comedy fans on three sides, and to make them laugh as I had been made to laugh all those years earlier, it was a surreal dream come true.

My career as a circuit comedian couldn't have gone much better. The great thing about the UK comedy scene is that it is possible to earn a good living without anybody really knowing who you are. You need to build a public profile to entice people to come and watch you on tour, but you only need to establish yourself with promoters and clubs as being a reliable pair of hands to fill your diary with club work.

I've been unbelievably lucky to get to work alongside so many incredible comedians over the years, some of whom are now household names, and many of whom you will likely never have heard of. The British comedy scene is so ridiculously abundant with talent and I sometimes can't believe that I've managed to elbow my way in and be a part of it all for the last two decades and counting.

The best comedian I worked with in the clubs over those years was probably Michael McIntyre. His ability to mix stand-up with crowd work and improv was unrivalled, and he was the only comic I would make sure to watch each evening as his set would be so different each time. I once watched him walk out onto the stage at the Glee Club in Cardiff with a pack of biscuits we had been sharing in the green room, then open his set with a blistering five minutes about the bizarre ingredients listed on the back of it.

For years I travelled the country performing to every type of room imaginable, and I loved it. I would jump in car-shares with other comedians or travel alone by train for the weekend clubs that required nights spent away. All of this travel wasn't easy without sight, but the reward of getting to be a comedian, of performing stand-up comedy, and of being part of the comedy community I loved so much kept those scales tipped in the right direction.

I got used to having to depend on others. When travelling away for a weekend's worth of shows, I had to depend on so many along the way that I would often feel like a relay baton being passed from pillar to post. If I was working in Leeds, for example, which had one of the very best Jongleurs clubs by the way, I would jump on the train from my local station into London and request assistance at the other end. A member of train staff would meet me off the train, hopefully, and escort me to the Underground. They would hand me over to a member of the Underground staff, who would show me down to the platform, put me on a tube train and radio through to the station I was heading to so that somebody could meet me there. A member of the Underground staff would meet me from the tube train, hopefully, escort me up to the main concourse and pass me on to a member of station staff, who would show me to the Leeds train and find me a seat. Leeds would be notified and a member of their staff would meet me off the train, hopefully, and show me to a taxi. I would get the taxi to the hotel and the driver would show me into Reception. The hotel receptionist would check me in and escort me to my room.

That's a lot of dependence, isn't it? It's a lot of having to rely on others and it could be exhausting. It's amazing that the infrastructure is there to facilitate this support, although in reality it would not often work as smoothly as that, and I would be left stood on a train platform waiting and waiting and waiting.

It wouldn't end there, though, as I would then contact whoever I was working with that weekend and arrange to head to the club with them that evening where a member of staff would be my guide to and from the stage.

I find it quite mad that for years I was able to do this and headline some of the biggest comedy clubs in the country, but if you'd asked me to go to my local supermarket and buy a loaf of bread I likely would have struggled. I had become accustomed to doing the big things, but the small things still felt way outside my comfort zone. They would stress me out and leave me feeling very self-conscious indeed.

For well over ten years now, Graham has been my regular driver, starting with a great deal of my club work but now working with me on my national tours. When we started working together Graham was a gas engineer, and he recently told me that if he ever wrote his own autobiography about his two jobs of fitting gas appliances and driving me about the place, he would call it *Travels with a Gas Bag* because it fits both jobs perfectly. Well, I'd just like to make it clear that I've taken out an injunction to stop any publication of stories about what life on the road with me is really like, so good luck with that, Graham.

It is Graham you will see walking me out onto the stage at my live shows, and he has made three appearances on *Live at the Apollo* doing just that.

The first TV I ever did was a kids' show. I was approached to play the part of a fruit-and-veg market stallholder in a new show that was being filmed up in Glasgow for the CBeebies channel, making the target audience of the show three- to five-year-olds. They wanted this character to be blind, which I thought was interesting because you don't get many blind fruit-and-veg market traders. I was twenty-eight years old, and aside from my two and a half years performing stand-up, I was not very comfortable with the idea of any other type of performing, especially not on kids' TV.

I decided to keep my options open and went to Glasgow to find out what it was all about, and after half a day of mucking about and acting like an idiot, I was kind of warming to the idea.

'This is it?' I asked. 'You want to pay me to be daft and silly?'

'Yep,' they said. 'Fancy it?'

Cut to the first week of filming and I'm stood there wearing an extravagant frock covered in teapots with a lampshade on my head. It might sound obvious, but once you've been on the telly wearing a frock covered in teapots with a lampshade on your head, it takes a hell of a lot more to make you feel embarrassed from that moment on, which I think went some way to making me a more confident performer onstage. Basically, my immunity to humiliation was supercharged during the making of that show.

The actual reason I did the show was because the creators did not want my character to be a stereotypical or clichéd representation of a blind person, as illustrated by the fact that they had made him a fruit-and-veg market stallholder. Even back then it was important to me that representation was done in a positive way and showed capability rather than cementing old tropes, especially for the kiddies.

Opportunities for more grown-up television did come my way over that period, but each time I would decline as they would always be entirely disability-focused and not what I thought representation should be. Twice I was asked to be a part of a comedy sketch show that was to be made up of disabled performers, but I declined the opportunities as I thought those shows would do absolutely nothing to move social attitudes or representation on in any positive way whatsoever. I strongly believed that broadcasters should be integrating, not segregating; that they should be representing across mainstream programming rather than grouping together and getting as many boxes ticked in one go as possible. Plus, although intentions might have been good, some of the ideas for these shows were bloody awful.

One of those sketch shows was to be called *Raspberry Ripple,* a Cockney rhyming slang term for 'cripple', while the other was to be called *I'm Spasticus,* the name taken from an Ian Dury song. I know. Both are horrific names for a TV show, and while the first was never made, I believe the second actually did go to air on Channel 4.

I was asked to be part of a *Big Brother*-type show for disabled contestants, and have also been approached about numerous group disability travel shows over the years. One producer even explained to me that he thought it would be good to show everybody at home how disabled people manage to get on and off trains because the public would be interested in things like that.

I felt that each of these shows sent out entirely the wrong message about disability, that disabled people only do disability-related things, and that we mainly prefer to do them with other disabled people. These opportunities just didn't align with how I wanted to represent myself, blindness or disability on the telly.

I was performing stand-up in the clubs and was still keeping my disability to a minimum, letting people in but, hopefully, always leaving them wanting to know more. It was important to me that audiences saw me as a comedian who just happened to be blind, rather than a blind comedian. To me there is a difference, as the latter feels like it would be my blindness that would define me as a comedian and so therefore would also define my comedy.

If I'd taken these opportunities earlier on in my career, I'm pretty damn sure that things would not have gone anywhere near as well for me as they have done. We are certainly moving in the right direction now in terms of integration across mainstream programming, and I think by holding out and playing the long game I have certainly benefited by being able to do TV and introduce myself to the British public on my own terms, and not by satisfying somebody else's clichéd agenda.

TV would come, but first, there's a couple of people I should probably introduce properly.

Chapter Thirty

I met Patricia during my first run up at the Edinburgh Fringe in 2005. Obviously I was very funny and she fell head over heels in love with me, and after repeated attempts to get her to leave me alone I decided it would be much easier to let her move in with me, although I think she remembers it differently to that.

We actually spent more than a year living together in that tiny little studio flat without killing each other, which is remarkable really when you think about it, because there aren't any other rooms you can storm off into after an argument without having to just go and sit on the toilet for a while.

She was working in TV back then, but her desire for a life behind the camera didn't last too long, as she wanted to make hard-hitting social documentaries that changed the world. Reality TV was becoming all the rage, though, and a fortnight cataloguing *Big Brother*'s sexiest moments had me trying to talk her in off a ledge.

It took years for her to retrain as a clinical psychologist, and I would like to say that the only thing worse than having to write a doctorate is having to live with someone who is writing a doctorate, but the truth is that living with a comedian is almost certainly much worse.

Comedian is not just a job, it's a hobby and an identity. As a result it can consume the life of the comedian and be a pain in the arse to whichever unfortunate soul has chosen to live with the comedian. It's a life of the most antisocial hours, working on weekends and over many a family or social gathering. It's a job that is not just brought home, but that lives and breathes at home. The comedian writes comedy, we perform comedy, we think about comedy and we talk about comedy. Oh my God, do we talk about comedy.

Being a comedian is not just something that can be accepted or tolerated, appreciated or respected, it has to be supported and facilitated, because without that backing the life and career of a comedian is just not compatible or even possible with a normal family life.

For well over a decade Patricia tolerated and supported my life as a circuit comedian, but when I entered the world of TV, she certainly facilitated me being able to take all of the opportunities that have come my way, which gave me the space and time to be able to chase the success that I have been able to enjoy. None of what was to come would have been possible without that backing and support, and certainly not *Strictly*, which pretty much consumed me for months on end.

Patricia's experience of being married to somebody who is blind means that, to some extent, there are parts of herself, or parts of a normal married life, that she has also had to relinquish to my blindness.

She can't share the beauty of her homeland with me, and by all accounts, Rio de Janeiro is a very beautiful place. All of the vibrant colours and intricate mosaic pavements, the ocean lapping against those golden sands, the mountains, the wildlife, those beautiful clear blue skies. I don't get any of that, so to me, it is just hot, really really hot – and I've had sunstroke at the Reading Festival, so you can imagine how I cope with that.

We can't go around an art gallery and admire all the paintings as other couples might, and discuss the clever usage of perspective, shade and all that fancy stuff.

She's never been able to take me to watch a ballet. So it's not all bad I suppose. Every cloud!

She is never really looked at by me with desire or lust, though, or held in a glance when she walks into a room. I kind of look through her, or slightly past her, like there is something much more interesting happening just over one shoulder. She is never on the receiving end of compliments from me about how she looks, because they would just be empty, wouldn't they?

She can't even ask me all those typical questions that wives ask husbands when getting ready to go out of an evening.

'Does my hair look okay?'

'Does this top match these shoes?'

'Does my bum look big in this?'

I mean, what do I say to that?

'I don't know, sweetheart. Things do tend to feel bigger than they look.'

She used to ask me what I thought she looked like, but

she doesn't ask me any more, because I never really had a satisfactory answer for her. I do know what she looks like, kind of, but it's not like a photograph in my mind that I can sit and describe in detail, even if I had the vocabulary to do so, which I don't.

When I try to imagine people's faces, it's like there is a photograph lurking somewhere just out of view, a photograph that I know I've seen, but one that refuses to be looked at. Like a reflection in a pond, I know it's there, but every time I turn to look at it, somebody tosses in a stone and it just breaks apart and dances away around my mind to defy any scrutiny.

We were married in 2012 and not long afterwards the two of us became three, our daughter Sophie being born in September 2013. The prospect of becoming a dad had caused me considerable anguish, if I'm honest, because I thought that my blindness would preclude me from being able to do the things I thought a proper dad should do. Yes, there are things I am unable to do as a husband, but Patricia has made her own choice there, whereas a child doesn't get to choose their parents, do they? When I was a kid my dad did loads of stuff with me. He read books to me, played board games, built Lego, took me to the park to play football, and treated me to fun days out. I remember us going to fairs and fetes, museums and exhibitions, and of course to watch the Mighty Reds play at Anfield. This was my baseline of what a proper dad should be, but I knew that many of those things would be beyond my capability. I worried that I was destined to be sub-par as a dad, and I felt both guilty and sorry for my child long before she even existed.

This is typical me, I think. I wasn't worried about the emotional stuff – I knew that my capacity to love would be no different from anybody else's, but it was the practical and logistical considerations of satisfying the job description of being a dad that weighed heavy. I like a challenge, but I like a challenge that allows me to try to do something to as high a standard as everybody else, to compete in the mainstream. I don't mind working five times harder to get there, but I need to feel that getting there is not entirely out of my grasp due to circumstances that are beyond my control. If I'd ever felt that my maximum potential to write and perform comedy was restricted by my blindness, that I would only ever be 50 per cent as funny as other comedians no matter how hard I tried, that I would be unable to live up to the idea I had of what I thought a comedian should be, then you can rest assured that I would have jacked in the jokes some considerable time ago and started looking for something else to do instead.

The prospect of becoming a dad was different, though, because I was doing just that. I was entering into something I knew I wouldn't be able to do to the level I thought it should be done, that I would only really ever be able to do 50 per cent of what I thought a proper dad should do, and that I would be for ever restricted by circumstances that were beyond my control.

My daughter has known no different than me being blind. She was born when I was blind and I'm still blind today, such is the simplicity of the plateau at which I finally arrived. I have got better at being blind every year that she has been alive, and I would say that a great deal of this adjustment and improvement is down to her.

The innocence of a child's mind is purifying. It filters out all of the shit and allows us to see ourselves through their eyes rather than from our own internal and jaded perspective. All of those worries and fears I'd had, well, I would come to realise that they were entirely in my own head, and not in hers. I'd had my own normal when I was a kid, but this was her normal and it was just different in some ways from what mine had been.

Even as young as two years old she was a very chatty, curious little girl, who was gaining a greater understanding of the world around her and that her daddy was blind. I don't think she understood what blind was, at that young age, just that there were differences in how Daddy looked at things compared to Mummy. When she wanted to show something to Mummy she could just wave it in front of her or point at it, but when she wanted to show something to Daddy she had to put his hand on it. I don't think she understood why that was. It was just the way things were. It was her normal.

On a very basic level I think she saw it as a difference in communication, no different from how some children might use two different languages depending on which parent they're speaking to. As Patricia is from Brazil, English and Portuguese have been part of Sophie's language learning from day one, but long before she understood that there were two separate languages in play, she just kind of knew that there were words and phrases she could say to Mummy that she couldn't say to Daddy, because Daddy was an idiot who didn't understand what she was talking about.

I don't think she understood why that was. It was just the way things were. It was her normal.

She would often repeat our explanation that Daddy's eyes don't work properly, but I think without really understanding what this meant. She would put my hand on a new dress to show me the frills and bows, but five minutes later she would run into the living room doing something silly and demanding my attention.

'Look at me, Daddy, look at me!' she would shout, causing me to react enthusiastically to her antics without really knowing what she was doing, and hoping she hadn't just run in carrying scissors with a carrier-bag over her head.

As she got a little older, her comprehension started to grow as she became more aware that these differences in communication were due to limitations. The first time I became aware of this shift was when I was in the kitchen trying to find one of her plastic cups that had fallen on the floor. Patricia was in the bedroom with Sophie and told her to go and help me find it.

'You can't find the cup, Daddy?' she asked. 'Because your eyes are broken? They don't work properly?'

This knocked me off my stride for a moment, as it was the first time she had made this connection with the understanding that I couldn't see. She was starting to realise that her daddy had flaws, which meant he couldn't do certain things very well that others could do, things that she could do, something as simple as finding a plastic cup on the floor.

I think that being able to see myself through her eyes changed my relationship to myself.

I had been performing stand-up in the clubs for over a decade by this point. I had been writing and performing stand-up that mostly had nothing to do with my blindness. I had taken and maintained this approach because I had wanted to surprise audiences, to challenge preconceptions, to let people into my world a little, but most importantly, to make them forget. The pursuit of what I saw as normal had been my driving force throughout all these years, and I honestly don't think I would have achieved as much progression and success as a comedian on the club circuit without it. I don't think I would have had the same appeal with audiences if I'd gone all in on blindness and made it my thing, and I really don't think I would have ended up as a headliner at the biggest clubs in the country if that had been the case.

In hindsight, though, I realised that there was probably another angle to this. That my approach to stand-up had not just been to make audiences forget about my blindness so that I could normalise it in their eyes, but that it had also been to make myself forget about it so that I could feel normal as well. Although I had shown huge practical adjustment over the years, I'm not sure that I had ever really been entirely comfortable in my own skin. Comedy had helped, comedy had given me an identity, but I think my identity as a comedian was still a way of denying a part of who I was.

I realised what my role was as a dad: to show my daughter that it's fine not to be able to do certain things, because it's not what we can't do but how we choose to face the obstacles that are placed in front of us. That my own neuroses were no longer my biggest concern, and that they paled into insignificance when viewed alongside her experience of me. It all sounds a bit wishy-washy, doesn't it? What I'm trying to say, I suppose, is that I learned to become comfortable in my own skin because that was now part of my job as her daddy.

The chance of me passing on my eyesight condition had been 50 per cent, a flip of a coin, and although I've had a good life, I so wanted my child not to have to live through the same deterioration that I'd had to. There was no way of testing to see if Sophie had inherited any of my genetic faults, because the results from my participation in that 100,000 Genomes Project had come back as inconclusive, so nobody really knew what those faults were in order to test for them. All we were able to do was take her for regular eye tests, and although these had come a long way since that specialist had dropped ball-bearings on the floor and told me to pick them up, they still weren't much more advanced than simply looking into her eyes and getting her to read from a series of eye charts.

It has now been several years since we passed the point at which the symptoms of my condition should have made themselves known, and I'm pleased to say that they never have. The coin landed favourably this time, and if she hasn't got it, she can't pass it on.

My daughter Sophie makes me laugh more than anybody I know. Her smile might be able to light up a room, but that's okay, because her giggles can power the whole place. There is lots I'm unable to do as her dad, but she doesn't care about that and neither do I any more. It's everything else that's important, after all.

These days I'm very comfortable with who I am, but it took time to get me here. It took my little girl to get me here. I still stand by the same approach I've always taken towards comedy, but even though I still think the greater benefit is in making audiences forget about disability more than I remind them about it, I no longer feel that I'm trying to make myself forget about it in the process.

Mainstream TV may have evaded me for many years of my career, but that would prove to be a blessing, because when those opportunities would finally arrive, I could not have been more ready to truly be myself.

Chapter Thirty-One

The first opportunity I got on proper telly was *Live at the Apollo,* a show that is an ambition for pretty much all comedians on the circuit. When I first did it, it was the only show that was solely dedicated to stand-up on terrestrial telly. Other shows have come and gone over the years but *Live at the Apollo* has been a consistent presence on our screens ever since I was taking my very first steps into comedy while still working in that call centre back in 2004.

The show is made by Open Mike Productions, and for a few years they had said that my name was on a list, that I was close but not quite close enough, that they did like me but that others were ahead of me that year. I felt within touching distance at times, but the vagueness of the rejections each year made it also feel like it might never happen.

Yeah, I was on a list. Was I really on a list?

Where was I on the list?

How big was the list?

Was there even a list?

Was the list literally every comedian who was working in the UK?

Was everybody on the list?

All you can do in comedy is keep your head down and play your own game. You can't sit about moping because others haven't given you opportunities. You've got shows to do, a living to earn, new material to write, and you always need to make sure that you're getting better and better with each passing year.

In 2015 I met the guy who would become my agent, Jacob Howe-Douglas. I was managing my own career at the time and Jacob had worked for comedy agencies in the past but was looking to set up on his own and wanted me to be his first signing. Something like this is always a gamble, for both of us really. Jacob had experience but his agency was brand-new and without a proven record. I had a profile on the club circuit but had not been able to prove myself much beyond it.

I like to think we found each other at the right time, both of us hungry and ready to make a name for ourselves in the industry. It's been a hell of a ride over the years that have followed, both being able to grow together. We've certainly changed each other's lives along the way, and long may it continue!

The first two years were slow, as was to be expected, but in early 2017 Jacob had me taking part in a run-through for a new TV show that was being pitched to the BBC. The show was never picked up for a series, but I had impressed enough for Jacob and I to be invited into the BBC for a meeting with the commissioner who had turned it down. Oh, and she was also the commissioner for none other than – yes, you guessed it – *Live at the Apollo*.

'I thought you were great on the run-through,' she said, 'and I think you should have a presence on the BBC.'

Well, she wasn't going to get any argument from me. Sign me up.

'I've had a chat with the guys at Open Mike,' she said, 'and told them I'd like you to be on the next series of *Live at the Apollo*.'

I think I tried to hold my breath in case I said anything stupid. As a result I just grinned at her for a bit too long without saying anything at all.

'Fantastic news,' said Jacob, in the professional way that agents talk in meetings.

'Yeah, brilliant,' I said eventually. 'That would be amazing,' I added. 'Thank you so, so much,' I waffled, then held my breath again to shut myself up so I could let Jacob take over.

'They said you're on their list and that they also want you on this next series, so everybody's happy.'

There was that list again. Had I actually made it to the top, or would I have been overlooked again if she hadn't intervened and requested that I be on the show? Who knows and who cares? Either way, I was doing *Live at the Apollo*, baby!

Her name is Pinki Chambers and I'll never know whether my opportunity on *Live at the Apollo* would have arrived without her support, but she would become an integral part of me being able to move my career on to TV and would go on to champion me for future opportunities that would be truly life-changing.

I was given this exciting *Live at the Apollo* news in May

and the series didn't record until September. That was four months to prepare, which in some ways was much too long. Four months to doubt myself and to question whether the set I put together was good enough, four months to pull it apart and put it back together again before ending up with what I'd been happy with in the first place. That is often the way: the more you unpick your work and rejig it, break it apart and rebuild it in numerous different shapes, the more likely you are to end up putting it back to how it was at the start of the process and deciding you probably had it right after all. God knows I've done it enough with bits of this book.

Prior to doing the actual TV recording, all of us comedians had to take part in a legal compliance show. This was so our sets could be seen by the lawyers to make sure that there were going to be no legal issues or repercussions from any of our material. The compliance show was bloody awful. It was extremely low-fi, held in the basement of a bar, and the audience was so minuscule that it was reminiscent of one of those terrible amateur comedy nights I had endured in the early days of my career. *Live at the Apollo* is impeccably produced, but all that was needed from the compliance show was the content of our sets to pass to the lawyers. What us comedians needed out of this show, however, was to leave with confidence in ourselves and in the material that we would be doing on the TV in just a few days' time. The tiny unenthusiastic audience wasn't even aware of the *Live at the Apollo* connection and just thought they were at a really low-budget comedy night, which didn't help.

There is a huge difference between a comedy club full of people all enthusiastically laughing, and a handful of miserable souls in a mainly empty basement barely tittering, and what that amounts to in terms of output is that it takes far less time to get through your material when there is barely any laughter.

We all walked into that room with twenty minutes of material that we hoped would work great on that glorious *Live at the Apollo* stage, but we walked out thinking we only had about twelve minutes of stuff that just wasn't very funny. I spent the next three days expecting a phone call to tell me there were no legal compliance issues with my set, but that they had decided to pull me from the show because it was all just a bit too shit for the telly.

Live at the Apollo is actually one of the easiest gigs you can do. For a start, the audience haven't paid a penny to be in there. I know I said that free gigs can often be trouble, but it's different when it's for TV. TV recordings are almost always free, but audiences feel excited and privileged to be a part of it all.

The Apollo is an incredible venue. There are three and a half thousand people all sat there facing in the right direction, the sound system is bananas, the stage and lighting look amazing. Everything that can be nudged in your favour has been nudged in your favour. It is only really your gig to lose. This is the problem, though. The gig might be easy on paper, but the opportunity is bloody massive, so it was entirely my own nerves and mindset that provided the biggest obstacle to success.

It wasn't really the fear of doing badly that brought all those nerves to the surface, but the fear of not doing amazing.

I could have walked out onto that stage and had a pretty decent gig, a gig I might have been happy with in any other circumstance, but I knew that pretty decent wasn't going to be good enough there. Anything less than making a statement would have left me feeling like I'd blown the opportunity that had been given to me.

I had been performing stand-up for fast approaching a decade and a half, and it felt like it now came down to this one moment. If I could make that statement, who knew what could be around the corner? If I only did pretty decent, though, maybe nothing would be forthcoming in the future. Maybe this was my only chance to show why I should be on the telly. Maybe this was literally make or break.

It's a wicked irony, isn't it, that the fear of not succeeding and achieving our potential can sometimes be the biggest threat to us being able to do just that? First, you must defeat yourself, young grasshopper.

Standing behind that *Live at the Apollo* sign, waiting to walk out onto the stage, was stressful. It can feel quite natural to want to give yourself a pep talk in high-pressure situations when you have to perform or deliver a presentation, to tell yourself that you're going to be amazing, to be your own hype-man and try to convince yourself that you're about to knock it out of the park. I had read that this can be counter-intuitive, though, just adding to the pressure we place upon ourselves to succeed. Apparently the best thing you can tell yourself in situations like these is that you're going to have fun, and that's it. So this was what I did. I stood behind that *Live at the Apollo* sign waiting for it to be raised and for my name to be called, just telling myself this one simple thing over and over again: 'I'm going to have fun! I'm going to have fun!'

I still do this now before any high-pressure performances, I just try to convince myself that this is all just fun, and I think it genuinely does send me out there in a far healthier state of mind and able to perform better than if I'd just hyped myself up with bravado and backslapping. I told myself this over and over again before every dance we did on *Strictly*. I'm going to have fun! I'm going to have fun!

Before every dance I would say it to Dianne. 'Dianne, let's go out there and have some fun.'

And, well, I think it worked, didn't it? It certainly didn't hurt, anyway.

My name was called and the sign started to rise, and for those first few steps, through the dry ice, I couldn't tell whether anybody was clapping at all. All I could hear was the song I had chosen to enter the Apollo stage to: 'The Boys Are Back In Town' by Thin Lizzy. I had noticed that a lot of comedians tended to avoid mainstream classics, often veering towards the niche or even pretty damn obscure. Maybe because a particular song meant something to them, or maybe just because they wanted to show everybody what a cool niche taste in music they had. I like a lot of weird obscure stuff that I could have chosen to walk out to, but I just wanted something that would be instantly recognisable by every single person in the room and by everybody watching at home when it was on the telly.

The song you choose has to be cleared for usage and there

are some bands that you just can't get the rights to use. The Beatles are an absolute no-no as Paul McCartney and the Beatles estate are incredibly protective over its usage and representation. I had asked if there was any chance of getting something by the Beatles cleared for usage, and I was rather comically informed that I had more chance of getting the BBC to approve a song by disgraced children's TV presenter Rolf Harris.

As I walked further onto the stage I became aware of the rapturous applause that had obviously been masked by the music as Graham walked me to the back of my stage stool, placed my hand on it and I was away.

I always use a barstool on stage, but I never really like to remain seated throughout an entire set. I like to be up and down, to use it as an anchor point to return to, to perch on and lean back against, to sometimes climb up onto and sit properly. It's a vital tool for me that facilitates confidence and performance on stage.

I can be up on my feet and move about, playing to the width of an entire room, but when I return to the stool I'm in no doubt that I'm where I should be and that where I'm facing is dead centre. Using a stool on stage frees my mind from having to keep track of my movements and angles, and enables me to just enjoy the act of performing.

When I was travelling the length and breadth of the country playing comedy clubs, I often had to use whatever stool was available at the venue. Barstools come in all shapes, sizes and weights, and some are far less ideal than others. I would find that sometimes if a stool was too short, or too light, it would affect how I was able to perform onstage. It would limit my movement if I couldn't perch on it and had to choose between sitting down or standing up in front of it, and it would affect my confidence in movement if the stool was so light that knocking into it would cause it to move and slide on the stage. How can I have confidence that I'm where I should be and that I'm staring down the dead centre of a room if the stool behind me has moved several times throughout my performance?

You often just have to work with what you've got, though, and I became used to changing my performance style and energy levels in clubs based on how comfortable and confident I felt with whatever stool I had behind me.

'We know you use a stool onstage so we'll make sure there's one here for you,' said the production team.

Of course it was very thoughtful and considerate of them to let me know they would be set up to enable me to work in the way they knew I liked to. To give yourself the chance of maximum success and to reduce your own stress levels, though, you often have to control as many of the variables as you can. I have already talked about how many of the major gains are made earlier in your career as you are learning how to write and perform, but as you climb up that ladder it becomes more about gaining those small margins to give yourself the best chance of getting your foot on the next rung.

With that in mind I arrived at the Apollo with my own stool, which was exactly what I needed. Why leave these things to chance or to what was available when I got there? The opportunity was too great and I was already stressed enough without having to worry about whether the bloody stool was going to be right for the job. I went online and bought the absolute perfect big heavy bastard of a stool that would enable me to be entirely comfortable on that stage and perform to my absolute best. That stool has now made three appearances on *Live at the Apollo* and has travelled the country with me on two mammoth tours. Money well spent, I think.

From the first gag through to the end, it honestly couldn't have gone any better. I ended with a story about my daughter doing a poo in the bath, and for some years this was the only piece of my stand-up she had seen.

She thought it was hilarious, and for quite some time she thought that was all I did for a living: that I went out and told roomfuls of people that she'd done a poo in the bath. There was a period of a few years when if you'd asked her what her daddy did for a job she would have answered, 'My daddy is a comedian. He goes onstage and he tells everybody that I did a poo in the bath.'

As she got older and began to associate the idea of work with earning money, I can only imagine that she must have felt quite relieved and pleased with herself. Thank God I did that poo in the bath, she probably thought, or my daddy wouldn't have a job and we'd be skint.

She asked me more recently when she could come and watch me performing onstage.

'When you're eighteen,' I told her, although it will likely be before then if I'm still lucky enough to be doing this.

'Okay,' she replied. 'And you can tell everybody I did that

poo in the bath, and then I can come out onto the stage and say, "Hey, everybody, it's me who did that poo in the bath!"'

This makes me laugh so much, although something tells me she might feel a bit different about that idea when she's eighteen.

I got very drunk after walking offstage that night at the Hammersmith Apollo, very drunk indeed. There was a free bar and the pressure I had placed on myself for the previous four months had been immense. How well it had gone had lifted all of that pressure in an instant and I doused myself in gin and red wine to maybe nullify some of that rush. I don't remember anything after a certain point that night, and woke up fully clothed at home with no memory of leaving the theatre. Graham had got me back and made sure that I at least reached my couch.

I was forty years old and had spent almost a quarter of a century with not the best relationship to alcohol, relying on its warmth and its comfort for over-indulgence, self-medication, and as the fuel I needed to facilitate a social life. In truth, the older I got, the worse the hangovers had been getting, and not only the unpleasant physical symptoms, but the quite self-destructive psychological ones. I would wake up after an indulgent or messy night with huge feelings of self-loathing. What the hell was I doing? I was forty years old, I should have my life far more sorted than I do right now. I'm such a useless waste of space. What a fucking loser!

Drinking had always been a part of my social life. It was all my friends and I did when we got together. I had never done a single month without drinking since the age of sixteen, never even attempted one and wasn't sure I could: it would likely mean not socialising at all. I wasn't sure I'd be able to socialise with friends and be around other people drinking and having a good time and have the willpower not to need to do the same. I wasn't mean or nasty when I was drunk. If anything I wanted to hug everybody and maybe occasionally take my clothes off in a busy bar and twirl them around my head. The meanness I inflicted on myself would come once the fog had started to lift.

One thing was very clear to me, though, in the aftermath of my Apollo binge: I had been given an opportunity that not every comedian gets. I had been given an opportunity to perform on *Live at the Apollo* and it couldn't have gone better. If nothing else ever came from that opportunity, if no other doors were opened, I would hate to be there in ten years' time lamenting that I had not put every last ounce of myself into making the most of that opportunity. I imagined being there in ten years' time, thinking that I really should have concentrated on work when that door was opened for me rather than continuing along the same path I always had.

I tried a month without alcohol and it actually passed easier than I'd thought, perhaps because there was a shift in my thinking: for the first time I actually didn't want to drink alcohol. A second month passed and I had a bit of a revelation: that life had become so much easier than it had been. People will ask whether you feel better for not drinking alcohol, and the truth is not exactly, but you certainly feel a lot less shit. My mornings became my own, I had more energy to be a dad, my work ethic outside simply travelling and performing stand-up increased into the spaces that would have been reserved for imbibing and recovering. I learned to socialise with a clear mind and around others who were indulging in alcohol. The biggest change, though, was that I stopped beating myself up and started to be a little kinder to myself.

That was eight years ago and I haven't touched alcohol since. I still enjoy a non-alcohol alternative, the taste and the ritual are nice, but I have kept a clear, focused mind since that first door was opened for me and it has done me the world of good.

Will I drink again in the future? Who knows? Maybe. I've got nothing against the stuff and would like to think that my relationship to it has changed significantly enough to allow me to enjoy a drop or two without veering into familiar overindulgence. I'm still a way off that yet, though. I've still got work to do.

I used my exposure on the nation's favourite stand-up comedy show to embark on a staggeringly humungous mammoth nineteen-date tour of some of this country's smallest studio rooms in theatres and arts centres.

Nigel Klarfeld runs Bound and Gagged Comedy, and if you are going to google that, then make sure you include the 'comedy' bit or you'll be deleting your internet history quicker than you can say 'that looks like it hurts!'

I had worked with Nigel for ten years by this point as he had produced five of my shows up at the Edinburgh Fringe, but this was the first move we would make into touring.

That nineteen-date tour was fun and it was valuable, but

it certainly wasn't profitable. I played some sold-out tiny rooms, some half-full rooms, and some that existed somewhere between the two. In Cheltenham I played to thirty people in a room that could have held four hundred. I arrived to find that it had been set up with the microphone on a fairly high stage, with eight massive cabaret tables spread around the vast space for what I could only imagine would seat three or four people each.

'We've spread them out,' said the stage manager at the venue, 'so it doesn't look so empty in here.'

'Okay,' I said, 'but it's going to be awful like this.'

I asked them to remove all of the tables, just put four rows of chairs down near the front, curtain off the stage completely and set the microphone on the floor in front of those rows.

'But it will look really empty and weird in here,' they argued.

'I'm not really fussed if it looks weird,' I said. 'It's going to be really empty, there's no getting away from that, but having them on the tables like this will be awful for comedy. Having those rows down the front and me on the floor in front of them will mean that it at least has the chance to be fun.'

It was fun. Being a comedian can be as much about learning how to make the most of a less than ideal environment, so that you can elicit the most enjoyment and laughter from an audience, as it is about simply writing and telling jokes.

In its home on BBC Two, *Live at the Apollo* might have provided only a fraction of the exposure it had once had in the glory days of BBC One, but I felt my appearance had given me a seal of approval, validation that I was on the right path and doing the right things, and I was pleased with myself for making the most of that opportunity.

I have since made two further appearances on *Live at the Apollo,* and thankfully on these occasions legal compliance was done in a more professional live-comedy environment that wasn't quite so damaging to my sense of self-worth as a comedian.

I appeared on a Christmas Special episode in 2019 for which I received only ten days' notice. Four months had been way too long for that first appearance and I had driven myself crazy over-preparing my set, but ten days was nowhere near long enough. I know, there's no pleasing me sometimes.

I quickly wrote some festive jokes about mince pies, sprouts and Michael Bublé, then had to rush into London to try them out during a heatwave in front of audiences who were too hot and wearing shorts. The problem with something like that is that the audience can laugh because of the incongruity and ridiculousness of the situation rather than because they think the jokes are funny. A guy doing Christmas-dinner jokes in this heat? That's hilarious, so you end up not knowing whether the jokes are any good or not.

My third appearance would see me host in 2022 as we were finally coming out of Covid. I'm very proud of having made three appearances on *Live at the Apollo* and am so grateful for those opportunities. Looking at the other comedians who have also made three appearances, it's a lovely club to be in. I mean, don't get me wrong, it would have been nice if it was when it was on BBC One and the viewing figures were eight million, but beggars can't be choosers.

Chapter Thirty-Two

With that first performance on *Live at the Apollo* under my belt, I readied myself for what was to come next. The opportunities, the panel shows, the . . . Well, nothing came next. Not for a while anyway.

I recorded *Live at the Apollo* in September 2017 and it went out on TV four months later in January 2018, but it would be almost two years before I'd be on the telly again.

I'm just trying to paint a picture here as to how slowly things can move in the world of TV, and also how unwilling people can be to take risks. I had done well on one show, but I was still seen very much as an unproven risk for many others. I had done really well in the particular corner of comedy that I was good at, with scripted material I had written myself, but that did nothing to showcase how I might perform in the very different and mostly improvised world of comedy panel shows.

Mock the Week was seen as a gateway to all other panel shows, but they weren't exactly falling over themselves to have me on the show. There were some visual components to *Mock the Week* that maybe played a part in keeping me from making an appearance during this period, or maybe they just thought I wasn't right for the show. Either way, that door seemed firmly closed to me at this time and there was no budging it open.

Ride to the rescue Pinki Chambers at the BBC. Imagine a bugle being blown as she gallops over the horizon on her sturdy licence-payer-funded stallion. 'I've had a word with the guys at *Would I Lie to You?*,' she said, 'and asked them to consider you for the next series and they said they'd love to have you on. Now go forth and conquer this opportunity and all future panel shows to which this will open doors!'

And with that she reared her horse in that majestic way that allows them to do that thing where they pedal their front legs in the air for a few seconds, before landing back on all fours and galloping off into the distance.

Just for full understanding, there was no horse. I know that so many people are anti the BBC and the idea of a licence fee that they'll be reading this and seething that they had in some way paid towards a horse. The horse was in my head. It was a Lamborghini.

This is where my book becomes a little difficult to write, because failure and misfortune are funny and endearing. I'm not sure anybody really wants to read about a stream of successes, and I'm not gonna lie, but things have gone very well indeed from this point on. At the point of writing I've done seven consecutive series of *Would I Lie to You?* and I've appeared on a ton of other panel shows along the way. I'm not sure anybody wants to read a book that goes on too much about all of this.

'And on my fifth appearance on *Would I Lie to You?* it went really, really well, and I was very funny again.'

So with that in mind, let me give you a brief introduction to a few of my first appearances on those shows and a little background info on how they all work, because I know that's probably what a lot of you are interested in.

Would I Lie to You? – or *WILTY* as we'll call it from now on, required that I did an initial research chat with them so that they could excavate my life for possible truths that they thought might work well on the show. Before Covid hit, this was done in person and a member of the production team came to my home for a chat that lasted a good few hours.

I told them everything funny that had ever happened to me, or so I thought, because just as we were wrapping up, Patricia came into the living room.

'Did you say about the deaf guy who lives downstairs?' she asked.

'Deaf guy?' asked the researcher.

'No,' I said. 'I didn't think that was worth mentioning.'

Well, it just goes to show what I know about comedy, because that particular story would go on to rack up millions and millions of views across various social-media platforms and immediately book me a seat for the next series as well.

People often ask me if it really was true and, yes, it was. In a nutshell, I had an Aussie neighbour downstairs who was deaf, but when he first moved in I didn't know he was deaf and he didn't know I was blind. This led to us both thinking the other was being rude: he never answered me when I said hello, but I ignored him whenever he waved at me.

All of this happened just as I relayed the story on the show, but in a horrible turn of events he moved back to Australia before the show was broadcast on the telly, which was really, really heartbreaking. This was because we had become accustomed to being able to make as much noise as we liked above him and now we would no longer have that luxury. How selfish of him to want to go home.

When you go into a recording for *WILTY,* you honestly have no idea what the card will say. You obviously know what your true stories are and the production team will let you know about the five or six they like the sound of, but until you turn that card over you have no idea if it will be a lie or truth, and if it is a truth, you have no idea which one it will be.

Lies are a complete surprise to the point at which, on one recording, I forgot what part of the lie was and contradicted it during the bullshitting that I was in the middle of undertaking. David Mitchell was on it straight away, though, and my story unravelled quicker than a jumper I'd knitted myself.

During the mystery-guest round, even if the mystery guest is on your team and you have a lie, you don't know which of your team mates is telling the truth: it is honestly on a need-to-know basis.

Aside from David Mitchell, Lee Mack and Rob Brydon, Bob Mortimer is the king of *WILTY* and I suppose the only downside to the successes I've had on this show is that I will never get to appear on the same episode as him. I've done it too much now for us to take up two seats on the same episode and Bob is still somebody I've never met, so I'll have to try to get to him through fishing. Nudge nudge, Paul.

At some point approaching the autumn of 2019, I was

invited along to a try-out for *Have I Got News for You?*, which was held at the Hat Trick headquarters in London. I have a feeling that Lady Pinki of the BBC may have been influential in this as well, and I'm honestly so grateful that she found the time to champion me for these opportunities between polishing her licence-payer-funded Lamborghini.

There was no Lamborghini.

It was a Bugatti.

We ran through some rounds of the topical news panel show in front of a small audience of show producers and Hat Trick employees, and if I'm honest, I came out of it not sure whether I'd done enough to secure a place on the show. It's always difficult to know how you've done when there isn't much of an audience because it seems nobody really does that well, but the producers obviously know what they're looking for and can see how we might fare if given a chance in that full studio environment.

I made my debut at the end of 2019 and I was really nervous about this one. It wasn't just the idea of not being funny that scared me but the idea of saying something stupid about politics or a subject I didn't know anything about, and then the tough take-no-prisoners Ian Hislop ripping me apart in the most hilarious way that would ensure it definitely made the edit.

First of all, Ian is lovely. He is so warm and generous with his laughter, and I've loved sitting either next to him or across the studio and being able to make him laugh, because he laughs hard and loud and will even slap the desk if you can catch him just right.

For that first appearance I was next to Paul Merton and this was another one of those pinch-me moments when I felt like I was actually inside the TV, inside a show that had been running since my childhood, inside an absolute staple of British comedy, inside my dad's favourite show on the telly. I'm not going to lie, sitting next to Paul as the theme tune started playing made my arse twitch a little more than I would ideally have liked.

The best way to approach *Have I Got News for You?* is actually to listen and play the game.

I'm not a political person, I'm not naturally politically motivated and often don't really give a shit about most of the stuff that makes it into the news. When I'm doing this show I have to do my homework. I'll read a lot of news for that week and try to give myself a good idea of what's gone on relating to the big stories, but also many of the more obscure happenings in the news as well.

They don't give you a heads-up on the contents of the show beyond the main category for the opening round: Conservative conference and tax cuts, something like that. All of the actual questions and other news stories are played in the moment.

What I will often do is write some jokes about loads of stuff, compile them into a neat and tidy list, read over them several times before we film, and then I'll immediately forget at least half of them. This is fine because it makes me feel prepared; it makes me feel like I have material in my back pocket if the moment should arise, but what I've learned from doing this show is that pretty much all of the really good stuff just happens in the moment anyway. It comes from just listening to what is going on around you and simply joining in the conversation, rather than just waiting to say your own prepared things.

Have I Got News for You? is visual and people have commented on this aspect of it when I'm on it, and about how unfair some of the elements of the show are to me if I can't see what everybody else can. There are a couple of aspects to this, though, what I will call game play, and supporting materials.

In terms of game play, there's not much point in showing me pictures and asking me to buzz in and say what they are. The production team have always been very good in this regard and made some small changes to the show whenever I've been on. During my first appearance, which was hosted by the wonderful actress Helen McCrory, who so sadly passed away a couple of years later, we had 'The Gramophone of News', which was an imaginative alternative to the usual spinning-picture round. The gramophone has never made a second appearance but we have always had some twist on the round that allows for a more accessible experience for me.

In terms of all the photos and videos that get played throughout an episode, the supporting materials as I call them, well, this is part of the show and it's down to me to meet them halfway in this regard. I always say to Ian, Paul and whoever is hosting that if they think something needs describing, then just describe it.

A few years back, I was a guest on a panel show that was hosted by my comedy friend and ITV chaser, Paul Sinha. The show was called *TV Showdown* and another comedy chum, Rob Beckett, was a team captain on it.

'What will we do about the videos in the show?' Rob tells me he was asked by one of the producers.

'What do you mean?' asked Rob.

'Well, how will Chris know what's in the video if it's not obvious from just listening to it?'

'I'll just fucking tell him,' said Rob.

It's as easy as that. Sometimes examples of things being described to me will make it into the edit, and I would imagine that sometimes they might not as they take up time. Yes, *Have I Got News for You?* is visual at times, but the world is visual and to pretend that it's not is a bit silly really, isn't it? It's much better to show everybody at home that somebody who is blind is all right existing in a visual world, if every so often you just fucking tell them what's going on.

I love appearing on *Have I Got News for You?*. The sense of accomplishment I feel if I have a good show is huge: to know that I've gone into it with almost nothing and been funny about things I often don't really know much about, that I've bounced off Paul and not said anything stupid in front of Ian and, most importantly, that I haven't ruined my dad's favourite show.

In early 2019 I was asked to appear on *8 Out of 10 Cats Does Countdown*, and this was the first panel show opportunity that came entirely from me doing well on the first two. *Cats Countdown* is produced by Xeppatron, who also make *WILTY*, so I was asked to do this show as a direct result of the story about my deaf neighbour going so well. Thanks, Patricia!

Countdown is visual. There's no getting away from

that. The game-play is visual. The numbers and the letters are pulled out and displayed for all to see while the clock counts down. Contestants can jot notes and workings as they attempt to solve the sum or build the biggest or daftest word they can.

I was not going to be able to do any of this. I would have the letters and numbers announced once to me as they were drawn out and placed on the board, and after that I would have only my own mind for the duration of the clock.

I think the production team were aware that this would obviously be an issue for me, but also aware that I would likely be able to make my limitations fairly funny under those circumstances. What I thought would be funnier, though, and much more impactful in terms of the message it sent out, would be if I was really, really good at playing *Countdown*.

I therefore embarked on a mission to train myself to play *Countdown* entirely in my mind and ended up watching about sixty episodes of regular *Countdown* over about two weeks. This was almost the end of my marriage, as the repeated theme tune of the show starting, the clock counting down fifteen times an episode, and the credits rolling at the end almost became too much for my wife to handle.

I mean I can see her point. That's over a thousand times it would have played over those two weeks. I'm surprised she stuck around.

All of that work paid off, though. I came up with ways of doing a half-decent job on both the numbers and the letters rounds. I would imagine the pattern that the numbers would make on a telephone keypad, just blocking off that particular square in my mind so that I was remembering the pattern, not the series of numbers. This method enabled me to access those numbers much quicker than if I'd remembered them in an ordered sequence.

For the letters I would build three-letter words or sounds as they came out, so that I had only to remember three things rather than nine. 'WET', 'ING' and 'BOO' are much easier to remember than 'WTGOEIBNO', and then something like 'BOOTING' just jumps right out at you.

The upshot was that I went on the show and battered everybody, and it was much funnier and more impactful than if I'd just gone on and been funny about how shit I was because I was blind.

The only bit I hadn't been able to practise was the conundrum, because it was never spoken out loud on the show so I couldn't play along during my *Countdown* marathons at home. I would always let the episode play out, though, because that meant two more theme tunes and I knew how much it was annoying my wife.

In the *Cats Countdown* studio, Jimmy Carr read out the two broken parts of the conundrum for me, and as the clock was about to hit the full thirty I got the answer in my head and almost lost my mind. Here is the thought process that got me to the answer. The conundrum spun around and Jimmy announced it as 'Bored Wank', then quickly spelled out the first part of that for me, so I knew which 'bored' it was.

By this point we were already five seconds into the

countdown. At some point I managed to make the word 'Break' out of those nine letters.

Oh, well, I thought, I've still got four letters left over, and I can make a word out of them too. Down. Well, that's as good as I can do, two words, Break Down. Break Down. Holy shit, 'Breakdown'!

I honestly didn't know what to do with my arms as I blurted out the answer just before the clock hit zero.

I have tried always to make this my approach to TV, to prepare, prepare, prepare, and to make sure that I'm representing well and showing the Great British Public that more is possible if you're blind or disabled than they may have thought. I don't see it as good enough to just turn up and hope I can hold my own on everything I do. I need to make sure that I'm able to play, compete or participate as close to fully as possible in whatever the format demands, and to try to make my performance stand out whenever possible.

I'm of the opinion that I can never prepare too much, and that I should always prepare way more than I think I need to. Yeah, sure I can end up going around in circles and driving myself a bit mad along the way, but over-preparing has proven to be so much more effective than under-preparing.

Following these initial panel-show appearances, we decided to put on another tour and see if they had done anything to increase my audience for stand-up comedy. This time we scheduled in forty dates in venues that were a little larger than last time around. That four-hundred-seater room in Cheltenham where I'd played to just thirty had been a bit of an outlier in terms of size on that last trip out, but this time we scheduled them all in at around that capacity and hoped I wouldn't be playing to thirty in each. The tour was scheduled to start in April 2020 and I was all set to hit the road, but the world was about to be closed for business and who the hell saw that coming?

Chapter Thirty-Three

In March 2020 I received news that they wanted me on *QI*. This was the full set for me at that point, the fourth of the big panel shows and all of my boxes now ticked in that regard.

A couple of weeks later, though, the country was closed down due to Covid, and with it went live stand-up. I was lucky that I'd been able to establish myself on TV just before Covid hit. I'd managed to squeeze one foot in the door and was now on the radar of producers and bookers when they were making shows. The TV work I was able to pick up during the various lockdowns enabled me to build my profile with the public over that period, and also to pay the bills while live performing was off the table or sporadic at best.

It wasn't the dream I had envisaged, making my debut on *QI* in an empty studio where the only laughter we could hear was what we could prompt from each other and the crew. My return to *WILTY* would be a bizarre experience compared to the first, with just forty audience members spread throughout a studio that could accommodate hundreds, and I made my second appearance on *Have I Got News for You?* remotely from my own living room.

The point was that I was there, though. I was lucky that

I had work and opportunity and that these had come to me before live comedy was taken away from us all. Plus, not many people can stake a claim to appearing on *Have I Got News for You?* wearing a lovely ironed shirt, a pair of dirty tracksuit bottoms and no shoes.

The creativity and perseverance of those who make television and radio was remarkable over this period, and the lengths that many went to in order to keep these industries creating and producing is to be applauded,

That also goes for the UK comedy scene as a whole, which took live stand-up online and found ways to bring the live circuit experience into people's homes. Comedy clubs were set up using Zoom in such creative ways, and many livelihoods were supported throughout the lockdowns.

There were even drive-in comedy shows, with punters having to remain in their own vehicles. I was asked if I wanted to do any of these and was told that you couldn't really hear anybody laughing from inside their cars, but that they did flash their lights if they found something funny. When the only signs that I wasn't dying on my arse were going to be visual flashes of light, I thought I'd best give these a miss as I really wasn't sure I could handle the not knowing.

I didn't realise how much I needed a break from stand-up until Covid hit. I had been relentlessly travelling the length and breadth of the country for seventeen years and had been trying my best to ignore the fatigue. As somebody who was self-employed, I would never have taken a chunk of time off work to sit at home and do absolutely nothing. I'd only really taken time off from work when there were personal things to do. Weddings, birthday bashes, trips to see family and so on, but never to sit on my own couch for a while.

I think I'd been running on fumes at times, becoming burned out but motoring on regardless, with stand-up becoming a functional thing that I did to pay the bills and put food on the table, regardless of how I was feeling. Having those breaks forced on me gave me the time to re-energise, to miss performing in front of an audience and to develop a new lust for it. That time away from the stage and the road was what I needed to fall back in love with stand-up. You don't realise what you've got until it's taken away from you.

My tour was rescheduled, rather optimistically it turned out, as nobody really anticipated the long and gruelling road out of Covid that lay ahead of us all. It would ultimately be rescheduled three times, but with each iteration becoming larger and grander than the previous due to the TV and radio exposure I was lucky to have throughout this time.

When I commenced the tour in 2022, it had grown to be more than a hundred and forty dates and would end at the legendary Shepherd's Bush Empire in London, which I would film for Channel 4.

As the country was returning to normal and we approached the end of 2021, I was invited to take part in that year's *Royal Variety Performance* at the Royal Albert Hall. What an honour that was. This was big, this was massive, this was literally the biggest most massive, most prestigious door that had been opened for me to walk through, and with my rescheduled, rescheduled, rescheduled tour starting soon in even bigger and bigger and bigger venues, and with tickets still available, it couldn't have come at a better time.

I had a brand-new charcoal suit in my wardrobe, which I had bought in a sale from a run-of-the-mill high-street chain, and I remember trying to convince Jacob that this would be fine. It was brand spanking new, what more did he want?

He insisted on taking me out to somewhere that sold suits that cost more than a MacBook Pro and made me spend a sum of money that gave this Scouser nightmares for weeks.

'Jacob?' I asked. 'How come whenever I earn money you take fifteen per cent of it, but whenever I need to spend money for work you don't chip in with the same?'

'That's not how it works,' he said. 'Now stop being so tight and try the bloody trousers on.'

Needless to say, he was right and the colourful tailored suit I ended up with not only lent itself to the occasion but made me feel a hell of a lot more confident about myself in that prestigious setting than my dreary high-street sale one would have done. I just hope he doesn't make it this far into the book and only reads the first 15 per cent to match his cut of the profits.

On the day before the actual show, I attended the Royal Albert Hall to perform a quick sound check and technical run-through. All performers have to run through their entire performance so that the production team can make sure that levels are correct and that the camera operators know what they have to do to capture the whole performance.

Most comedians don't really need this as there is just one sound source to consider, and many of us barely move.

Also, unlike an all-singing, all-dancing hit from a West End musical, or a flying-trapeze circus act, a comedian's set is awful if performed in an empty room. A song still sounds like a song, and a circus performance still looks impressive, but a comedian's set just sounds rubbish when nobody's there to laugh at it.

Similar to that legal compliance show for my first appearance on *Live at the Apollo,* something like this would just suck all of the confidence out of me, which would not be ideal before I had to do literally the biggest show of my career. I therefore did my opening gag, told them that I'd then stand there talking for seven minutes in the same place or possibly sat on a stool, then gave them my last gag so they knew how I'd be ending the whole thing. I got to leave with confidence intact, and excited about the show the next day rather than expecting a phone call to cancel my involvement.

A highlight of that rehearsal day was getting to sit in an empty Royal Albert Hall and watch Keala Settle performing her big hit 'This Is Me' from the film *The Greatest Showman.* My daughter was a bit obsessed with *The Greatest Showman* around this time and I had sat through the film more times than I could count, with the album playing pretty much on loop at home and in the car.

Now, I know I may possibly have slagged off musicals a bit during *Strictly's* Musicals Week. 'If they're made for kids then great, but if they're made by adults for adults then grow up.' Or something to that effect. I may also have elicited some complaints about these comments. Look, I'm a comedian and I often say things to try to be funny. Sometimes these things are things I don't believe, and sometimes they're exaggerations, me doubling down on genuine beliefs to get a laugh.

I'm genuinely not a musicals fan, but I suppose that *The Greatest Showman* falls into the first category of being for kids so it doesn't matter: my rules mean I'm allowed to enjoy it.

This was one of the most privileged experiences I've had as a comedian, though, to sit there in an empty Royal Albert Hall and hear Keala Settle perform that song with a choir and a band of drummers positioned around the auditorium. I've seen some noisy bands in my life, many with names that you couldn't get away with saying on TV before the watershed, but this was probably one of the most powerful performances I'd ever seen. It was joyous, it was emotional, and it knocked my bloody socks off. I remember sitting there with goosebumps, trying to hold back a tear or two, thinking, What the hell am I doing here sharing a stage with something as remarkable as that?

The Royal Albert Hall is an incredible venue, but it just doesn't have the dressing-room facilities for the amount of performers that the *Royal Variety* brings with it. Nowhere probably does. Myself and my fellow comedians Josh Widdicombe and Bill Bailey shared a makeshift dressing room, which was basically just the dark end of a corridor somewhere in the bowels of the building with a few little curtained-off cubicles resembling a wartime hospital ward.

Bill had done the *Royal Variety* before but, like me, this

was Josh's first time on the show and I don't think it's an understatement to say that the two of us were shitting ourselves. *The Royal Variety Performance* has a reputation for being a really difficult show if you're a comedian. You're among such high-energy, bells-and-whistles show-stopping performances that just a single person with a microphone can seem a little out of place and underwhelming amid such an exhilarating show.

That's just the start of it, though. *The Royal Variety Performance* also attracts a good, solid returning audience who are mostly nowhere near the kind of people who would attend a contemporary comedy night. Demographically there is a hardcore *Royal Variety* audience that are quite well to do, who probably always drink tea with a saucer underneath, and who are probably sporting at least one fake hip each.

Whoever the royal guests are for the show are also sat in clear view for all to see, and it is known that often a good bulk of that audience will wait to see how the royals react before allowing themselves to follow suit. The list of established household comedy names that have apparently died on their arse on a *Royal Variety Performance* is exhaustive, and when you're preparing to take part on the show other comedians feel it their duty to regale you with stories of modern-day comedy legends who have had hideous deaths on that stage, and who have left nothing but the sound of their own footsteps.

For our performance we had the Duke and Duchess of Cambridge, William and Kate, sat up in the Royal Box. Maybe having the younger royals to entertain made it easier for us all to do well, as I would imagine that surely it must be easier to make them laugh with contemporary stand-up than it would have been the Queen and Prince Philip.

The show is not broadcast in the order it takes place in the room, so on the night itself I remember Josh had to follow the cast of *Matilda*, which he was having kittens about, and I was following four German strong men who performed incredible feats of strength and circus skills, or so I found out later.

I was waiting in the wings to come on and all I could hear from out in the auditorium was the music that the German strong men were performing to, and the sound of five thousand people in the audience screaming and losing their minds at what they were seeing in front of them.

Jesus Christ, how was I meant to walk out there now?

Apparently one of the strong men would lift the other three into the air and have them balancing and spinning on top of him like he hadn't even noticed they were up there, but I wouldn't find that out until afterwards.

Jesus Christ, what the hell were they doing out there?

They finished their set and the audience screamed and cheered, like they'd just witnessed a real-life magic trick performed by the Son of God Himself.

Jesus Christ.

How the hell was I meant to walk out there now and just talk into a microphone? 'Hello, ladies and gentlemen. It's nice to be here.'

What a nose-dive in excitement I would be. What a disappointment to be a bloke sat on a stool after they've just witnessed whatever the hell they'd just witnessed.

Thankfully, there was a bit of clean-up to do on the stage

after my German fellow entertainers had finished doing the thing that everybody else saw but I didn't, so while this was happening they played a charity video about the hideous effects of Alzheimer's.

Well, thank God for that, I thought, because now I only need to be funnier than Alzheimer's.

Usually if performing at a charity night, a miserable depressing video that illustrates some of the work that the charity does can be the kiss of death if played before a comedian is introduced, but on this occasion I would have taken anything that put a little distance between me and those incredible spinning muscle men.

A video about dead puppies? Stick it on, thank you very much, and make it quick.

Soon, though, the Alzheimer's video was over and it was my turn. A voice announced my name and out I went.

In the technical rehearsal the day before I had done only my first and last jokes, but it seems that my opening gag had caused a little concern among the higher echelons of the Royal Variety charity. It was a joke that introduced the fact that I was blind for anybody who didn't know that already, and it was about a toilet. Here is the joke . . .

I would start by sitting on the stool and telling the audience I hadn't always been blind and that I used to be able to see. I'd then explain that you do get used to it but that it's the little things in life that I miss the most. 'Like the ability to be able to stand up off the toilet,' I would say.

I would stand from the stool.

'Take a small step away from the toilet,' I would continue.

I would take a small step away from the stool.

'And then just look back and admire your work.'

I would peer back over my right shoulder pretending to look down into an imaginary toilet. The audience would laugh at this moment, before I added the tag line. 'It's not the same when you've got to put your hand in.'

I would then mime reaching down into the bowl to admire what was in there.

The feedback I was getting was that certain people thought this was unsuitable chat for the presence of royalty.

Would I have opened with it if the royal guests were the Queen and Prince Phillip? Most likely not. Would I have done it if the royal guests were Charles and Camilla? Maybe, who knows? Probably.

But William and Kate? Come on, they'd find it funny, I knew they would. So I walked out onto that stage, sat on the stool, and opened with that exact joke and it couldn't have gone better.

William and Kate laughed big at it and the joke made the edit. Well, it had to really as it was the only mention of the fact that I was blind, so they had to leave it in, didn't they? Cheeky of me, eh?

What they did edit out, though, was the final part to that joke where I mimed pulling my hand back out of the toilet and spoke to the audience. 'The big question now, though, is . . .'

I looked up to the Royal Box.

'Will His Royal Highness shake hands with me in the line-up afterwards? Or will he try to tiptoe past?'

I mimed William sneaking past me in the post-show line-up.

'Shhh,' I said, pretending to be the prince. 'Tell him I've gone home.'

The audience bloody loved this and I would later find out that Prince William had been laughing loudly for all to see. He found it all hilarious. I just don't think they were comfortable showing the future king of the United Kingdom laughing too much at a joke about poo.

This was only the second bit of my stand-up that my daughter had seen, and again it was about poo. If she didn't still think I only talked about her doing a poo in the bath, she was certainly convinced that poo was all I talked about.

The show was incredible, and not just for me, but for Josh, Bill, and Judi Love, who was also on the bill, although she was not sharing our end-of-corridor wartime-hospital changing facilities. Everybody had a great time and nobody had walked off to the sound of their own footsteps.

Later on I was stood in the line-up next to Josh waiting to meet our royals in attendance, and Josh was caught up in the horror of what this moment would have been like if we'd done badly. 'Oh, my God, Chris,' he said. 'Imagine how awkward this bit would be now if we'd died on our arses.'

'Yeah, but we didn't,' I said.

'I know we didn't,' Josh answered back, 'but if we had done, this bit now would be fucking awful.'

And I think that perfectly reflects the psychology of the British stand-up comedian. Anxious about doing badly on such a high-profile show, but then still anxious about how awful it would have been if we'd done badly, which we hadn't. It's difficult existing in the mind of a comedian sometimes but, as I've already said, imagine having to live with one of us – it must be a nightmare.

Chapter Thirty-Four

The last few years have been a bit of a whirlwind. I've had plenty of opportunities come my way and with a lot of hard work, and all of that over-preparation, I'm happy to say that I think I've made the most of each of them.

The natural progression of TV and radio is that once you establish yourself on pre-existing shows, opportunities will arrive to start doing your own projects as well. One of the things I've been most proud of over the past few years is creating and hosting *You Heard It Here First,* a comedy panel show I made with BBC Studios for Radio 4, which has had two series to date and hopefully more to come in the future. The format is perfect for radio as it invites my comedy guests to live in an audio-only world and, by extension of the format and the medium, it allows the audience at home to do the same. It's a daft, chaotic show that has everybody playing and improvising in the moment with no idea what's coming up next, trying to decipher obscure TV adverts just from their audio, or playing ridiculous games like Guess What This Cat's Feeling from cat miaows alone.

Because I don't ask my guests to turn up with anything they've prepared, aside from a short anecdote to introduce themselves, I have to make sure I write the show in a way that allows them to have fun and be funny, and the biggest compliment has been how many of my guests have said they've had fun during the recordings. That was always the aim for me, to create an environment that allowed my guests to have a laugh, because then it would surely be entertaining to listen to at home.

I've had some great guests on, but nothing made me feel more like I was living in a surreal fever dream than having Su Pollard bring bucket loads of chaos to proceedings. I had been on *WILTY* with Su and had the best time getting to share the screen with her, so I asked her on to my radio show and she was utterly brilliant.

I made a travel show for Channel 4 with Open Mike, the *Live at the Apollo* guys, which saw me travel to some of the most visually stunning sights in the world to find out if it was really worth all the effort if you can't see them. The show is called *Wonders of the World I Can't See* because we visited the wonders of the world and I can't see. It's the Ronseal Quick Drying Wood Stain of show titles, it . . . 'does exactly what it says on the tin'.

I went fishing in the Mediterranean with comedy hero Harry Hill and two proper Greek fishermen, who quite clearly didn't want Harry or me getting in the way of their fishing. Harry is brilliant when onstage in his big-collar persona, but he's a different type of brilliant when he's being himself. Harry doesn't do himself for just anybody so this was a real honour and a treat for me to have him on my show.

I went to Jordan with the absolute bullshit merchant Guz

Khan who I think made up most of the facts he tried to pass off as knowledge. In fact, Guz was so hilariously full of shit at times that I wasn't entirely sure we were in Jordan at all. Guz is such a spiritual and calming presence to be around that I hated having to give him back and wished I could have taken him home and kept him in my house.

I travelled to Rome with the sartorially elegant Tom Allen who braved ridiculous heat in knee-high socks, a tie and a blazer. Honestly, have a day off, Tom! Tom is one of the most naturally funny comedians working today, and even on my own show I often just had to step back and let him make my show funny while I became a viewer.

My favourite, though, had to be heading to Niagara Falls with broadcasting legend Liza Tarbuck, and travelling into the falls with her as the wonder overwhelmed all of our senses. Despite the point of the show being to see if travelling to these places was worthwhile for me, it's difficult to come to a genuine conclusion when you're on holiday with Liza Tarbuck, isn't it? I mean, who gets to go on holiday with Liza Tarbuck? I rest my case.

2024 was an incredibly busy and crazy year for me. In January I started a brand-new national tour and spent the first five months of the year performing sixty dates while also recording the second series of my radio show, and writing and filming a Christmas comedy movie for Sky.

The Christmas movie was something I'd pitched to Sky at least a year earlier, and during that time the idea had passed through the various phases of commissioning, planning and writing before the bosses in control of the purse strings gave us the green light to go ahead. The film is called *Bad Tidings* and it's a Christmas comedy caper about two feuding neighbours who have to defend their empty street from a family of criminals on Christmas Eve, and any similarities to *Home Alone* are entirely coincidental. In fact, I had never actually heard of *Home Alone* until the similarity was pointed out to me some time later.

I think that to do the best job you can do and achieve the most success in your various ventures you also have to know your limits and seek help when you think you might need it. I had no experience of planning or writing scripts, or delivering one to a deadline but, lucky for me, I knew a couple of guys who did. I wrote this script with Laurence Rickard and Martha Howe-Douglas (yes, Jacob's sister), who appear in and write the absolute runaway hit BBC sitcom *Ghosts*. *Ghosts* is brilliant and daft, and Martha and Larry were able to work with me to produce a script that was exactly the kind of comedy I had envisaged when I'd had this totally unique idea for a Christmas movie that was nothing like *Home Alone,* whatever that is.

I asked Lee Mack if he fancied starring alongside me in the movie and he agreed straight away without even seeing the script. He really liked the premise and said he'd always wanted to be in something like *Home Alone,* although I obviously didn't know what he meant by this and didn't think to ask.

So why Lee Mack? Well, let me take you back in time a little to explain.

In around April 2022 I received an invitation to present a

BAFTA at the upcoming BAFTA television awards ceremony at London's Royal Festival Hall. The award they wanted me to present was for the best female comedy performance, which is a big one to be asked to hand out.

All of these things, although honours in their own way, come with a lot of pressure, especially when you're a comedian and are expected to bring the funnies. The BAFTAs is on live TV, pretty much. It runs in the room slightly ahead of broadcast, but that's really just so they can edit out any swearing or overly political diatribes that may be part of any acceptance speech. It's not to edit anybody to look good: that bit is down to the individuals in question, and if a joke doesn't land in the room, it goes out on the telly regardless.

I suppose you could always just shout, 'Shit bastard tits!' at the end of any joke that doesn't get a laugh in the room, therefore forcing them to have to pay it a visit in the edit. The problem with that strategy, though, is that you're then going to look slightly deranged in front of the entire TV industry and anybody that could ever give you a job in the future.

'Shall we get Chris McCausland in to host the new super show we're making that's going to be amazing?'

'Hmm. I'm not sure about that. Do you remember when he just kept shouting, "Shit bastard tits!" at the BAFTAs whenever he didn't get a laugh?'

'Oh, yeah, good point. Let's maybe avoid him, then. That was weird.'

As a comedian you have to be funny at an awards ceremony, but anything you prepare is bespoke for the occasion, so it's pretty much new material that comes with the risk that it might only be funny in your head and not when spoken out loud. Many try to be funny at awards ceremonies and some succeed, but far more fail in their pursuit of a laugh, which is fine when you're an Olympic pole-vaulter or a member of a boy band. Nobody really gives a shit. The award gets handed out and the world moves on.

BAFTA wanted me to present this award with Lee, I would imagine because I'd made several appearances on WILTY and we obviously had good comedic chemistry. Now, the thing about Lee is that he's just as obsessive about over-preparation as I am, so rather than us turning up on the day and figuring something out when we got there, I went around to his house during the week so that we could plan something properly over a coffee or three.

We came up with this idea where Lee would have to tell me my lines from the autocue, but then hilarity would ensue, hopefully, when I would start confusing lines meant for me with lines Lee was saying for himself. It was in essence a sketch, a good old-fashioned double-act sketch.

As I've already said, though, the longer you look at something you thought was funny the less funny it can start to seem, and this became the case here as well. We wrote this sketch on the Wednesday and we thought it was hilarious. I committed it to memory over the next couple of days and we FaceTimed each other on the Saturday to run through it a couple of times. By then I'd started to wonder whether it was as funny as we'd first thought. By the time we arrived on the Sunday, I was concerned that it might not be funny at all.

Also playing into my nerves was that Lee had been firmly

cemented at the very top of British television comedy for some time, while I was still very much proving myself there. If this didn't work, I would be known for ever as the guy who'd made Lee Mack not funny, and I didn't want to be known as that guy.

All of this wasn't helped much by the rehearsal we had on Sunday on the stage. By some ironic twist of Fate, or terrible planning on Lee's part, Lee had decided to have laser treatment on his eyes and couldn't read the autocue. The sketch was about me not being able to see it and him having to tell me what it said, but he couldn't see the bloody thing either. Our rehearsal was a bit of a shambles while Lee got the autocue man to make the text larger than he'd ever had to make it before, which of course meant that not much could fit on it at any one time, a bit like that old computer magnification software of mine. Combine our shoddy run-through with the fact that we did it in an empty room to no laughter, and my nerves were ramping up to eleven as we were stood at the side of the stage waiting to be introduced so that we could do this brand-new material on almost-live TV in front of the entire TV industry.

'Lee,' I said, 'how about we just forget all the autocue stuff, tell them what the nominations are and get out of there?'

'Don't you bail on me now,' said Lee. 'We've got this.'

To a comedian, the first laugh always settles the nerves. I knew that if the first gag got a laugh we would be golden, but our first laugh came before even that. As soon as I set up the premise, the audience immediately grasped that something funny was about to happen and a huge glorious laugh of anticipation rippled throughout the room. This is gonna be all right, I thought, as Lee and I cracked on with it.

It might sound completely obvious to say, but an audience makes all the difference to comedy, not just in terms of providing the laughter but in setting the pace. When you're running through a piece of comedy with no audience, you're playing to the beat of a drum that is entirely in your own head. The laughter of the audience, though, the volume, the intensity, the length and roll of a laugh, the rounds of applause and the gentle titters on set-ups, well, these all set an entirely different beat that you can't really play to until you're in that moment.

The people laughed, the beat was a joy to play to, the bit couldn't have really gone any better and, thankfully, I hadn't made TV's Lee Mack not funny, which was a relief. The industry audience in the room loved it. One of either Ant or Dec told us that it was the funniest thing they'd seen there in years, and I had to bite my lip about the McDonald's toilet fiasco all those years earlier as I'd always kind of blamed them for it.

The audience at home went mad for it and that video went viral around the world several times over, with millions upon millions of people watching it across all the various social-media platforms. I can't imagine that many performers of Lee's standing would have happily ignored the gap between our relative differences in TV experience and profile to do something as comedically risky as this, but Lee is an incredibly generous performer and is more than happy to take those risks and share any limelight, just so long as he thinks it's funny, and you pay him enough.

I then got Lee to appear on my radio show, and Lee asked

me if I would do an episode of his sitcom with him. I said no to that at first as I wasn't sure how it would even be possible, and I didn't want potentially to mess up something I was such a huge fan of.

Not Going Out is one of the last of the British studio sitcoms. It's long-running, brilliantly daft and funny, and I've genuinely watched most if not all of its episodes over the years. It's filmed in front of a live audience, though, and to be honest, I just didn't know how I'd be able to do it without sight. In my mind, it didn't matter if a character was blind: if you're filming in a live studio environment, surely you would still need to be able to see to hit your marks at specific points so that you were in exactly the right places at the right times for the action and the cameras.

'It'll be fine,' said Lee. 'We'll do each small scene separately and film them two or three times each so that we get it right before moving on to the next scene. We do that anyway so it'll be no different from normal.'

Okay, this was feeling like a safety net, plus Lee was starting to get insistent, and Lee can be quite annoying when he's insistent. Lee and I set about putting a premise together that would accommodate the whole cast. We came up with the idea of a whodunit set on an old-style train. What came out the other end was an episode that all occurred in real time and so was just one long scene that we would have to film from start to finish in one go, completely ripping a hole right through the safety net Lee had promised me when I had agreed to do it. Thankfully, though, the other thing we had inadvertently done was to create a scenario that had quite an enclosed environment so my movements on the set were greatly restricted by the confinement of the train carriage.

I turned up for one of our writing sessions with reams of notes I'd made and printed out just for Lee. As I arrived I handed him the hefty wad. Lee took it and started thumbing through the stack of pages.

'Bloody hell,' he said, slightly taken aback by the amount of notes. 'Now I know what it must be like having to work with me.'

All in all my appearance worked out great, and I loved it, but Lee was winning as TV sitcom definitely trumped radio panel show. I needed a way of gaining the advantage back in this regard. I wanted my Christmas movie to be daft, slapstick and suitable for the whole family, and Lee was perfect for the job. And movie trumps TV sitcom, so I knew this would hand the advantage back to me.

'Just don't write me naked in any scenes,' he said to me. 'I'll do almost anything but not naked. Nobody needs to see that.'

We filmed the movie between two main locations, a street in Essex, and a soundstage at Sky Studios in Borehamwood, which made me feel like I was operating way above my station with this little Christmas TV movie. That's because we were among some very illustrious company during filming at the studios. Not only were we occupying the soundstage that had most recently been vacated by a little movie called *Wicked*, but we had the latest Bridget Jones movie shooting alongside us, while an enormous set was also being built for the new *Jurassic World*.

First, though, Essex, and Sky had hired an entire almost-empty street from its developers. As it had just one resident living there, they paid him to go on holiday for a few weeks so that we could have the whole place entirely to ourselves. Sky did an incredible job of dressing the street in April for Christmas, and they even brought in their own moon on a crane so that the intensity and angle of moonlight could be controlled for all of the night shoots. I found it insane that an idea I had written down on a piece of A4 paper more than a year earlier had led to all these people making it Christmas in April and me literally being given the moon on a stick.

Because a great deal of the movie was set at night, on Christmas Eve, and because it was only April, we had to do most of the outside filming between the ungodly hours of 10 p.m. and 6 a.m. These were our working hours for two weeks, and even though we were approaching the summer months, it could get pretty damn cold at around 3 a.m. in Chigwell.

One night, we were waiting for them to set the cameras for a particular scene out in the street and Lee was bloody freezing in just a pair of pyjamas. 'Do you know when we were stood at the side of the stage waiting to come on at the BAFTAS?' he said. 'And you said shall we just not bother with the sketch and do the nominations? Well, if I'd known then that it would lead to freezing my tits off at three a.m, in Chigwell, I might have said, "Yeah, let's just leave the sketch, do the nominations and piss off."'

One thing I was insistent about during filming was doing my own stunts. I thought it was important that viewers at home could see that it was actually me being kicked head over heels into a car, or diving across a room, or falling off a roof. I wanted the viewers at home to see my face in these moments, not just the back of a stunt double's head. Part of the comedy of the film was obviously based around my character being blind and ultimately being a part of the hero duo that defies expectations to bring down this family of criminals on Christmas Eve. My character was petty and childish, but it was a positive representation that showed disability and blindness in a capable and very normal light. For me, though, I also wanted to show that more is possible for somebody blind who is acting in a movie with plenty of slapstick and action, and that meant viewers needed to see that it was me doing everything.

For a scene in which Lee had to kick me up the arse so that I tumbled head over heels into an old rust-bucket Sierra, I let him kick me up the arse so that I tumbled head over heels into an old rust-bucket Sierra. The first time I landed on the handbrake and almost cracked a rib. They covered it with a bit of foam and we went again, and again, and again. I did this twelve times in total, each time Lee's kicks getting a little harder until by the end he was pretty much launching me into that car.

For a scene where I had to dive across the room and take out a dressmaker's doll, they threw a couple of crash mats onto the floor and I just dived across the room and took out a dressmaker's doll.

For a scene in which I had to fall down a roof I gave the production team two options. Either strap me to the top of a house, or build me a replica roof in the studio that I can fall down.

'Erm, we've spoken to our insurance team and we think we'll build a roof in the studio,' they said.

Hey presto! We had a roof for me to fall off.

The replica roof was massive, the size of the proper roof, and they attached me via a harness to the top of it. On 'Action!' the harness was released so that I slid down the entire height of the roof on my chest, and I'm not gonna lie, it hurt. What I hadn't anticipated was that the roof would obviously be covered with row upon row of Christmas lights, and that sliding over them would be really quite painful. I reached the bottom and tried to pretend it hadn't hurt at all, because I couldn't let them know it had, could I? Not after I'd insisted on doing it myself.

'Okay, are you ready to go again, Chris?' asked the director, Tim Kirkby.

'Erm, yes,' I said, secretly wincing inside and wishing I'd just let them use the stunt double and bollocks to everybody seeing my face as I fell.

I think I slid down that roof six times, and I could feel it for about a week afterwards, but six is better than twelve, I suppose. Through some jiggery-pokery me falling down that roof was CGI'd to the top of the proper house, and I believe it looked really great, like I'm actually up there, so it was worth all the effort and pain, I suppose.

I was delighted with how the film turned out. It was exactly as daft and silly and slapstick as I'd hoped it could be when I first took the idea to Sky. The film ended up being their second most watched release of the year, only behind *The Day of the Jackal,* and that's not bad, is it?

Plus, movie definitely beats sitcom, not sure if I've mentioned that yet.

Once the first leg of the tour was over and filming had wrapped on *Bad Tidings,* I hosted my own Saturday-morning chat show for ITV over the summer. I was so proud of what the team and I were able to create and bring into people's living rooms every morning for several months. I made the show with Cactus TV who make *Saturday Kitchen* and that book-club show I got to do with Ade Edmondson. I specifically asked that we maybe take it slow when it came to guests I would be interviewing on the show as I'd never done anything like that before. I quite clearly said that we should start off with a couple of my contemporaries, comedians I already knew and didn't feel overwhelmed by. I had to learn how to host a show without any autocue, and I also had to learn how to interview somebody because I'd never done that either.

'Yes, of course,' replied Amanda Ross, who was running that ship, 'not a problem. We'll take it slow.'

Cut to episode one and my first guest is none other than absolute comedy legend Paul Whitehouse. I had to figure out how to host a chat show without any autocue and learn how to interview somebody with Paul Whitehouse sat right in front of me.

'What are you trying to do to me?' I asked Amanda.

'Yeah, I know,' she said, 'but Paul is free and we can't turn him down because you're a bit nervous, can we? You'll be fine. He's lovely!'

She was right, of course. Paul is bloody lovely! However, I spent much of that first episode trying to listen to what he was saying to me while my own brain shouted over the top of him, 'You're interviewing Paul Whitehouse! You're interviewing Paul Whitehouse!'

'I know I am,' I tried to tell my brain. 'Can you please shut up? I can't hear Paul Whitehouse!'

'Yeah, that's him right in front of you now. Hey, do your Smashie impression, go on, he'll love that!'

I'm pleased to report that I did not do my Smashie impression in front of Paul Whitehouse while I was interviewing him. However, I'm ashamed to admit that I did it once we'd wrapped on the show. I don't know what came over me and it just came tumbling out of my stupid mouth.

'Popadoodloo Gherkins! Mad Mike Bonkers Smash here, quite literally the world's most popadabadobulous DJ!'

Now imagine that in a terrible Smashie voice, or check out the audio book to hear it for yourself, I suppose.

I don't think there's any chance of Paul inviting me along to do any fishing with him and Bob after that.

What the hell is wrong with me?

Every week we would create new and daft games to play with my guests, and I would be on cloud nine as I would have a band play live in the studio. We had some noisy British bands that would bring a dose of rock, punk and even a bit of metal into people's Saturday-morning breakfast time. The big hitters of the series were Shed Seven – you know, those guys who were part of the Britpop movement that I didn't give a shit about when it happened. Well, these guys were so brilliant and humble and I loved them. Obviously I got to incorporate my love of music into my own show, but really this was a way of me also getting to hang out with the cool kids, and maybe pretend I was a little part of the music scene that I loved and respected so much.

The series ended with me interviewing Ben Elton, another of those pinch-me moments. From the teenager who was falling in love with comedy and who was in awe of Ben Elton, now here he was on my own TV show. It might only have been Saturday-morning TV, but you could have stuck a fork in me there and then – I felt done in the very best sense of the word.

So, eight months into 2024, I'd started a brand-new tour, recorded my radio series, made a movie for Sky and hosted an ITV chat show, not to mention getting to do all of the usual stuff, like filming episodes of *WILTY*, *Have I Got News for You?*, *QI*, *The Last Leg*, *The Wheel*, *Gogglebox* and others.

I told you it was a busy year, and in September I should have been heading straight back out on the road for the second leg of my tour, but something else came up.

You may have heard about it.

Chapter Thirty-Five

It's no secret that I said no to doing *Strictly* a few times before I finally relented. I honestly thought it could be an absolute disaster. I first said no to taking part in the previous year's series: 2023 just wasn't a good time for me to commit the time and the headspace to give it my all. I was due to head out on tour early in 2024 and I had this time blocked off to get my tour show up and running, with a series of warm-up shows in small theatres and arts centres. If I'd done *Strictly* then, I likely would have started a national stand-up tour with an undercooked show, and the stress of that would have brought me close to a nervous breakdown.

I was then asked to do the Christmas special instead, and to be honest, I just didn't see the point. I was aware that the idea of me doing *Strictly* would be a curiosity, but I didn't feel that a one-off episode would allow me to stretch the premise beyond that.

My unavailability for the 2023 series and my sound reasoning regarding that Christmas special was perfect for me, though, as it meant I didn't really have to think about it. It was an airtight excuse, a way of sticking my fingers in my ears and not paying much attention to what anybody was saying to me about it.

'No, no, no. Not happening, not even giving it another thought. Thanks for calling, have a nice day.'

Before the 2023 series had even started, I was asked if I would do the 2024 one – these guys were relentless – but again I said no. Now my excuse was that I would be on a full national tour. I had tour shows in the diary and they couldn't be moved for a TV show. In truth, the idea of doing *Strictly* absolutely terrified me. It was so far out of my comfort zone that I just couldn't comprehend how I would do it, or even what I was being asked to do.

If I am asked to do any other TV show, unless it's the first series, I can pop online and have a listen to past episodes to see how the show works and what I'd be getting myself into. TV might be visual, but there's usually more than enough going on for me to get a good understanding of the mechanics or comedy of a format from listening to the audio alone. If I'm asked to do a show that's brand-new and there are no past episodes to dip into, most shows can be pretty well explained using words.

Strictly fit into neither of these camps. It had plenty of past episodes online, but listening to people dancing would tell me absolutely nothing about what was being asked of me. It also wasn't something that words alone could properly explain.

Yeah, okay, it's a dancing show, I get that, but can you explain the dancing? Like actually explain the dancing so that I can imagine it in my head properly? Of course not.

What kind of dancing?

What do you mean Latin? What's that?

What the hell is a samba?

How good are the good people at the dancing?

How rubbish are the rubbish people at the dancing?

When you say tricks and lifts, what exactly are they?

How intricate are the dances?

How much do people move on that dance-floor?

Are they moving fast? How fast?

All of these questions could very easily be answered by showing a video or two, but couldn't be answered with words in a way that gave me any real understanding of what I was being asked to do and ultimately, I suppose, decide whether it was something I would be able to do.

What was being asked of me was such an unknown quantity, and so far out of my grasp for me to picture in my mind, that the idea of doing the show seemed completely preposterous. I honestly couldn't believe that there were actually people who thought it was even remotely possible.

'No, no,' I kept saying. 'Got that tour remember, I can't move it.'

'Erm, I think we should move the tour,' said my agent Jacob.

'Be quiet, Jacob. This isn't helpful. It can't be moved, it's booked in.'

'Ahem, I think we can move it,' said my tour promoter, Nigel.

'Hang on a minute. You guys are meant to be on my side here.'

'Yes, I think absolutely this is the right thing for you to do,' said my publicist Amanda.

'Right that's it, you're all fired!'

The thing is that, although the three of them are lovely and wonderful and I pay them all to have my best interests at heart, their jobs are to boost my profile and ultimately to help sell more tickets. This was not what was at the forefront of my mind here. My aim was to avoid a potential disaster, public humiliation, career suicide.

This may seem a bit extreme – career suicide? But I honestly thought it could be a possibility, and I was thinking about self-preservation, about maintaining the standing and the profile I'd been able to build up to that point, and about not risking all of that on something as preposterous as this, something I didn't even understand.

For me, the risk was massive. Me doing *Strictly* had a huge chance of ending badly, and I'm not just talking about 'a bit of goofy dancing and being voted off in the first couple of weeks' badly, but actual 'catastrophic failure in front of the nation on live TV' badly.

On my appearance on *Blankety Blank* the previous year, I had been the only celebrity guest of the six who hadn't been on *Strictly*. Well, four of the others had been on it and *Strictly*'s head judge Shirley Ballas was sat in the seat above me.

'Fancy having a go on *Strictly*?' asked the host Bradley Walsh.

'No, Brad,' I said. 'I'd probably end up taking out several cameras. I'm not sure they could afford the insurance.'

It was a joke, but the sentiment was 100 per cent true.

'Badly' for me on *Strictly* could involve any number of catastrophic incidents.

I went on YouTube and showed a clip of *Strictly* to my daughter and asked her whether she thought I should do the show.

'No, Daddy,' she said, almost immediately. 'You'll fall off the stage and break your leg.'

She was being funny, but underlying her gallows humour was a real concern that I would hurt or humiliate myself attempting what she was watching on the screen in front of her.

'Do you not think I'd be able to do that?' I asked her.

'No, Daddy. You're blind. You won't be able to see to do this. It's too difficult if you're blind.'

At this point I had just completed a 140-date national tour, which had sold out venues up to and over a thousand seats. I had built up this audience over my exposure on the various comedy and entertainment shows I had been a part of over the previous five years or so, by doing well on them, by being funny, by being a comedian. If I did *Strictly* and it was a disaster I risked maybe losing part of this audience. If I was simply unable to do what was required of me or experienced a catastrophe in front of the nation because of my blindness then *Strictly* had the potential to make people feel sorry for me, to elicit sympathy in response to failure, and who wants to go and watch a comedian they feel sorry for?

So what changed?

I've done a lot of shows for the BBC, so I think it's fair to say that I wouldn't have been on their radar if it wasn't for the fact that I'd proven myself across many of their flagship shows over the previous years. I had built a profile that meant I was a recognisable face within TV comedy and would be a recognisable face for a big enough proportion of the *Strictly* audience. All of these things are important and they wouldn't have asked me without them. However, it would be daft to pretend that me also being blind wasn't a significant factor in the BBC and *Strictly* bosses wanting me on the show over any other straight white male comic.

Strictly has a track record of pushing boundaries when it comes to representation, and it was fairly obvious to me that they wanted their first blind contestant on the show. I was obviously the front runner, and probably by some distance, judging by their relentless insistence.

I think representation is important. I think it is actually more important for everybody else to see the group being represented than it is for the group being represented to see somebody like themselves. I understand the idea behind 'If you can't see it you can't be it,' which means that if an under-represented group or minority doesn't see people like themselves achieving or being represented in various roles and positions, then they may never be inspired to believe that they can do that job or chase those dreams. I get the value in that, but I believe there is greater value in everybody else having exposure to representation and seeing people who are not like themselves, seeing groups who are marginalised and under-represented being portrayed and represented in a positive and normal way, and for those under-represented groups to feel seen by everybody else. This, for me, is where the real value in representation lies because this is how societal attitudes are changed. In terms of blindness or disability, it shows everybody who is sighted or able-bodied that we are no different from them, and that we are capable of so much more than they may have thought. For me, positive representation is more about exposure and education.

I have always tried to conduct myself and represent in this manner when I'm on TV, to be funny because I am funny and not because I'm only good at being funny about being blind. I try to let people into my world and show them that blindness and disability are more normal than they may have thought, and finally to make them forget whenever possible in order to normalise the idea of blindness or other disability even further. I believe I've done this well across the shows I've appeared on or made throughout the TV years of my career, but I have always felt that doing this was very much within my control. I did not feel that doing this on *Strictly* was in my control because I didn't know if what they were asking me to do was possible to the standard that would be required. My daughter certainly didn't think so.

The risk was that if I did it and I was rubbish, it would have done nobody any good, not me, not others who are blind or disabled, and certainly not the attitudes of the general population. Aside from the dancing, though, representing positively was something I felt I could do well. I knew I wouldn't go in there with a sob story and cement the idea that having a disability is something to be sad about. I knew I could go into that show and represent in a humorous and relatable way. In fact, I thought I might be the best person to do that. I was obviously their front runner for a reason, and that was because I was in an extremely privileged position.

To be considered for *Strictly* made me privileged, not because of *Strictly* itself, but because of the career I'd been able to build from all of the opportunities I'd been given along the way. I'm privileged to be somebody with a disability who had been able to build a career that came with a public profile that placed me in a position where I was being offered the opportunity to represent myself and others on the biggest television show in the country.

I'm very aware that my appearances on some of the most popular shows on TV might be the only exposure that many people will have to somebody blind or even disabled: part of what I'd always tried to do was to make people like myself feel seen in a way that moved attitudes forward. *Strictly* was an opportunity to do that, far beyond anything I'd done before.

The problem was still the dancing, though, which could still be a disaster, but who the hell would they get to do it if I kept saying no?

I knew I'd be annoyed if somebody else who was blind ended up doing it, but was boring, or overly sentimental, or just didn't put in the effort to show that more can be possible. Basically, I knew that I would be really fucking annoyed if they didn't represent blindness in exactly the way I wanted it to be represented, and if I knew exactly how I wanted blindness to be represented, why didn't I just do it myself?

Jesus, I was talking myself into it, and the fact remained

that I couldn't dance and still didn't really know exactly what was being asked of me or if it was even possible.

Wow, what a position to be in, terrified of a high chance of disaster on national TV in front of millions, or annoyed with myself for the rest of my life for being a chicken shit and allowing somebody else to do it differently from how I would have done it.

I'm a complex bastard sometimes and even manage to get on my own nerves.

I knew by this point that I was going to do it. Of course I was. Otherwise why was I giving it so much thought?

How does that saying go? It's better to regret something you do rather than something you don't do, blah blah blah. I mean that's not always true, is it? Murder for one thing, unless you're really happy you murdered somebody, or joining a parents' WhatsApp group, which is always instantly regrettable. It's one of those sayings that probably has more exceptions to the rule than proof in the pudding, but all it means is that, yeah, you might regret doing it, you might regret doing it big-time, but the wondering of what could have been will eat you alive.

'Okay, I'll do it,' I said to Jacob.

'Good stuff. I'll let them know. They'll be over the moon.'

'But if this goes horribly wrong,' I added, 'then be it on your head.'

'It won't,' he said. 'You'll be great.'

Once I had agreed to take part there was absolutely nothing to do for ages. I was told that I was the earliest signing they had ever made, signing up while the previous series was still taking place.

The 2023 series finished, there was Christmas, the start of a new year, and the start of my new tour. I hit the road for a series of sixty theatre shows all over the place. *Strictly* was a secret and I'm pretty good at keeping secrets.

Just a handful of people knew I'd be doing it.

Patricia obviously knew. She didn't watch the show either and had no idea what I was getting myself into.

My parents and my sister knew, because I'd talked to them about it while trying to decide, but they had no idea how I could make it work and were just as nervous about the whole thing as I was.

Those within my close working circle knew, because they had to. The only others I had told were Neil and his wife Fiona. Fiona is a *Strictly* super-fan and she knew I'd said no to it in the past. Only Neil knew I'd been genuinely considering it this time around, though, and it is to his credit that he was able to keep this from her until we were into the new year.

Telling Fiona I was going to be doing her favourite show was one of the funniest and most emotional moments. I hadn't planned on telling her, mainly because I had no faith that she'd be able to keep it a secret. Sorry, Fi. She loves *Strictly*. She loves *Strictly* so much. She loves watching it and talking about it. She loves thinking about it and, well, mainly talking about it. How could I heap this on top of her and ask that she keep it a secret?

We were over at their house in the new year, and I just decided there and then to burden her with this information. It felt like the right moment. Fiona was talking about something in her own work life that was stressing her out.

'Do you want me to tell you something that'll cheer you up?' I asked her.

'Yeah, go on, then,' she said.

'I'm doing *Strictly* this year.'

It was as simple as that. No drum roll, no building up to the big announcement, just completely matter of fact, like I was telling her any old random bit of news. If I could have bottled a reaction to me doing the show, it would have been this one. The poor girl didn't know what to do with herself as her arms flapped about the place and she babbled questions without leaving any room for answers.

'What? How? What? Are you joking? I don't understand? Oh, my God! What? Please. How? Oh, my God!' She looked at Neil for confirmation. 'Neil, is this true?'

Neil confirmed that it was, at which point she nearly hyperventilated right there in the living room before she started screaming with excitement and crying at the same time.

This should have been my first indication of just what *Strictly* meant to people, but if I'm honest, I just wrote it off as being Fi – she's a bit nuts like that. I mean, what normal person would cry about a dancing show? Well, what the hell did I know? As I was to find out, it would be so much more emotional than I ever could have imagined.

Part of Fiona's reaction was due to the fact that her very close friend was going to be taking part in her favourite ever TV show. I can imagine that was a lot to deal with. The truth was also that she now knew she'd get tickets to go and watch her favourite ever TV show live in the studio and get to be a part of it all from the inside. In a way, I was just the mechanism that was enabling that to happen. I know this because she pretty much said so through a babbled stream of consciousness that she couldn't quite seem to control.

'Oh, my God, I'm going to get to watch it live.'

'Oh, my God, I'm going to meet all the dancers.'

'Oh, my God, I'm going to meet Johannes.'

'Oh, my God, Johannes, Johannes, Johannes!'

What came out of Fiona's mouth next perfectly sums up the level of belief that all of my friends and family would have regarding my prospects on the show.

She paused as if she'd had a sudden moment of realisation that had caused her some trouble. 'Can I just ask?'

A silence fell across the room. We all knew this was going to be important.

'Ask what?' I asked back.

'If you get eliminated . . .' she said, psyching herself up to finish the question '. . . do you still get the audience tickets?'

'I wouldn't imagine so,' I replied.

'Shit,' she said.

Finally, though, I had somebody who knew the show, who understood the show, and who could explain it to me in a way that would help me understand how I might be able to do what was soon going to be asked of me. I now had somebody who could help me build my confidence for what was to come.

'Honestly, Chris, I've got no idea,' she said. 'I mean how are you gonna know where you are on the floor? Know what direction you're facing? Know where your dance partner is? How will you be able to learn any of it? It's so visual.'

'Okay, put a sock in it, Fi. This isn't helping!'

The truth is that nobody really understood how it would be possible or if it was even going to be possible. There is a difference between doing some ballroom dancing and being able to reach the standards required not to be a token participant on the show, and I still didn't really understand what that standard was.

Do you know how many of my friends and family put a bet on me to win? None of them. Not my parents or sister. Not an auntie or uncle or one single cousin. Not Neil or Kev, or Gary, Steve or Haydn. Not Graham who drives me around or Jacob my agent. Not my tour promoter Nigel or my publicist Amanda. Not any wife, husband, boyfriend or girlfriend of any friend, cousin or colleague. Literally none of them. Nobody had even the tiniest amount of confidence in me to risk a tenner at 25–1. Instead they all thought exactly the same thing . . .

'How the hell is this going to work?'

And . . .

'Well, it won't last long.'

Aside from those few family and friends, and those I worked alongside, I had done a really good job of keeping my involvement in *Strictly* a secret. At the beginning of June it was leaked into the papers, though, and my hunch is that this may have – possibly, maybe – come from somewhere within BBC or Strictly Towers. Maybe possibly a little bit, maybe as a way of possibly maybe deflecting a little attention from certain slightly negative stories that had been consuming quite a few column inches during that time. Possibly maybe. Who knows? Just saying. Did I cover myself enough there, legal team?

If I'm honest, I preferred it when nobody knew about it: once it was out there it was all anybody wanted to talk about. As it was only a leak I was still contractually obligated to publicly deny all knowledge, although in private conversations I didn't pretend it wasn't happening. Still, though, the number-one thing people wanted to know was: how the hell is that going to work? Which didn't do a great deal to boost my confidence as I still didn't have a clue.

'Is it true?' asked my postman John.

'Yeah,' I said. 'I'm not allowed to publicly acknowledge it but it's true.'

'Bloody hell' he said.

'The problem is,' I explained, 'that because I can't see it, I don't know how good the dancing is that I'll be expected to do on the show.'

'I'm not gonna lie,' said John, 'it's fucking good.' And with that he thrust a parcel into my hands and was away.

Cheers for that, John.

I think the producers of the show have obviously got a good idea of who they think might work well together, but they keep that firmly to themselves. In August I attended an event in north London where all of us contestants got to meet each other, and also where we got to meet all of the professional dancers for the first time.

This was an opportunity for the producers to see us all paired with every dancer, to see who looked good together and who looked like they might have some chemistry. Think of it as speed-dating for *Strictly*.

I met all of the dancers in the space of about ten minutes and it was quite overwhelming. A cacophony of accents and names coming at me that mostly flew in one ear and right out the other. My future dance partner, Dianne Buswell, was about to embark on her eighth series; she was thirty-five years old and from Australia, although I didn't know any of this then.

The first thing she asked me was to guess where she was from, and I guessed Essex. Yes, her Aussie accent might have been fairly watered down, but I don't think it's possible to overstate how little I knew about the show at this point and the dancers who appeared on it – oh, and also how outraged she was by my answer.

We were all taught the most rudimentary of ballroom steps, basically just forward a step and back a step in exactly the same way Bez from the Happy Mondays might dance ballroom, if given the chance. Incidentally, Bez would make a brilliant contestant on *Strictly,* but I don't think his unpredictable and post-watershed mouth could survive on early evening TV without the BBC receiving fines from Ofcom that would likely make him the most expensive contestant ever to have taken part. The public would bloody love him, though.

All of us contestants stood in a big circle, facing outwards, and just repeated this simple basic ballroom step over and over, as the professional dancers formed a slightly larger circle facing inwards and rotated every time the whistle blew so they moved on to the next person.

This ballroom step was basic even for me, so I don't think

they were forming any opinions here that were based on actual style or technique. It must have been as simple as who is the right height for each other, and whose faces look best in close proximity. Maybe Lauren Oakley and I just looked a bit odd together. Who knows?

I think with me, though, they must have had a good idea that Dianne might be the best person for the job, because what a job it would be. If I was in those production meetings in Strictly Towers I would have said that Chris needs one of our absolute best, most-experienced dancers. She has to be a good communicator because visuals aren't an option here, and it would work better if it was somebody who was a bit daft and had a good sense of humour. Dianne more than ticks the boxes in all of these areas so I think she was probably their front runner for the short straw quite early on.

The producers genuinely did keep it a secret about who we had been paired with. They wanted the on-camera reveal to be natural and for both contestant and dancer to be surprised, and hopefully pleased when they were revealed to each other.

After the Dianne–Essex incident, I requested a list of all the professional dancers along with their nationalities so that I could do my homework and have a good idea of who was who and where they were from. I wanted to be excited to meet my dance partner properly for the first time, rather than trying to figure out exactly which one she was.

I know that the pairings were kept a secret from the dancers because I spoke to them about it, and although they had hunches and maybe two or three that they thought were more likely than the rest, they said they genuinely didn't know for sure until they opened the door and saw who was standing in front of them.

I thought this probably wasn't the case for Dianne, though. Yeah, it's fine to keep it a secret and not actually tell her who she'd been paired with, but at some point somebody had to have had a word in her ear about what to do when walking through that door.

'Look, we're not telling you who you're paired with, Dianne, but when you walk through that door, can you make sure you say your name, please, so he knows who you are?'

I think it's fair to say that Dianne and I hit it off straight away. She's smart, funny, and just so incredibly down to earth that we found ourselves able to have a laugh from the start.

'You made it to the final last year, didn't you?' I asked her, having done a bit more homework than just reading that list.

'I did,' she confirmed.

'Well, that won't be happening again this year,' I joked.

'Never say never, Chris,' she said.

I told you she was smart.

Chapter Thirty-Six

Aside from the results shows, that very first opening episode of *Strictly* is the only one that is pre-recorded. This is where the partnerships are revealed to the public for the first time and where everybody has to perform a big group dance together.

Dianne and I really did have to start from absolute zero with everything. I had no previous dance experience and no reference points that she could use to help explain any of the moves, and this became very apparent before we even had to start learning a proper dance on our own.

We had a couple of days to learn and practise the group dance and straight away my limitations and my shortcomings were pretty obvious to all. The dance moves were taught in group sessions and, due to the short time frame, the sessions pelted along at quite a pace. Everybody else was able to watch and copy the dance moves that were being shown to them, but I needed about five times longer while Dianne tried to describe to me what I had to do, and we very quickly found ourselves playing catch-up with everybody else. Dianne would later tell me that she did have a bit of a panic at this point about how anything in the future would even be possible. After all, the opening dance number was amateur by comparison to what was to come, and I was distinctly amateur at the amateur.

First of all, my posture was appalling. A lifetime of slouching on the couch and hunching over a computer had not left me with the most upright of natural frames. I think that losing my sight had affected my posture in multiple ways. For a start I had spent most of my life having to lean forward to see things better, hunching closer to computer monitors and TVs. On top of that I had also walked with the constant possibility of being whacked in the head by those overhanging garden branches I mentioned earlier. Get them cut! So, my posture was bloody awful and Dianne was suddenly reassessing the seemingly impossible task and realising that the straw she had drawn was possibly a lot shorter than she had first thought.

I should say here that Dianne swears she wanted to be paired with me from the moment she saw I was confirmed as taking part. Maybe she fancied a project, maybe she fancied November off: either way, this opening episode certainly had her reassessing just what she thought might be possible.

There was a moment in that opening dance where we all lined up in two rows facing each other. We would then take turns to skip into the centre and meet our opposing counterpart for a hip-bump before returning to our place in the line-up. Opposite me was Arsenal legend Paul Merson, and the first three times we tried this I missed Paul completely. Paul ended up where he was meant to be but I went off at a bit of a mad angle and ended up somewhere behind him. If I couldn't even walk in a straight line, how was I going to do anything a bit more challenging on live TV?

The evening of the recording came around and, to be honest, I kind of felt all right about it. I didn't feel much pressure at all. The limelight was very much shared between everybody, and it was pre-recorded, so what was the worst that could happen? Yeah, I mess it all up but we just do it again, and only five hundred people see it happen. I've embarrassed myself in front of five hundred people before now so that wasn't a problem. I actually found the whole thing quite exciting. There weren't any strict rules to the dancing, they would sure come soon, it just felt like a gang of entertainers getting together and having a laugh to mark the start of this journey.

Just on that 'journey' word, by the way. It's one of those words that people turn their nose up at. They tut. They sigh. Oh, not another journey, they think.

I'm guilty of this. The word has gained a bit of a reputation for being overused, emblematic of something a bit eggy and overly sentimental, a sappy expression of an experience that comes with emotional baggage and moments of self-discovery along the way. The problem is that when you get to the point of a sentence where 'journey' is looking like it might make an appearance, there isn't another word that does the job. What else are you meant to say? Expedition? Excursion? Jaunt? There's nothing, so let's just swallow any bits of mouth-sick together and agree to put up with it as I will be using it again, and pretty soon.

Even though the group dance was to be featured at the end of the opening episode, it was actually the first thing we filmed in front of the studio audience. Yes, the whole of TV is a lie. This means the studio audience first learned of the partnerships when we walked out onto the floor for the very first time to take our places.

Big Stu Holden is the warm-up guy for *Strictly*. He keeps the audience energised and laughing before filming starts and throughout some quite mammoth studio days, and he's incredible at it. It was Stu who announced Dianne and me to the studio audience as we walked out there for the first time as a partnership, and the noise from the room was deafening.

As audiences go, five hundred people is not massive, but the way the studio is set up has the audience split along its two longer edges, and this creates two walls of noise, which makes it feel like it's all around you.

The audience went absolutely nuts when Dianne and I emerged together, and I honestly felt quite taken aback. I found it very emotional, even at that early stage, to hear and feel how much these people loved the show and how much they obviously loved Dianne. It was quite overwhelming. It suddenly hit me that I was part of something that meant a lot to people, not just my *Strictly*-obsessed friend Fiona. There were a lot of Fionas out there who were crazy about this show.

The dance went well enough. I was happy, the producers were happy, and Dianne seemed happy, but the improvement I would show throughout the series would highlight my poor standard on this opening show when it was compared side by side at a later date.

When training began for that first live episode I made it clear to Dianne that I didn't want her dumbing anything down for me. The only reason for me being there was to surprise people about what was possible, and for that to be the case I needed to be attempting everything that every-body else would be attempting, and perhaps even more. I wanted us to try to find ways of making impressive and seemingly impossible things happen, to try to blow people's minds and make a statement rather than just being there as a token inclusion. Dianne was so on board with this from the very start that I never felt I was in any danger of looking like I was there to tick a box. We were both on exactly the same page in this regard: we were either going to shock people from that very first live episode or go out in a blaze of glory trying.

'Okay,' said Dianne. 'I'm gonna do a cartwheel, you're gonna catch my leg, pull it down, then play air guitar on it.'

The precision involved to achieve this took a lot of practice. The first time we tried Dianne ended up in a heap on the floor. The second time we both ended up in a heap on the floor, and on one attempt Dianne cartwheeled in towards me and kicked me straight in the face. If Dianne had any doubts that I wasn't completely blind, if there was a small part of her that thought I might be able to see at least something but was keeping that to myself, it was very quickly extinguished as I stood there and took her foot in the face without the subtlest of flinches or even the slightest sign of any anticipation whatsoever.

The one thing we had from the very beginning was trust. We wouldn't have been able to pull any of it off if we hadn't. I had to trust Dianne implicitly that she would be exactly where she was meant to be at all times, and she had to trust that I would put 100 per cent into absolutely everything. I couldn't be holding back because I was nervous or wary of my movements or surroundings, any less than full commitment on my part just wouldn't have worked. This would be especially true when we started incorporating lifts into our dances in future weeks as they simply wouldn't have been possible without sufficient momentum. Doing all of this in the dark meant I had to trust Dianne implicitly so I could move with that momentum.

I would imagine usually in *Strictly* the journey belongs to the celebrity contestant, and that their professional dance partner is there to get the best out of them and to facilitate their journey. In the case of Dianne and me, the journey was both of ours. I was learning how to dance on live TV, overcoming fears and limitations, stretching myself far outside my comfort zone and ultimately surprising myself as well as the nation about just what was possible. Dianne was facing the biggest challenges she'd faced during her time on the show, having to find entirely new ways to teach and problem-solve every single week and to be so incredibly creative in the face of these limitations.

That first live episode was the most terrifying thing I've ever done in my life, even more so than that first gig all those years back in Balham. Waiting to go out onto that dance-floor felt truly horrific. I knew from the pre-recorded group dance on the opening show that the live band and the noise from the audience would completely change my environment compared to what I had been used to in training. We trained in an empty room, and even immediately prior to walking out on the dance-floor we got to run through our dance in an empty marquee that was attached to the studio.

In these environments I had an awareness of the open space around me just from the sound that empty space tends to make when you're present in it. I could hear Dianne existing, breathing, counting steps, and would often have a good idea of where she was even if we weren't in contact.

I knew in the live show everything would change. The cacophony of the noisy, enthusiastic audience would cause the open space around me to shrink in so tight that everywhere would suddenly feel a lot smaller, and I knew that it would completely drown out any awareness I had of Dianne, which would make her invisible to me in more ways than just the one.

I was about to enter an environment that I hadn't been able to prepare for. Would I even be able to do any of the tricks or set-pieces under these conditions? Would I be able to grab Dianne's leg down and play guitar on it as we had practised in that empty room, when it would all sound and feel so different in the packed studio?

The production team asked me if I wanted the audience in the studio to remain quiet during our dances so that I could have a better awareness of my surroundings. It was a thoughtful gesture but I immediately said no. *Strictly* was a party for those lucky enough to be in the studio and I wanted to do this thing properly or not at all. I wanted that energy, I wanted that noise, I wanted to participate in that full electric atmosphere and try to prove that this was possible without concessions. I just wasn't yet sure if I would be able to. We were about to find out on live TV in front of millions. It was make or break and I was absolutely shitting myself.

When our names were called from that marquee, we

made the walk through the back corridors of Elstree Studios to the floor. It felt like the dead man's walk, like I was walking the green mile to my execution. Dianne would tell me later that I had gone a peculiar shade of grey with all of the colour draining from my face, and that she was the most nervous she had ever been going into a dance because she didn't know if this was going to work either.

'Are you okay, Chris?' she asked.

Such was the delay in me answering that her words might as well have been beamed up into space, processed by a satellite, then bounced around a few more before being beamed back down to me stood right next to her. Even then I would answer in the form of a grunt of acknowledgement of the question and nothing more. I was sick with nerves.

We were dancing a cha-cha-cha to 'Twist and Shout' by the Beatles, and our set was a mock-up of the Cavern Club in Liverpool where the Beatles famously played before taking over the world. We entered the studio while everybody at home was watching a video insert that chronicled our first week in training. My starting position was behind a microphone while Dianne was stood at a table nearby.

I tend to withdraw when under huge amounts of stress or pressure: it's my way of being able to process it all and compartmentalise. I need to look at it all logically in my head rather than letting the nerves or the emotion take over. I went so quiet and withdrawn, though, that Dianne was worried I might be about to completely freeze on live television.

'Thirty seconds to go,' said Al the floor manager.

I wasn't concerned about freezing. I knew I was ready

to give it my all. I was just getting myself mentally into the position where I was able to do that. I'm pretty good at going into performance mode when I have to. As a comedian I might not always be feeling in the right frame of mind for comedy, but I have to flick those switches in my head and put on a show regardless of how I may feel. That was something I definitely had going in my favour here, that one transferable skill from comedy, of being able to bottle things up, shove them to one side and put on a smile and a show.

'Twenty seconds,' said Al.

That training-room video was nearing its end now. It was almost time. I pumped my arms in the air to get the audience going. If they were going to make noise here, let's get them to make as much noise as possible. The audience went bananas.

'Ten seconds,' said Al.

I'm an idiot, I always have been, and by that I mean I've never really grown up in lots of ways. I feel comfortable with comedy and often use it as a way of dealing with difficult emotions or stress. I'm a comedian and I'm addicted to making audiences laugh. It makes me feel good, it makes me feel confident, it makes me feel like I'm succeeding.

So, with just ten seconds to go before we went live, I decided to go for the laugh, to show the audience in the studio that I was nervous but that I was also able to find this funny. I turned from the microphone where Dianne had set me in position, took a few steps away and comically pretended to stick my fingers down my throat and throw up in the corner.

The audience laughed.

I felt good.

Dianne panicked because I was no longer where I was meant to be for the start of our dance. I felt so out of my depth, though, so about to enter the unknown, that I needed to do something on my terms, something that made me feel like me, something that allowed me to get a laugh.

It worked. It made me feel a little better, a little more like me, so I turned around and trod back to find that microphone and my starting point again as Al counted us in.

'Live in five, four, three,' he said, before Dianne and I were there for everybody to see at home.

'Dancing the cha-cha-cha, Chris McCausland and Dianne Buswell,' said the studio announcement.

I took a deep breath and flicked those switches. Performance mode on. One hundred per cent. Nothing else will do.

The opening strums of the guitar jangled and I was away, bopping my head and swinging my hips behind the microphone as the audience responded with screams and cheers.

I broke from the microphone and wandered over to where Dianne was meant to be, and there she was, so far so good. We went sweeping down the dance-floor with our cha-cha-cha step and the audience in the studio went even crazier. This was bloody working.

We pulled apart from each other, coming back in to meet in the middle, our hands finding each other and pushing as we spun to face the opposite direction, pulling away from each other again. The audience was loving it.

A little more footwork and dancing before we were approaching that risky guitar leg bit. This was make or break, grab hold of the leg and we were on the home straight. If we messed it up, the chances were it was game over and there would be no recovering from a foot in the head or us both landing in a heap on the floor.

We cha-cha-cha'd some more and danced into position for the big moment. Dianne disappeared from my hold momentarily and I filled the moment with a bit of quick footwork before sticking out my hands hopefully to grab her leg, which should have been coming through any moment. Oh, my goodness! The relief and joy I felt when I took hold of her leg, pulled it down into the guitar position and started strumming. The audience went absolutely nuts.

I flung myself forward into a knee slide towards the cameras as everybody screamed. We were through it, and almost at the home straight.

I waited until I thought Dianne had probably kicked her leg over my head then jumped up to find her hands right in front of me as we had practised, before we immediately went into a bit of fast-paced synchronised footwork. I slid her through my legs and caught her behind me, and back we danced before the final big moment.

The plan was that Dianne would spin around and drop backwards into my arms and I would drag her backwards towards the centre of the studio floor before swinging her body around and stepping over her legs as they passed beneath me in a sweeping circle. This was another moment that had been hit-and-miss during training, but over time I had learned to read the shifts in her body weight and antici-pate where her legs would be so that I could step over them without stumbling and losing that momentum. It was insane that we were attempting it, to be honest, but we really had set out to make a statement and blow people's minds with just what could be possible. This final trick was the icing on the cake.

I dragged her back and started swinging. Over one, two, three and four, yes! The noise was deafening now as we ran back to the microphone, Dianne leaping into my arms for our final victory pose.

I have been on the receiving end of some lovely audience responses during my twenty-odd years performing stand-up. I know I've talked about some of the trickier gigs during my early years, but the vast majority I've done throughout my career have been lovely. I have told you about doing well on *Live at the Apollo* and *The Royal Variety Perform-ance*, and how both of these experiences couldn't have gone much better. I've been lucky enough to play some of the most prestigious and amazing theatres up and down the country while on tour, and I've had amazing shows in front of packed houses along the way. All that considered, though, I had never experienced an audience reaction quite like the one that Dianne and I got from those five hundred people in that studio. It wasn't just appreciation, and it wasn't just well done. It felt like the audience were celebrating a last-minute goal being scored in an FA Cup final. It was raw and it was primal and it was so incredibly emotional.

My emotions would ultimately come out in a lot of ways at the end of a dance throughout the following weeks. There was just something about the release of all those nerves, the overwhelming sense of relief of getting through the dance on live television, the knowledge that millions were watching it in that moment, and the noise of the studio audience hitting me in the face from both sides that would all combine into a perfect storm that would place a lump in my throat, water in my eyes, and would rip me open just a little bit more each week.

On this first occasion my emotions poured out of me in utter joy and celebration. I was meant to put Dianne on the floor, but I didn't. I kept hold of her in my arms and ran out into the dance-floor as we screamed with utter joy. Twenty-three points out of a possible forty might not seem like a great result, but what that first dance represented was so much more than a score. It taught me straight away from Episode One that things did not have to be perfect for them to be a success on the show. Just over 50 per cent from the judges, but for everything that it was and everything it represented, it could not have been more of a statement and it could not have been more meaningful.

Social media went mad. We might have impressed the judges with our bravery and energy, but had been lacking in posture and technique, but it was only week one and the viewers at home were blown away. The gamble had paid off and we had done exactly what we'd hoped we could do.

After the show I phoned home to see how my family had found it on the TV.

Patricia was relieved and utterly gobsmacked at what we had just done and was on cloud nine while she absorbed the social-media frenzy.

My beautiful daughter had cried so much that she had

missed the whole thing. She had been so nervous for me, so nervous that I would hurt or embarrass myself on the TV, so worried that I wouldn't be able to do the dancing because I'm blind, that when Dianne and I had first set off in that sweeping cha-cha-cha down the centre of the dance floor, the emotion and the relief had been too much for her and she had immediately burst out in tears and hadn't been able to stop. They would have to rewind the show and watch it again, but it would take a few goes for her to manage it without all those tears. I know that this outburst of emotion and tears came partly from relief that I was dancing, actually dancing, but I know that it also came from a lot of pride. She was so incredibly proud of what I had done that night and she just found it difficult to deal with it all.

I returned home at about 11 p.m. on that Saturday night and was immediately attacked at the front door for the longest hug I'd ever been on the receiving end of. Sophie had watched that dance over and over and over again. She was one extremely happy and proud little girl and that meant so much more than any comments or scores from the judges.

That first live episode was such a success, and I honestly felt we had been able to do something quite remarkable. There was just one big worry in the back of my mind . . . How the hell were we going to do something like that again?

Chapter Thirty-Seven

As the weeks progressed we did manage to do it again, and again and again, and with so many moments along the way that felt magical to be a part of. With each dance Dianne choreographed something truly spectacular, and with a lot of hard work and trust, we were able to deliver a real wow factor each week and surprise people in so many ways.

This has been a difficult chapter to write as I didn't know how much to cover of my time on the show. Yes, there will be people reading this who don't care much about the meat and gravy of *Strictly*, but there will be others who are only doing so because I was on the show. I went back and forth and round in circles. My plan was to cover just the first five live shows as each allowed us to bring something different to the table, to shock and surprise in different ways, then to cherry-pick a few key moments beyond that before we get to the climax. I also couldn't miss out on the opportunity to slag off some of my Latin experiences, and by the time I'd done all that I'd kind of covered the lot, although I could have written ten times more so count yourself lucky. So, whether you're a *Strictly* fan or not, here is a little bit of everything.

Our cha-cha-cha in week one had been fairly high energy

and in your face, but the foxtrot that followed felt graceful and elegant, like proper olde-worlde dancing, a romantic echo of a time gone by. The gliding across the floor, the change in speed and acceleration as the footwork changed from quick to slow and back again. The hold as Dianne and I moved together, a single entity. This was my introduction to ballroom and I loved it. The ballroom hold is a strange one, though, bodies as close as possible but with heads as far away as you can manage, like you want to dance with each other but just can't bear the stench of each other's breath.

Our foxtrot ended with Dianne climbing onto a bench while I held her hand, and me walking around to the end as she stepped up onto its arm before falling off into my arms. The noise in the room when we executed this move flawlessly was staggering. It felt impressive, it felt magical, and it felt like it perfectly illustrated the level of trust that we had had to place in each other. Here we were, Dianne a professional dancer, who had never taught or even danced with anybody who was blind before, trusting that I would catch her in that exact moment on live television in front of millions.

We weren't done yet, though: after I had raised her back up onto the bench, I stepped straight up onto its arm and joined her there, before we gazed at each other for a brief moment and dropped down on the final beat to end up sat side by side next to each other. These final moves took so much practice and precision to pull off, but for it to work as it did made all of that effort and risk so worthwhile.

The audience erupted around us. Again I found the emotion overwhelming and this time had to take a brief moment on that bench to gather a little composure before heading over to the judges. I would often require a moment or two at the end of a dance and would just cling to Dianne for dear life until I felt able to speak without choking up.

Over the next two weeks the jive and the salsa had us back in high-energy performance mode. The jive was fast and it was relentless, and I think I spent at least half of that week's rehearsal time just lying on the floor trying to breathe. It felt like I was trying to keep hold of a runaway horse, and my thighs burned as if I'd been doing just that.

The footwork was so incredibly fast-paced and I worried that any mistake would leave me unable to rejoin the routine and find the rhythm again. That was often one of my real concerns each week, that if I did make a mistake, I wouldn't be able to see what Dianne was doing so that I could just join in with her again and would be left to try to figure it out in my head. That's why I prioritised the footwork each and every week. I would spend two days just making sure we had all of the footwork down before we started adding anything as fancy as arms or hips. For me, the footwork was so much more important than everything else because if I messed it up there was a good chance that the dance could be over for me.

We did our jive in the guise of Wayne and Garth from *Wayne's World*, and aside from it feeling like that wig had been screwed directly into my brain with six-inch anchor bolts, it was fun to bring a bit of comedy from my youth into movie week and, of course, some head-banging to 'Bohemian Rhapsody' as that wig wasn't going anywhere.

The reaction at the end of our jive was raucous but felt more like one of congratulations. Almost like the audience couldn't believe I'd managed to get through it without cocking it up.

Our salsa was one of my favourite moments of the whole series as this was where we first incorporated lifts. We danced to Men At Work's 'Land Down Under' and Dianne was in her element, getting to celebrate her homeland with an Aussie anthem and more kangaroos than you could shake a didgeridoo at.

Every time we performed a lift or a trick the audience in the studio would go nuts. Despite how well we had done in those previous weeks, I think that many people carried a concern or a doubt that maybe lifts would be a problem for me. On that floor it honestly felt like we were shocking the audience in the studio and, by extension, the viewers at home with every lift and trick we executed with confidence and pizzazz. The screaming was loud and intense and the noise when we finished with Dianne hanging upside down on top of me was simply astonishing. Emotionally, I was being ripped open a little more each week: there was the relief and the joy and the pride in what we were doing, the appreciation from the audience in the studio, and the knowledge that my family and friends and millions of others were watching at home. It was all a lot to handle.

I stood there for a moment holding that pose with Dianne hanging upside down, and I thought about Sophie watching at home and likely screaming at the TV. About her watching me do this right now, about her being able to see me overcoming all those nerves and allaying our fears, about the cuddle I would get when I returned home later that night. I swung Dianne around a little and, rather ungracefully, set her back on her feet. Then I just held on to her until I felt able to talk on the telly.

I never really recovered from the emotion of that moment all the way through my Sunday at home. I would think back to what we had managed to accomplish in the studio on the previous night and the reaction from the audience that told us as much, and it would cause my throat to close and my eyes to fill with water from the joy and the pride. The truth was that I wasn't just surprising everybody in the studio or watching at home, but I was surprising myself in ways I had never thought possible and it was all just a lot to handle.

I carried this fragility with me into training for our next dance, our waltz to the emotionally charged anthem of my beloved Liverpool Football Club, 'You'll Never Walk Alone'.

Tommy Blaze is also from Liverpool and has sung on *Strictly* since its first series. Listening to his incredible soulful rendition of this personally meaningful song over and over again throughout that week had me wobbling more than a few times every day, and this was only amplified when combined with Dianne's choreography, which was simply outstanding. I don't mind admitting that I wasn't sold on her idea when she first ran it by me. There was a moment in the dance where she broke away from me and left me to do a few ballroom steps without her, before I would walk down the centre of the dance-floor alone to meet her in a collision that would spin and spin and spin.

I thought that maybe the idea of walking alone to 'You'll Never Walk Alone' might be a bit on the nose, a literal interpretation of the song that was maybe a bit too eggy, but I couldn't have been more wrong. When we started training for it, I could instantly feel the emotion as we met in that collision and started to spin, and I had to use all the tricks in the book to curtail any tears.

I felt a hell of a lot of pressure going into that dance as I was worried about messing up or doing a bad job to a song that meant so much to so many, but that dance would ultimately prove to be such a big moment for us. In the previous four weeks we had shocked and surprised, we had done what had felt elegant and magical, we had done fast, energetic and impressive, but now we would show vulnerability and sincerity in our dance. I knew we'd done a good job when even Everton and Manchester United fans were sending me messages on social media to say we had made them cry.

Before entering the show I had no idea that dancing would be emotional. This had caught me completely off guard. I was surprised to feel so much of it in what we were doing, but also that it would connect with people and move them in the way that it did. I didn't expect it to be that powerful.

Every week Dianne would have to start from absolute scratch with me. My fellow contestants might have had a good idea of what each dance was before they arrived at training on any given Monday morning, but I would usually have none. Obviously I couldn't watch past *Strictly* performances on YouTube, or absorb everybody else's dances week by week to build up an idea of what made a decent or a passable

Charleston for when my turn would finally come around. Every Saturday I would stand up there in Claudia's area and lend a bit of enthusiasm to proceedings, but without really knowing what anybody else was doing on that dance-floor beyond the basic premise.

This meant that Dianne would have to start each Monday morning facing a blank slate by trying to describe the very basics of the dance we would be doing that week. She would start by talking me through the style, the posture and the movement, before explaining her ideas to me. Before the series started people would ask us how we were going to do the training, and the truth was that we just didn't know. This was a brand-new experience for both of us so we were just going to have to wing it, we said. We would figure it out as we went along.

She would start with words, describing certain positions or moves, but often I would then have to feel her body position to get a better idea of what she wanted from me. Sometimes I would have to get on my hands and knees and feel what her legs and feet were doing so that I could try to replicate it. And if that failed she would just manhandle me into position, picking my foot up and putting it where she wanted it, like I was one of those bendy toy figures that you can manipulate into strange and bizarre positions. I used to have a Spider-Man like that, and sometimes I felt a bit like my old bendy Spider-Man.

While others might have used the visuals of the room for orientation, I had to learn how to read Dianne's body movements and positioning. The amount of practice and precision we needed for some of this was enormous. If I was going to lead and drive Dianne through the centre of the dance-floor at a fast pace with momentum, we had to make sure that we were always 100 per cent landing in the right place and at the right angle for that to happen. In order to make this work the way we did, we often had to commit such disproportionate amounts of training time to tiny details that others would have barely had to consider.

I was very aware that anything less than absolute 100 per cent commitment was not an option. I was there to surprise people and to prove that more was possible. Slacking off or cutting corners in any regard just wasn't an option.

I thought that if anybody else made mistakes, or was a bit sloppy or uncoordinated, that would likely only reflect on them in that moment and as an individual. For me, I felt that any of my shortcomings would reflect on the abilities and capabilities of the wider community I represented. It wouldn't just be the case that Chris is a bit rubbish at dancing, or that he can't do intricate footwork, or that he struggles with lifts and tricks, but that blind people can't do these things and it was ridiculous to have suggested that they could.

'It's political correctness gone mad!' people would shout.

I know that in some way I was guilty of this assumption before agreeing to do the show, but a little of this was down to the fact that I didn't know what I was being asked to do. Part of the contract I made with myself when I agreed to take part was that I would put every last ounce of myself into doing the best job that I was able: I couldn't have any lack of effort or desire on my part reflecting badly on an entire community of others.

It was because of the amount of commitment and trust that Dianne and I had to have to make this work, and because of how seriously I was taking the training each week, that I then felt I was allowed to have some fun and undercut the whole experience wherever possible. I entered the show with one single mantra, I suppose, and that was to take the dancing seriously, but not to take myself or the show outside of the dancing too seriously. This was an entertainment show, after all, and I just thought that once the dancing bit was over, there was room for me to try to entertain and represent myself in a way that I felt a lot more comfortable with.

There was no point in pretending that *Strictly* had always been a dream. It hadn't and I'd had to be asked several times before finally agreeing to take part. There was no point in pretending I knew anything about dancing. I knew nothing and that was obvious to everybody. There was no point in pretending that I was loving every single moment because it was really, really hard, and at times I wasn't, but that was fine: that was why it was such a challenge. Just so long as I was happy I had put every last bit of myself into that dance on a Saturday night, then as soon as that dance was over, it was time to have a laugh.

Comedy was a place of familiarity and comfort, a place of confidence. Much in the same way that I had pretended to throw up before the first dance to get a laugh in the studio, comedy was how I represented myself in a way that made me feel like myself in an environment that had me so out of my depth.

Long-time judge Craig Revel Horwood became my

on-screen adversary from that very first live show. Craig's role on the show is as the pantomime villain, so I thought it would be good television if I revelled in his villainy and gave him back as good as he dished out. Our back-and-forths very quickly became a highlight for many viewers, and the thing I loved most about them is that they were all transmitted live and in the moment, and never subject to approval from producers or at risk of an edit.

I knew where the lines lay in terms of what is appropriate for family viewing on an early Saturday evening, but I also knew how to push this slightly into territory that the producers might not have been quite so keen on if I'd given them a heads-up. I would often keep ideas to myself until we were in the live show.

Dropping to our knees at the end of our *Wayne's World* jive to perform our 'We're not worthy' bows to the judges took everybody by surprise but brought a little anarchy to proceedings. Giving Dianne a piggy-back over to the judges after our Charleston would likely have got everybody concerned about health and safety and risk assessments, if they'd known in advance, so we left that out of studio rehearsals and kept it for the live show.

Dianne was always brilliant in these moments, willing to be daft and silly, and always up for having a laugh if she felt we'd earned the right on that dance floor.

It's no secret that I preferred ballroom over Latin. I mean, I went on about it enough. Ballroom felt like proper dancing, like how couples used to dance for fun, actual fun. Latin didn't feel like anything anybody had ever done for fun.

Latin was very performative: it felt more like something that people would do only in competition or to show off.

'Hey, everybody look at me! Look how fast I can dance! Look at the weird shapes I can contort my body into while dancing! Look how I can get my hips and my arms and my legs doing completely different and unnatural things all at the same time! Aren't I amazing?'

The cha-cha-cha had been Latin, but it had earned a special place in my heart because of what that first dance had meant. The jive was Latin and it very nearly killed me but *Wayne's World* had made it fun.

The samba was bloody horrible. Its only saving grace was that we got to perform this during Halloween week so could bring a little tongue-in-cheek zombie horror into the performance. Part of my problem with the samba was that we had to open this episode, which changed the routine I had enjoyed up to that point. On the first five episodes I had been able to have a practice run through of our dance in that marquee, but going on first meant that this wasn't possible as we needed to be lined up waiting to enter the studio for the start of the show.

While waiting to enter the studio, I was trying to think through the dance, think through what the opening moves were, I was trying to practise it in my head. The problem is, though, that a lot of what you learn over the week becomes muscle memory, and the footwork is so intricate that it's actually really difficult to think through it without actually doing it. I couldn't think even how the dance started and I had a panic.

'I can't remember how it starts,' I said to Dianne, while we were waiting to be introduced down those stairs.

'You know it,' she assured me.

'I don't think I do,' I said. 'I can't even remember what the first thing is.'

Dianne dragged me out of the line-up and quickly went over those first few steps with me before we jumped back in line just as we were being introduced.

I didn't make a mistake in our samba, but I certainly over-compensated for nerves with a bit too much energy. Apparently the top half of my body was having a bit too much fun and the judges didn't like that. This is what I mean about the samba, though: the bottom half of your body has to do so much all at the same time, but your top half has to pretend nothing's happening. It's a stupid dance!

There was a move in this stupid dance where I was behind Dianne and she would drop down onto my outstretched arms while kicking her foot high over her head, and on one occasion in rehearsals I leaned too far forward as she kicked too far back, and she caught me so hard in the face that I almost threw up and had to lie down for twenty minutes to recover. If I'd thought that guitar leg kick in the head had been hard, well, this was on another level: I took the entire impact of her flying foot right on one eyeball. It's honestly a good job they didn't work already or I would have been doing that dance half blind anyway and *Strictly* would have had an insurance payout like no other.

That was the start of a tricky two-week period as they had us doing a tango next, and the tango was hands down the most difficult of all the ballroom dances. It wasn't even like I could pretend I was enjoying it, because you're not allowed to smile during the tango, you have to look bloody furious about it, that's the rules.

My nerves fluctuated from week to week depending on the dance and the amount of confidence I had in it, but nerves were always a huge presence. That first live episode might have been hands down the most terrifying thing I'd ever done in my life, but if I were to compile a list of the ten most terrifying things I've ever faced, then episodes of *Strictly* would populate the other nine spots as each week would bring an anxiety and a level of nerves like nothing I'd encountered previously.

Each week I would try to allay some of my family's nerves by sharing training videos with Patricia and Sophie to show them what we had in store for the Saturday night, or I'd bring them along to the training room so they could watch us do a run-through or two of our dance.

My dad couldn't handle watching it live for maybe the first seven weeks or so. My mum would watch on the telly with live audio description being provided by the BBC, which was a nice touch, but my dad would have to disappear until she told him it had gone well or at least hadn't been a disaster, at which point he would emerge back into the room, rewind the TV and watch it with the comfort of that knowledge. My poor mum never once got to see whoever was dancing immediately after me because that would be when my dad was watching me. Can you believe he even had the gall to moan to me about how nervous he got before each of my dances when it was me that was doing it?

If at any point in the future those boffins with the white coats, safety goggles and clipboards manage to restore my sight, or at least to the eyeball that she didn't fling her big toe into at a thousand miles an hour, I'll certainly have to sit down with Dianne, to watch our dances and actually see what we were able to accomplish each week. It was a bizarre experience for me at times, if I'm honest, as I had never been part of anything that had such an intense sense of camaraderie and togetherness, of such a well-oiled machine with so many working towards the same goal of putting on an incredible show every Saturday night, but I had also never felt so left out of what I was a part of creating. The show is so completely visual, and to have been there every Saturday night but still not really to have much idea of what anybody else was doing on that dance-floor, or even what Dianne and I were a part of and what it looked like for the audience at home, well, it's a weird juxtaposition to feel.

Our blackout moment during our Couple's Choice dance to John Lennon's 'Instant Karma' was not really intended to bring Dianne into my world, but rather to bring the studio audience and the viewers at home into it. The idea was to show everybody just what is possible in the darkness by surprising them with what we were doing as we came out of it. We went from me standing behind Dianne and covering her eyes as the lights went out, to the lights coming back on moments later to reveal me in a fast spin with her lying across my shoulders and my outstretched arms as the pyrotechnics went off. The only downside to this dance for us was that Dianne had been really ill all day, so we hadn't been able to enjoy it as much as we would have liked. She had been unable to keep anything down and had spent a lot of that day in or near a toilet, so we were just grateful that it was only the pyrotechnics that went off, or that fast spin out of the darkness could have been a very different surprise.

In week nine and for one night only, the show left Elstree Studios for the Blackpool Tower, the home of ballroom dancing. Blackpool was incredible. To get to dance with an ensemble around us, to be able to put on a performance like we did, to be able to make Dianne so happy and proud in a place that is so special to her and all of the other professional dancers, well, it was maybe the highlight of all of the high-lights for me.

I knew I'd nailed our American smooth when, as we approached the last few moments of the dance, Dianne spun away from me and let out a shriek of delight before spinning back in for our final pose. We celebrated at the end of that one because we knew it was good, that we'd done ourselves proud, and I knew from the studio reaction around us that everybody else thought so as well. Blackpool gave us our highest judges' scores up to that point in the series, and with them came our first tens, which immediately reduced Dianne to tears.

After our waltz in week five I felt we had accomplished so much more than I'd ever thought would be possible, and if we'd gone out in week six, I would have been so proud of what we had achieved. To be receiving tens at Blackpool in week nine, though, well, it was mind-blowing.

Every week we had only four days to learn each dance, as on a Friday we would have to perform it several times in the studio for the cameras so that they could figure out how they were going to shoot it on the night.

Although I had no frame of reference for any of the dances when the series started, as we progressed I was accumulating more and more knowledge and experience that Dianne could refer back to when teaching me new positions or moves. A lot of the dances would borrow from each other or share similarities, but the *paso doble* would prove to be a particularly difficult one for Dianne to teach me as it was unlike anything else we had done. So bizarre was its frame and movement that poor Dianne was still trying to describe some of its basics to me on the Wednesday evening while I was questioning whether she really knew what she was talking about.

'Are you absolutely sure?' I would ask her. 'It's just that this doesn't feel like it could possibly be a real dance. Are you sure you know what a *paso doble* is?'

The problem was that it didn't really feel like dancing, it felt like some kind of over-the-top historical battle re-enactment performed by people who really couldn't act. I just couldn't imagine why anybody would ever choose to do one unless they were being forced to for a competition or a TV show. It felt ridiculous, but it was Latin, so of course it did. I was getting used to that at least.

Dianne's parents had landed from Australia and this was the first time they had been able to watch their daughter dance live in eight years. Their trip had been booked for some time, and to have remained in the competition long enough for this to happen made me feel good, as if I was able to give Dianne something back for everything she had given me. It was just a shame that it was our *paso doble* week and they were going to have to watch us do this weird amateur-dramatics performance piece instead of an actual dance.

'Dianne,' I said, 'we really need to try to stay in one more week so at least they can watch us do a proper dance and not just this weird shit one.'

'It looks a lot better than you think it does,' she said.

'I'll have to take your word for that,' I replied, 'but it's ridiculous and I don't like it.'

I have still got no idea how we were able to pull off some of those dances when I had never seen what they were meant to look like. Dianne's teaching was honestly off the chart, but more than that, she had the patience of a saint, because if you think I've moaned a bit too much about Latin in these few pages, then imagine what it was like trying to teach it to me.

Chapter Thirty-Eight

After the emotion and the sense of accomplishment at the end of that first live show, I had wondered how the hell I would be able to do it again. It had felt a bit like a fluke, like a one-off, like something I'd got away with, to some extent, and that surely couldn't be bottled up and reopened week after week.

Well, what did I know, because we managed to do it another ten times to secure us a place in the semi-final, earning our place in the penultimate live show with a quick-step for Musicals Week, which again allowed us the opportunity to dance with an ensemble around us,

It felt nuts to say it out loud, that after all of the nerves and the fear, and after wandering into such a complete unknown a few months earlier, we were in the *Strictly* semi-final.

Making the semi-final had been such a ridiculous notion to me that I had other commitments in my diary for that week. I was due to film festive pre-records for Jimmy Carr's *Big Fat Quiz of the Year*, *The Last Leg New Year's Eve Special*, and was also due to make an appearance on that week's episode of *Have I Got News for You?*.

When I had put these shows in the diary I was advised that

they fell on the *Strictly* semi-final week, but I had brushed off this advice as not being my concern: I had assumed I would be at home twiddling my thumbs long before this.

I kept my commitment to the two festive pre-records as they were once-a-year shows and didn't really require much in the way of preparation, even for my tendency to over-prepare for everything. I had to bow out of *Have I Got News for You?*, though, as I knew I just wouldn't be able to do the work in advance of turning up.

'I can be there in body,' I told them, 'but I won't have the faintest clue what's gone on in the world unless the question is about dancing.'

'Yeah, there's nothing on dancing,' they told me. 'Maybe next time might be better.'

Those final two weeks ran straight through without a day off and were the most intensive and exhausting working weeks of my life. I've worked longer streaks than that without a day off many times in the past, but the demands of the show and my schedule around it meant that I was putting in minimum sixteen-hour days and pretty much just running on coffee and fumes.

We had to learn three brand-new dances over those two weeks while also relearning two of our previous ones, and I couldn't have been happier with the songs and the dances we got to do over that final run-in.

The semi-final saw us doing a joyous and somewhat comical Charleston to 'When You're Smiling', although the Charleston almost rivalled the *paso doble* when it came to difficulty in Dianne trying to describe it to me. It's such a goofy dance, with hugely exaggerated moves, that it took a lot of repetition before I got anywhere near what she wanted from me.

Our Viennese waltz to the darkly beautiful and brooding 'Nothing Else Matters' by Metallica was one of my highlights of the series. I had actually included 'Nothing Else Matters' on my list of totally awesome songs that I'd submitted to the production team before the series started. And I had even written next to it that I thought it might suit one of those lovely spinning twirly dances. I might not have known the name of the spinning twirly dance back at that point but how right I was, because our Viennese waltz to Metallica would prove to be a real high point and the final key that would unlock my emotional resilience and leave me a blubbering wreck for the final week that was to come.

Dianne's choreography for that dance was stunning and the ending was incredibly powerful. We ended by embracing each other in a hug on the final note of the song, a simple gesture that represented so much about what we had been able to overcome and achieve together to be there on the cusp of the final. As the song crashed to an end and we flung our arms around each other, the audience in the studio screamed and I was finally ripped open completely.

That was me for the entire final week, a blubbering mess who just couldn't turn the tap off now that it had been turned on. Those three months had taken their toll. I was tired and I felt physically and emotionally drained. I joked that I'd been poked with a stick for twelve weeks until I finally cried on the telly, but once I started I couldn't stop.

What had *Strictly* done to me? I remembered being a thick-skinned northern bloke, who'd last cried when Liverpool had beaten Barcelona 4–0 in the Champions League semi-final, because it was miraculous and wonderful and it had been completely unexpected. Now I was an emotional wreck who would leak uncontrollably from his eyeballs if anybody so much as said a kind word to me or touched me affectionately on the arm.

I had so many emotions but no longer had the resilience to keep a lid on any of them. When I had started out on *Strictly* I hadn't wanted to be there as a token gesture of inclusion, and I had worried about whether the show was even something I'd be able to do. As we earned our place in the final, though, I was incredibly proud to say that Dianne and I had made it through every single one of those previous eleven weeks of elimination without once receiving fewer points from the judges than whoever had been eliminated following the audience vote. We had held our own at every stage along the way.

In training for the final, I injured myself attempting an insane lift that Dianne had seen somebody doing on TikTok. It felt as if it almost tore me completely in two from my left arse cheek to my right shoulder-blade. There was no healing it in time, but the physio gaffer-taped me up so that I held together enough to get through the show. I did that final with five lengthy pieces of physio tape that pretty much kept my arse attached to my back. People would ask me if I was feeling healthier with all the exercise, and I would laugh. I had lost weight and was sure I'd feel healthier at some point in the future, once I'd been able to rest and heal, but as we went into that final I felt a bit like the walking dead.

The amount of energy I must have been burning each week was insane. I ate like it was the end of the world and I still managed to lose weight. I was a forty-seven-year-old man who was eating a burger and chips for a Tuesday lunch, for God's sake, then maybe even on a Wednesday and a Thursday as well. I was eating bars of chocolate like it was Christmas, and soon it would be Christmas. That was the danger, that I would continue the eating once the dancing had stopped and suddenly balloon like never before.

For the final, we revisited our Couple's Choice and blackout moment to John Lennon's 'Instant Karma', a chance for us both to enjoy the dance this time without illness marring it. Our new dance for the final was a show dance to 'Get What You Give' by New Radicals, and Dianne choreographed a homage to everything I'd loved about ballroom.

For some reason I was meant to emerge out of a massive box. I don't know why this was the case, nobody could tell me, but the production team wanted me in a massive box, so a massive box was built and I was loaded into it for the start of the dance. The plan was that I would strut out of the box as the front of it collapsed open, but I decided to leap out of it with full energy like I had a rocket up my arse. If they wanted me to come out of a box, I was going to come flying out of a box!

We chose to end our time on the show by revisiting our waltz to 'You'll Never Walk Alone'. Of course we did. Our waltz was the last thing we were to do on the show, and I was failing to hold back tears before we even started it. Earlier that week Dianne and I had recorded one of those video inserts to be played in before this last dance. We had sat on a couch in the training room and told each other what the last three months had meant to us, and we had cried a lot.

I was stood in that studio waiting to start our waltz while that video played, and all I could hear was Dianne and me crying on that couch. This set me off in the studio, and all of a sudden I was crying at the sound of us crying. It wasn't really the thought of everything we had done to get there that had made me emotional, but the thought that this was now the end of it all. Yes, I needed to sleep, and yes, I needed to rest, but the thought that this was to be the last dance we would do together at the end of this incredible journey was something that this new emotional me was finding it difficult to come to terms with.

In the training marquee, just ten minutes earlier, I'd had a panic that I couldn't remember the start of our waltz. I think the occasion and the tiredness finally overcame me. This was our third dance of the show and it had been a really long day. We had been in the studio since seven that morning and done an eleven-hour working day before we had to perform live gymnastics on the telly in front of millions. My mind went blank and I panicked, but Dianne just worked through the opening sequence a few times with me so I knew how to start: everything else would naturally follow from muscle memory once we were into it.

Our waltz couldn't have gone any better and I wrapped up my time on the show with my best performance. Dianne left me on my own to do my ballroom steps without her, I walked through the centre of the dance floor and we met in that collision that just spun and spun and spun. As we came to a rest, we linked arms to walk from the floor for those final notes of the song, but the moment got the best of both of us and we never made it all the way, instead ending the dance in an embrace that was so full of tears.

We had scored thirty-eight points from the judges for each of our first two dances that evening, but for our final waltz we received a perfect forty with tens across the board. I was the only one of the finalists that had no previous dance experience, and all I wanted was not to show myself up and let Dianne down, not to end up so far behind the others in the scoring that my inclusion might be seen as a joke. Over those three dances we were awarded no less than ten tens, and we ended up just four points off a maximum score for the entire evening. To hold our own and end in the way we did, it felt like such an achievement and the perfect way to wrap up what had been such an incredible journey.

Our final visit to the judges was eventful and emotional. Head judge Shirley Ballas embraced Dianne and lavished her with the praise she deserved for everything she had managed to get out of me throughout the series. Motsi Mabuse and Anton Du Beke were so generous with their parting words that the tears had no chance of subsiding. My adversary throughout it all, resident villain Craig Revel Horwood, surprised everybody by wrapping up his judge's comments with a poem he had written about me, and I got him to come out from behind his desk to end our entertaining *Strictly* feud with a fairytale hug. It was now all down to the audience at home.

I knew we had a lot of public support, but how the public would mobilise for the final vote was still a mystery. It had been such a joy to get to do this with every single one of the other contestants throughout the series, the only sadness being that we'd had to say goodbye to one of them each week.

My fellow finalists were all incredible dancers, and such lovely people to share that final moment with. Tasha Ghouri had been hands down the best dancer throughout the series but I suppose that had given her the least room to improve. Sarah Hadland had probably had the best combination of dance experience and personal journey out of all of us. JB Gill was an incredible dancer and had a huge JLS fan base out there, who could make a massive difference in a national vote. Then there was me, who had started with nothing and never been the best, but had surprised and shocked so many along the way.

We all wandered out onto the dance-floor and took our positions for the result to be announced while the viewers at home were watching a video insert.

'Ninety seconds,' said floor manager Al.

Ninety seconds is a long time to just be stood there waiting, so we broke from our positions and gave hugs all round. This had been the highest-scoring final in the show's history and we had done that together as a team.

'Thirty seconds,' said Al.

Back to our positions we all went, feeling better for that final moment of camaraderie that we had just shared unbeknown to the millions watching at home.

'Ten seconds,' said Al.

I felt remarkably calm but my mind was busy.

'And five, four, three . . .'

The final count passed silently before Tess began. She spoke but I didn't really hear her: my mind was working overtime, processing everything that had happened to lead to this utterly bizarre moment, stood there with Dianne in the *Strictly* final.

Dianne squeezed my hand and I squeezed back. This was it.

'Your *Strictly* 2024 winners are . . .' said Tess.

Tension music started playing in the studio. Like a heartbeat it thudded and the audience in the studio joined in with a clap.

Whatever happened now, this had truly been an experience and an achievement that I would for ever be proud of. What we had been able to overcome to be there in that moment, well, it all kind of felt like a dream, to be honest, a ridiculous surreal fantasy ending in something that had seemed so implausible a few months earlier.

The tension music continued for what felt like an extraordinarily long time, before Tess finally put us out of our misery.

'Chris and Dianne!' she shouted, as the room around us erupted for that final time.

I know now that the support we had up and down the

country was phenomenal. I know now that it wasn't just the studio around us that erupted, but people's living rooms in every town and village and city across the country. I know now that our fellow finalists erupted around us, Sarah and Vito, Tasha and Aljaž, JB and Lauren.

I'll tell you who didn't erupt in celebration, though, Dianne and me. The release of the tension in that moment, the appreciation for what we had managed to accomplish, and the realisation of what it had meant to so many people, well, it was a lot to take in.

Dianne immediately crumpled into tears and I followed a fraction of a second later, and as the noise of celebration continued in the studio around us, the two of us just clung to each other for dear life as we sobbed and sobbed and sobbed.

Four months earlier I had met Dianne for the first time and thought she was from Essex, but now I felt a bond and a sense of pride that was so phenomenally overwhelming. It's silly, isn't it? It's just a TV show. It's just a TV show about dancing.

Strictly was so far out of my comfort zone, such an un-known quantity, and so terrifying a prospect. It was the scariest, most consuming, most exhausting, most mentally demanding, emotionally depleting thing I have ever done. I will never be part of anything like it again, though. Something that connects with so many in the exact same moment. Some-thing that brings so much emotion out of people, something that brought so much emotion out of me.

I had said no to doing *Strictly* several times, but my

partnership with Dianne was the most remarkable thing I've been a part of throughout my entire career. She was able to find things within me that I didn't even know were there, and what we were able to achieve together, well, it's hands down the proudest I've ever been of anything I've done in my life.

To Dianne. We did it partner!

Epilogue

I have been writing this book while on tour throughout the first half of 2025. I have written this book while performing over a hundred and forty shows in only slightly more than as many days. It has been written on half the motorways of these united kingdoms, in theatre dressing rooms before and in between shows, in hotels too numerous to mention, and at home during any small amounts of time off from touring I've had. If this book achieves nothing else, I would at least like it to win an award for the book that has been written in the most places or travelled the most miles during its creation.

The most difficult thing about writing this book over this period has been the complete lack of downtime afforded to me while on tour. The process has been quite consuming and a constant presence that, if not provoking my fingers to rattle away on this keyboard, has caused my mind to whir away in the background on its behalf. As I said, though, when the thing I can't stop thinking about and the thing I need to be thinking about overlap, well that's when I can actually get things done.

I have ended up dedicating four chapters to my *Strictly* experience, probably around fifteen per cent of the total word count. Fifteen per cent of forty-eight years for something that took only several months to complete. I appreciate this is likely too much for some, and nowhere near enough for others. It is certainly disproportionate, and that is because without *Strictly* there would be no book. Let's be honest, my success on *Strictly* is why my publisher asked me to write it, and might even be the only reason you are reading it right now.

More than that, though, I think my experience on *Strictly* has made it possible for me to be able to write this book. I have always felt crippled by perfectionism, and that's not to say that I feel everything I have dared to put out there is anything like perfect, but that this anxiety has restricted my output in the past through the fear that what I have to say just might not be interesting enough, funny enough, or good enough.

'Things don't have to be perfect to be a success' is a sentiment Dianne and I voiced a few times throughout *Strictly*, but it is something that I honestly learned for myself during my time on the show. What we did together was nowhere near perfect, but it couldn't really have been more of a success.

What I learned is that it is much more important to connect with people and to give a piece of yourself that you might have otherwise kept hidden away. I learned the importance of sharing vulnerability and of letting people in, and so I hope I've been able to do that a little throughout these pages in a way that I don't think I would have been able to do if I'd tried to write this book previously.

I'm a northern bloke who grew up in Liverpool in the

eighties, and that, combined with the experience of losing my sight over such a long drawn-out period of time, has meant I have moved through life with a tendency to bottle up my emotions, to dig a hole and bury them deep. I think my natural instinct has been to keep myself closed off emotionally and try to be self-sufficient to some extent, so that a façade can be maintained and presented for others to see.

Those few months at the end of 2024 ripped me open on live TV in front of the nation, they ripped me open and left my emotions scattered about the place amidst tears for everybody to see. So surely this is the best time to get everything down in a book, then? To share my story, before I am able to gather them all and stitch myself back up again.

I'm also a needy comedian, though, so I hope I've managed to entertain and undercut my life experiences enough to paint myself as the idiot I am and to make you laugh sufficiently along the way.

A year ago I would have also felt that I was sharing a story without a good enough ending, but what Dianne and I were able to accomplish together, well *that* feels like an ending to this part of my story that I couldn't be prouder of. There is no doubt in my mind that *Strictly* will stand alone as the most insanely ridiculous thing I will ever achieve in my life, but I'm good with that. I'm good for it to be an island on its own, something I can be proud of taking on and accomplishing in the way that we did together.

Three days after the final, I was at a local restaurant with Patricia and Sophie and some friends. The seven of us had enjoyed our meal in peace. Nobody came over to speak to me, nobody shouted anything about *Strictly* from another table, nobody in that restaurant said a single word, until I put my coat on to leave and the entire restaurant gave me a round of applause. I honestly didn't know what to do with myself. I felt like I was in a movie, and I was extremely touched and embarrassed by the attention in equal measure. But what a privilege, to have been part of something that has made it into so many living rooms and that has connected with so many people in the way that it did – it honestly blows my mind.

As if the year needed anything else, I ended 2024 with an honour that goes to one person each year, and sometimes they aren't even real. I was asked to present Channel 4's *Alternative Christmas Message*, which has placed my name on a very exclusive list alongside some very real people indeed, such as the Reverend Jesse Jackson and Sir Stephen Fry, and some equally recognisable but significantly less real people, such as Ali G and Marge Simpson.

I used this Christmas message to call for improved government support for disabled people in the workplace, and to remind the nation of our strengths. At the end of *Strictly* I said that with opportunity, support and hard work, anything can happen. So much untapped potential is locked up in so many like myself who are often underestimated due to disability. Opportunity and support are the keys that unlock that potential, and all the hard work, well, that's down to us. There are so many out there who are eager to prove that more is possible than you might think.

In May 2025, while I was writing this book, Dianne and I received the BAFTA for TV's most memorable moment of the year, for our waltz to 'You'll Never Walk Alone'. It was the only BAFTA voted for by the British public, which brought home to us just how many people we'd had along with us for the ride. The cake was full and plenty already, but this was certainly the big fat cherry to be placed on top.

I wasn't able to be at the awards ceremony as I was on tour performing shows that had already been moved once to accommodate my participation in *Strictly*, and so certainly couldn't be moved again. Plus, we were up against the cultural phenomenon that is *Gavin & Stacey*, for God's sake, so I honestly didn't think we would win. It turns out, though, that not turning up to collect a BAFTA is inadvertently the coolest thing I've ever done in my life.

I'm grateful for every opportunity that has come my way since that first appearance on *Live at the Apollo* back in 2017. There have been a lot, and although I have worked hard, the best decision I made along the way was to stop drinking, as it allowed me to be kinder to myself and to make the most of each and every one of those opportunities.

I feel very lucky. Lucky for the family and friends I have, lucky for all those I get to work alongside, and lucky for the audience I have been able to reach.

If I can proffer any parting words of fortune-cookie semi-wisdom before I give this keyboard a rest, they would be to be kind to yourself, because it is the one thing that will make the biggest difference to everything. To do things that scare you, because it's the scary things that are often the most rewarding. And, of course, to keep laughing, because it is, after all, the best medicine.

Thanks for reading my book.

Lots of love,
Chris X

Acknowledgements

This is the bit at the end of the film where the credits roll to some rousing music, although as this is a book, you'll have to imagine the music in your head.

I would like to thank my publisher and editor, Rowland White, for holding my hand throughout this process, even though he doesn't like holding hands. I didn't really know what I was doing at times, but he made me believe that I did, before asking that I stop trying to hold his hand all the time.

Katya Browne, for spending days of her life on the phone to me going through editorial changes because I couldn't do it visually. She has more patience than all the saints combined, but I think she has still blocked my number.

Also Nick Lowndes, Bea McIntyre, Ruth Atkins and Jess Minter, for doing editorial things that are way above my station, but that made everything better.

Louise Moore is the MD of Michael Joseph, so I would like to thank her for giving all of these people jobs. I think they deserve a pay rise – just saying.

Of course a book is nothing if it doesn't sell any copies, so thanks to Christina Ellicott, Rachel Myers, Kelly Mason, Laura Garrod, Hannah Padgham and the whole of the

Penguin sales team. I am writing this in the book, though, without knowing whether they did actually manage to sell any copies, but let's just assume that they did.

The sales team would have a much harder job if there was no marketing and publicity team, so thanks to Clare Parker, Sriya Varadharajan, Alice Gordge, Elizabeth Smith, Vicky Photiou, Colin Brush (second cousin of Basil) and Mubarak Elmubarak, for all of their work in this regard.

Design and production were handled by Lee Motley and Helen Eka, and I believe it looks great!

The audiobook is being produced by Lottie Chesterman and Helen Sheffield, who I don't think will ever have a tougher job than trying to get a blind man to read a book out loud. A portion of every copy sold will be going straight towards helping to pay for their therapy.

Thanks to my copy-editor Hazel Orme for your kind words, and for taking all of my commas and putting them in the right places.

I hope you're still imagining the music in your head.

The book wouldn't even be possible, though, if I didn't have the right people around me. So thanks to . . .

My agent, Jacob Howe-Douglas of HD Management, for the last ten years and the next ten to come. Oh, and for agreeing to reduce his commission rate from fifteen per cent down to just six. That's in a book now, so it has to be true.

Nigel Klarfeld and Rebecca Pakdel at Bound and Gagged Comedy, for all of your hard work in producing my tours, and for everything that came before. Special thanks comes from my wife Patricia for having me out of the house and on the road as much as you do – she wants me to let you know that she appreciates it.

Amanda Emery of Emery PR, for being the absolute best publicist I could wish for! Even though I am terrible at replying to emails.

To Graham, for all of the driving and the good company over the last thirteen years and counting. We are two peas in a pod, which is why it works so well. If he wants to write that book, I won't sue. Well, maybe.

To Debbie, for all the driving that came before Graham, and for making so much of my early career possible.

To comedian Jon Long, for being brilliantly funny and great company, and for joining me out on tour and opening my shows as much as he has over the past six years.

And to both Graham and Jon for letting me read so much of this to them in the car while we were on tour. I mean, it's not like they had much choice, but thanks for not leaping from a moving vehicle and leaving me on my own in there.

I have worked with too many to mention over the years, but thanks to everyone I've worked with at the BBC, ITV, Channel 4 and Sky, and for all of the opportunities you have thrown my way. Special thanks obviously go to Pinki Chambers for championing me for the very first of these opportunities, as without her support, the last third of this book may not have happened.

To everyone at Zeppotron, Hat Trick and Thames TV, for those early opportunities, and for making me a regular face on some of the biggest and funniest shows on the telly.

To everyone at BBC Studios, Open Mike Productions, Cactus TV and Sky Studios, for having faith in me to front my own shows and for being great people to work with.

Huge thanks go to the whole *Strictly* team, for an experience that was truly life-changing.

And of course, to my dance partner Dianne Buswell, for finding things within me that I didn't know were there, and for being the absolute best!

Nearly done, I hope you're still doing the music.

I wouldn't even have a story to tell if it wasn't for the following people, though . . .

So thanks to Neil, for being the best mate a guy could hope for over the past four and a half decades. For the memories, for the love and support, and for bringing those tapes back from America and sharing in a life of kick-ass music with me!

To Kev, for being the most genuine guy I know, and for the last thirty-odd years and counting. I would also like to apologise for the Hanson Christmas album bit and the bird-shit story.

To Haydn, Steve and Gary, for all of the friendship, laughs and support over the years. For all the gigs they have tagged along to, and for making uni the right decision all those years back.

To Colin, for being both family and friend. For your support in my early career, and for always remaining close even over huge distances.

To the Liverpool rabble. All of my aunties, uncles and cousins who have always come out to support me in everything I've done. From tiny club rooms to selling out Liverpool's Philharmonic Hall – it is appreciated more than they will know.

To my sister Louise for all of her encouragement and support over the years, for being so invested in my career, and for helping me navigate the Edinburgh Fringe as she did. Also for being the best little sis I could wish for, even though she did keep on sitting on my side of the telly.

To my mum and dad, for never wrapping me up in cotton wool, for always encouraging me to do what feels right, and for being proud of my achievements long before I was on the telly. And to my dad for all that driving to north-west clubs in terrible weather.

Most importantly though, thank you to my wife Patricia and my daughter Sophie for allowing me to do all of this and enabling me to chase those dreams. To Patricia, for all of her encouragement and for facilitating everything. To Sophie, for the hugs at the door when I get home. And to both of them, for giving it all a purpose.

Okay, you can stop doing the music now. I'm done.